Entre el Sur y el Norte

Margarita Machado-Casas and Yolanda Medina
General Editors

Vol. 23

The Critical Studies of Latinxs in the Americas series
is part of the Peter Lang Trade Academic and Textbook list.
Every volume is peer reviewed and meets
the highest quality standards for content and production.

PETER LANG
New York • Berlin • Brussels • Lausanne • Oxford

Entre el Sur y el Norte

Decolonizing Education through Critical Readings of Chicana/x/o, Mexican, and Indigenous Music

Edited by
Marco Cervantes and
Lilliana P. Saldaña

PETER LANG
New York • Berlin • Brussels • Lausanne • Oxford

Library of Congress Cataloging-in-Publication Control Number: 2022001643

Bibliographic information published by **Die Deutsche Nationalbibliothek**.
Die Deutsche Nationalbibliothek lists this publication in the "Deutsche Nationalbibliografie"; detailed bibliographic data are available on the Internet at http://dnb.d-nb.de/.

ISSN 2372-6822 (print)
ISSN 2372-6830 (online)
ISBN 978-1-4331-9333-0 (hardcover)
ISBN 978-1-4331-9334-7 (paperback)
ISBN 978-1-4331-6066-0 (ebook pdf)
ISBN 978-1-4331-6067-7 (epub)
DOI 10.3726/b19537

© 2022 Peter Lang Publishing, Inc., New York
80 Broad Street, 5th floor, New York, NY 10004
www.peterlang.com

All rights reserved.
Reprint or reproduction, even partially, in all forms such as microfilm, xerography, microfiche, microcard, and offset strictly prohibited.

To all of the activistas and artistas working to disrupt the colonial project.

Table of Contents

List of Figures — ix

Acknowledgments — xi

1. *Decolonizing Pedagogies entre el Sur y el Norte: Healing, Resistance and Social Change through Music* — 1
   MARCO CERVANTES AND LILLIANA P. SALDAÑA

Transborder Movements

2. *Mujeres del Viento Florido: First Transborder Gathering of Indigenous Women Musicians in Santa María Tlahuitoltepec, Mixe Oaxaca* — 23
   XÓCHITL CHÁVEZ AND MERCEDES ALEJANDRA PAYÁN RAMÍREZ

3. *El Tallercito de Son SATX: Creando Comunidad a Través de la Cultura* — 55
   KELI ROSA CABUNOC

4. *Decolonizing, Healing and Evoking Resistance through Music: Crossing Ideological and Colonial Borders Using Transmedia and Experiential Educational Approaches* — 81
   IRIS RODRIGUEZ

Decolonization Within the Walls Higher Education

5. *Towards a Decolonial Feminist Hip-Hop* — 103
   MELISSA CASTILLO PLANAS AND AUDRY FUNK

6. Toward Decolonial Teaching in Ethnomusicology: Learning Elements of Afro-Caribbean and Mexican Traditional Music as Participatory Pedagogy 127
ALEXANDRO D. HERNÁNDEZ

7. Mapping el Movimiento: Decolonizing the Classroom through Chicano Musical Performance Pedagogy 145
NOE RAMIREZ

Reflections on the Path to Decolonial Pedagogies

8. Reconstructing Music Education: One Chicana's Journey 167
RACHEL YVONNE CRUZ

9. "Has Algo": Reading and Writing in a Chicanx Punk Pedagogy 187
OLIVIA JEAN HERNÁNDEZ

10. Unsettling Social Justice Teacher Education: An Intergenerational Exploration of Music as Healing, Survivance, and Pedagogy 211
SEAN D. HERNÁNDEZ ADKINS, LUCÍA I. MOCK MUÑOZ DE LUNA, TANIA VARGAS, AND BYLASAN AHMAD

Index 233

List of Figures

Figure 2.1: SEQ Fotografía*ARABIC 1 Directora y Maestra Leticia Gallardo en su viaje a Los Ángeles, California en el 2015. Source: Xóchitl Chávez   30

Figure 2.2: SEQ Fotografía*ARABIC 2 Workshop 1. Identity. Source: Xóchitl Chávez   40

Figure 2.3: SEQ Fotografía*ARABIC 3 Proceso de composición colectiva de la letra de la canción "Tocamos como mujer". Source: Mercedes Alejandra Payán Ramírez   42

Figure 2.4: SEQ Fotografía*ARABIC 4 Workshop 4. Conducting a band tips. Source: Mercedes Alejandra Payán Ramírez   44

Figure 2.5: SEQ Fotografía*ARABIC 5 Despedida del First Transborder Gathering of Indigenous Women Musician in Santa María Tlahuitoltepec Mixe, Oaxaca. Source: Miguel Angel Santiago Martinez   45

Figure 4.1: Yacatsol. Source: Iris Rodriguez   98

Acknowledgments

Much gratitude to all the contributors for being a part of this book project which started during one of the most violent administrations in recent memory and was completed in the midst of a pandemic that has ravaged Black, Brown, and Indigenous communities in Turtle Island and around the globe. We honor your intellectual work and creative vision to decolonize teaching/learning spaces and are grateful to learn from you on this journey. Thank you Peter Lang for your support in publishing this important contribution to decolonial studies, education, and Chicana/x/o Studies. A special thank you to the editor of this series, Margarita Machado-Casas, for your incredible guidance and support in bringing this book to life. We also thank our mentors – Marie "Keta" Miranda and Josie Méndez-Negrete for nurturing our activism and scholarship throughout the years – and students and colleagues in the Mexican American Studies program for affirming music in academia. And mil gracias to our SOMOS MAS family in San Antonio for building a community of activist scholars-teachers-cultural workers who are decolonizing education and transforming the culture of schooling in San Antonio and beyond.

Decolonizing Pedagogies entre el Sur y el Norte: Healing, Resistance and Social Change through Music

MARCO CERVANTES AND LILLIANA P. SALDAÑA

The life-giving power of music has sustained the survival of Chicana/x/o, Mexican, and Indigenous communities over five centuries of conquest, occupation, colonization, and resistance. Within the spirit of the creation-resistance (Rodriguez, 2014), this book examines music as a site of anti-colonial struggle and decolonial praxis in schools and communities within and beyond the colonial border that divides Mexico and the U.S. Premised on the emancipatory notion that schools–part and parcel of the "colonial matrix of power" (Quijano, 2000) – can engender a decolonial imaginary and praxis (Pérez, 1999), we compiled this reader to provoke consciousness and cultivate decolonial approaches to teaching and learning through the critical study, performance, and creation of musical expressions. Moreover, this reader examines music as a site of healing, remembering, revitalizing, restoring, celebrating, returning, connecting, and envisioning possibilities for humanization in schools and community-based teaching/learning spaces (Smith, 2012).

As scholars committed to decolonization as a political, epistemic, spiritual, and cultural project across the continent, we examine transcultural understandings and solidarity between and across subaltern peoples of the Global North and the Global South, with particular attention to Chicana/x/o music. Music provides ways to critically explore epistemic erasures, disrupt colonial narratives, and create spaces for transformative consciousness among children and youth, particularly around issues of economic domination, migrant rights, transborder resistance, institutionalized racism, epistemic and cultural erasure, and educational inequity. We hope this collection can add to the growing possibilities towards decoloniality in our communities and abroad.

There currently is not a text that focuses solely on decolonizing education through Chicana/x/o, Mexican and Indigenous music, though scholars of Chicana/x/o music have worked to interrogate, question, and analyze music in ways that have established groundwork to further push for decolonial readings of Chicana/x/o musical expression. The contributors in this volume engage various decolonial schools of thought and connect these with Chicana/x/o borderlands epistemologies to offer new insights on how teacher-scholar-musician-activists can decolonize, indigenize, and challenge Western imperialist practices inside schools and community spaces, from K-12 classrooms, academia, and communal learning/teaching spaces. We offer new articulations on music, pedagogy, and decoloniality that take place within and across the political locations of what post-development scholars refer to as the "Global South" and the "Global North." Scholars like Boaventura de Sousa Santos argue that coloniality is reinscribed through global capitalism within and across southern territories and nations, which are often referred to as the Global South, and northern territories and nations, which are often referred to as the Global North. Within this framework, the "Global South" includes those countries and territories that are victimized by the Global North's "voracity of capitalism, colonialism, patriarchy and all their satellite-oppressions" (Santos, p. 3–4, 2014). In challenging these dehumanizing relations of power, we call for a "decolonial turn"—a paradigm shift that requires us to center our own epistemologies in our collective efforts to dismantle coloniality (Maldonado-Torres, 2011).

It's important to note that the contributors in this book do not analyze coloniality from a place of a disembodied knowledge; on the contrary, they write from their own lived experiences as Chicana/x/o and Indigenous educators, transborder activists, musicians, and scholars who create, research, sustain, and teach music to cultivate consciousness and decolonized subjectivities, and offer new ways of coming to knowledge through sound, voice, and movement of the bodyspiritmind. Martha Gonzalez (2020) writes about the artistic and activist work of Chicana/x/o "artivistas" and the importance of *"convivencia,"* or "being present and engaging together in mind, body and spirit via participatory music and art practice" (p. 13). We acknowledge that decolonization is not an abstract in the global imaginary, nor a metaphor for other social justice projects (Tuck & Yang, 2012), but realized in our communities' creative expressions. Creating music, whether for spiritual, political, or pedagogical purposes, is a part of what Raza Studies scholar Roberto "Cintli" Rodriguez (2015) calls creation-resistance, where the act of creating and resisting (reacting against) are both equally important strategies for humanization and social justice.[1]

Decolonization and Decoloniality

As Chicana/x/o studies scholars committed to decolonization as a political-spiritual-epistemic project, we center the perspectives, cosmologies, and worldviews of critical thinkers from the U.S.-Mexico borderlands. In this sense, the work of Chicana feminist and queer theorists like Gloria Anzaldúa and Emma Pérez are important in offering new epistemologies that emerge from their subalternized racial/ethnic critiques of Western epistemology. In her essay, "Nepantla, el lugar de la frontera," Gloria Anzaldúa (2015) writes on the importance of border artists and border arte in decolonial movements. As Anzaldúa notes, border artists who inhabit the transitional spaces of nepantla "cambian el punto de referencia" or change the frame of reference (p. 49) and create possibilities for "shifting identities, border crossings, and hybridism --- all strategies for decolonization" (p. 63). Like border artists, educators who create, preserve, and teach through music, decolonize occupied teaching/learning spaces (Anzaldúa, p. 49). This is particularly important for Chicanas/xs/os and Indigenous people who have "been stripped of our history, language, identity, and pride" as "we attempt again and again to find what we have lost by digging into our cultural roots imaginatively and making art from our findings" (p. 48).

Anzaldúa reminds us that the process of decolonization is also full of contradictions, tensions, and ambiguities that require constant self-reflection in our praxis, particularly for those living in cultural, spiritual, and linguistic, and psychological borderlands where we are at once fighting against oppressive "traditions" while creating oppositional ways of knowing that counter Western approaches to learning, teaching, and being—what Anzaldúa (1999) called "new mestiza consciousness." For Anzaldúa, decolonization is a political, spiritual, and creative process that happens within the self before it materializes at the institutional and structural levels and within our communities of practice.

Historian Emma Pérez critiques traditional approaches to history that ignore transborder migrations, diasporas, gender, and sexuality in colonial heteropatriarchal historiography, and proposes a "decolonial imaginary" to challenge Western and androcentric perspectives that leave queer and transborder women out of writing. Through a "decolonial imaginary," Chicana/x/o scholars are able to create an "interstitial space where differential politics and social dilemmas are negotiated" and where colonial narratives are disrupted (p. 6). Within this spirit, educators-musicians-activists draw from music to create a rupturing space where they and their students alike can bring forth new interpretations of their world – where they can breakdown binaries of oppressed/victimized and oppressor/victimizer to "[negotiate] … a decolonizing otherness where all identities are at work in one way or another" (p. 6). In other words, teaching with and through music can create another consciousness – an oppositional consciousness which, as Chela Sandoval notes in her work, can serve as "politically effective means for transforming dominant power relations" (p. 43).

We also turn to the work of Maori scholar Linda Smith (2012) who defines decolonization as the long-term process of dismantling colonial power at the bureaucratic, cultural, linguistic, and psychological levels. For Chicana/x/o, Indigenous and Black people in present-day U.S., decolonization has been linked to past and contemporary struggles to abolish la migra, end the inhumane and cruel practice of separating children from their parents (a form of cultural genocide), and demolish the U.S.-Mexico border wall – what Gloria Anzaldúa describes as "a 1,950 mile-long open wound, *dividing* a pueblo, a culture" (p. 24, 2007). As Roberto "Cintli" Rodriguez (2015) notes, our struggle to end this colonial violence, and by that extension, to affirm our humanity, has been a 500-year struggle that can be traced to 1492. Like many decolonial struggles around the world, these political projects have been rooted in the spiritual activist practices of artists who use their creative vision to wage these struggles within and across settler colonial borders in efforts to sustain cultural practices, epistemologies, and communal approaches to learning/teaching.

In creating this volume, we also look to the work of decolonial scholars from Latin America who have written extensively on "coloniality" – the oppressive, inhumane, and hegemonic practices of colonial domination which have been masked by the language of salvation, progress, and development (Mignolo, 2011). According to Ramón Grosfuguel, "Coloniality allows us to understand continuity of colonial forms of domination after the end of colonial administrations, produced by colonial cultures and structures in the modern/colonial capitalist/patriarchal world-system" (2010, p. 73). Scholars like Walter Mignolo and Arturo Escobar (2010) offer the idea of engaging in "epistemic decolonization" or de-coloniality – the imagining and creation of "intercultural communication and towards an-other nationality that puts life first and that places institutions at its service, rather than the other way around" (i).

It's important to note that Peruvian sociologist Anibal Quijano (2000) was the first to theorize the interlocking, systemic and historic patterns of colonial oppression through a concept he referred to as "el patrón colonial del poder," or the "colonial matrix of power." According to Quijano, coloniality is articulated in four major domains of the human experience: economic, in terms of appropriating land, controlling finance, and exploiting labor; political, in terms of maintaining authority; civic life, where gender and sexuality are controlled within Western heteropatriarchal discursive practices; and the epistemological realm, an aspect of coloniality that Quijano (2000) regards as the most insidious since it shapes subjectivity, consciousness, identity, and the control, distortion, and erasure of knowledge. We understand that decolonization cannot be reduced to only one dimension of social life – political, epistemic, economic, or social. The "coloniality of power" challenges us to think more expansively about liberation, agency, and the ways in which educators-scholars-musicians-activists can engage in creative-political expression to decolonize.

Literary scholar, David Saldívar (2010), links the coloniality of power to pensamiento fronterizo or border thinking in Chicana/x/o Studies. Pensamiento fronterizo emerges from the critical reflection of those who live on the margins – undocumented immigrants, refugees, women, children, and working-class and queer people who live and think within the major structures of dominance and subordination. Saldívar's pensamiento fronterizo provides a theoretical framework for understanding the ways in which music serves as a spiritual, ceremonial, affective, political, epistemic, expressive, performative intervention – from the classroom to the streets. Saldívar argues that Quijano's concept of coloniality of power can "help us begin to account for the entangled relations of power between the global division of labor, racial and ethnic hierarchy, identity formation and Eurocentric epistemologies" (p. 193). This concept also helps us "trace the continuous forms of hegemonic dominance produced by colonial cultures and structures" (p. 193) as we deploy strategies for decolonization. It is this interrogation of the coloniality of power that has produced what Anzaldúa calls "la conciencia de la nueva mestiza" – a Chicana/x who is in-between cultures and embraces her multiple cultures and identities to engender decolonial solidarities and social change (p. 99).

Mignolo's (2010) concept of "geopolitics of knowledge" is also useful in examining the persistence of Western hegemonic thought in institutions of knowledge production which continue to uphold Eurocentric thinking as "universal" while relegating non-Western forms of thinking as "folkloric." (p. 71) The authors in this book speak to this "geopolitics of knowledge" and address the ways in which Indigenous, Chicana/x/o, and Mexican music scholars-teachers-performers-activists sustain musical knowledge and traditions to heal from colonial trauma, nurture ethnic identity and critical consciousness, and restore communal approaches to music creation and teaching/learning. While the Latin American decolonial school of thought helps us think about structures of coloniality and processes of decolonization and while we see tremendous value in the work of these scholars, we trace our genealogy to Chicana/x/o epistemologies and Indigenous schools of thought to inform our activism, pedagogies, and creation resistance. As Chicanas/xs/os, we not only think from the confluences of multiple colonialities, but also multiple resistances against Spanish colonial violence and the everyday impact of U.S. settler colonialism on Black, Indigenous, and Brown people. Struggles for decolonization are not only epistemic or political (Walsh, p. 86); as Anzaldúa reminds us, they are also cultural and spiritual. In sum, the decolonial music projects in this volume are anchored in the embodied and self-reflexive knowledge and creative practices that recover, heal, humanize, and transform our communities.

The contributors in this volume confront the colonial matrix of power and fight against the epistemological, spiritual, cultural and linguistic assaults of the modern/colonial educational systems that deny us our stories and cultural knowledge. Like other decolonial scholar-activists, we push for an epistemic shift in centering Chicana/x/o, Indigenous, and transborder perspectives on decoloniality, and center their pedagogical interventions in their classrooms, community spaces, and across imposed geopolitical borders. Moreover, these pieces reflect the language in which Chicana/x/o and other people living within and across these borders develop decolonial curricula, strategies, social movements, projects, and creative/artistic production to confront coloniality, its borders and the epistemic suppression that continues to take place in our worlds. We not only believe that it is possible to create decolonial worlds, we create these worlds in our classrooms, community talleres/workshops, and performances, and disrupt through lyrics, movement of the body, critical analysis, and dialogue.

Decolonial Pedagogies: Confronting the Colonial Matrix of Power

Our conceptualization of decolonial pedagogies is intimately connected to our lived experiences growing up in occupied territory known as Texas, and the identities of resistance we embody as scholar activists, educators, artists, and cultural workers. Our experiences navigating the epistemic violence of a Texas settler colonial curricula and the deliberate erasure of our histories as Indigenous and Mexican people, along with the gross institutional negligence of Black and Brown students – all of which are part and parcel of the settler colonial schooling project – have informed our pedagogical praxis. As such, we continue to learn from our students (who are our teachers), fellow educators, activists, and cultural workers to confront oppressive education and the political, legal, economic, and social systems that are a part of the "colonial matrix of power." As curriculum studies scholar Miguel Zavala notes, we must continue to "center colonized people's survival and recovery" and create "spaces for students to critically reframe their lives in ways that counter the neocolonial situation that limits their rehumanization" (p. 53–54). In sum, a decolonial pedagogy must provide students with opportunities to examine their colonial reality and how it "operates on all levels, from the micro practices of the body to the macro-structurations that position them as workers and racially marginalized beings" (p. 54). The essays in this volume, which are written in the self-reflexive tradition of testimonio, offer pedagogical principles rooted in their Chicana/x/o, Mexican, Indigenous standpoints, political stances, and spiritual activism in their communities of praxis. They write from their memories of colonial violence in educational institutions and their struggles to undo the harm of colonial practices. It's also important to note that their decolonial pedagogies are emergent, in process as they themselves become critically conscious and create teaching/learning approaches that interrogate, challenge, and de-link from the damaging effects of Eurocentric epistemologies and pedagogies.

Decolonial pedagogies speak to some of the same principles as other transformative teaching/learning approaches, while centering the past and present impact of colonialism in Chicana/x/o, Indigenous, and Mexican communities. As Zavala (2018) notes, decolonizing pedagogies "represent an expansion and departure from broader critical pedagogical strands" like feminist, Indigenous, anti-racist, critical, and humanist approaches (p. 59). Decolonizing pedagogies explicitly engage colonialism as a historical process and expose the logics of coloniality – the existing colonial patterns that continue to inform our lives – within and across geopolitical borders, in our classrooms, and community spaces of conviviality and teaching/learning. For Chicana/x/o studies pedagogues, decolonial pedagogy should necessarily engage the historical process of colonialism, survival, and recovery for Raza communities today (Zavala, 2018). Raza Studies teachers-scholars like Rodriguez (2014), Arce (2016), and Gonzalez (2018) propose teaching through Maya-Nahua epistemologies like the four movements represented in the Nahui Ollin and maíz-based principles like in lak'ech and panche be as a way to affirm our ancestral knowledge and activate that precious knowledge to social action. According to Zavala, these decolonial frameworks, which are part of ethnic studies grassroots movements across the U.S., re-frame the ethnic studies movement as a "500-year struggle against the colonizing logic of erasure." (p. 3). Likewise, music also generates awareness on the experience of colonization and the struggle of Chicana/x/o, Mexican, and Indigenous communities and creates opportunities for collaborations that center Indigenous values like mutuality, community, recovery of knowledge, affirmation of identities, and healing.

As we imagine a decolonial pedagogy using music as an instrument of social transformation, we employ approaches to sustain musical expressions that align with Django Paris and H. Samy Alim's (2017) "culturally sustaining pedagogies" (CSP) framework. Paris and Alim define culturally sustaining pedagogies as teaching/learning approaches that "[seek] to perpetuate and foster--to sustain--linguistic, literate, and cultural pluralism as part of schooling for positive social transformation. CSP positions dynamic cultural dexterity as a necessary good for positive social transformation" (p. 1, 2017). Culturally sustaining approaches are particularly relevant in teacher education where prospective teachers are forging their political identities as educators and learning how to intentionally challenge colonial ideologies and practices in their pedagogical praxis. As Michael Dominguez writes, "Teacher education continues to struggle at disrupting those White middle-class norms in our own prevailing discourses. We continue to promote systems that claim justice and equity, but remain firmly rooted in a framework of coloniality. As a result, our own ability to produce the types of teachers needed to enact CSP has been, and remains, limited" (2017, p. 229). This is in part due to the "Othering" of students and what Dominguez describes as "an ontological difference between the colonizer and the colonized that makes school-and societal institutions in general--challenging for youth of color" (p. 228). As decolonial educators-scholars-activists, we are intentional about dismantling, or at least putting a dent, on the colonial structures to heal from centuries of settler colonial violence that have plagued our K-12 schools and institutions of higher education. To understand why inequity exists in Yanawana/San Antonio, Texas, which is where we're situated, for instance, it is necessary to look at how Spanish conquest uprooted indigenous familial units, economies, languages, foodways, and governments. The implementation of casta systems and its imposing colorisms that still impact our current society must be studied if we are to understand current Chicana/x/o populations in the US. Music can offer routes to understand and act on the damaging effects of colonization on Chicana/x/o and Latina/x/o communities.

The work of the contributors in this volume speak to the concerns of borderlands people who have been largely excluded from theoretical, pedagogical, and political concerns in decolonial studies. They speak to the persistent condition of living between worlds and the need to build bridges between academia and community, music and social change. The decolonial educators in this volume also serve as nepantleras/xs/os – border thinkers who make connections for social change. To borrow from Chela Sandoval's (2000) concept of "technologies of crossing" – music is a technology of crossing as they help students shift to decolonial modes of consciousness to take action – whether it's to sustain Indigenous expressions or create new hybrid forms that refuse to be subsumed by coloniality.

Foundational Scholarship in Chicana/x/o and Mexican Music

Chicana/x/o cultural studies scholars have helped to lay the groundwork in applying decolonial readings to Chicana/x/o cultural production. Arturo J. Aldama and Naomi Quiñonez's (2002) reader *Decolonial Voices: Chicana and Chicano Cultural Studies in the 21st Century*, examines how "subaltern cultural productions of the U.S.-Mexico borderlands (film, art, music, lit, pop culture, and alternate historiographies) speak to what Walter Mignolo (2000) considers the intersections of 'local,' 'hemispheric,' and 'globalized' power relations of the border imaginary" (pp. 2–3). Luz Calvo and Catriona Rueda Esquibel (2015) have proposed ways to "decolonize" our diet by reclaiming Indigenous foodways and decolonizing food systems. The study, teaching and performance of Chicana/x/o music presents possibilities towards further dismantling coloniality.

Music provides a forum for colonized people to transform oppressive conditions within colonial spaces. Folklorist Américo Paredes was one the first Mexican American scholars to document and study music of the US/Texas borderlands, with a focus on the genre of the corrido. Paredes's (1958) work, *With a Pistol in his Hand*, documents how corridos in South Texas spoke against Texas/Anglo settler colonialism. However, the corrido also reflects Chicana/x/o histories and experiences that are often complex and at times contradictory as the music draws from European instrumentation and song structure. Also, some early corridos celebrate Mexican colonial efforts over Indigenous populations. Further, in the text there are moments Paredes expresses anti-Indigenous rhetoric and the romanticizing of the Spanish settlement of Nuevo Santander in the Rio Grande. This shows the very real elements of coloniality, early in the Mexican American cultural memory. Moments like this present opportunities to reflect, analyze, interrogate, and act against uncritical celebrations of anti-Indigeneity within Mexican American poetics. As Chicana/x/o pedagogues, musicians, and activists, we believe it's important to interrogate the racism imbedded in settler narratives as we work to decolonize education and the practices attached to so-called traditional music. An examination of corridos can still point to the ways the genre symbolizes resistance against U.S. colonialism by speaking against lost land, critiquing the police state, and calling for the end of the U.S./Texas settler colonial occupation. Thus, the genre has also helped Chicana/x/os preserve a historical memory of struggle and survival. As Anzaldúa writes, corridos have "narrated one hundred years of border history, bringing news of events as well as entertaining..." and have "made our hard lives seem bearable" (p. 41). Through music, histories, culture, chords, words, and melodies, Chicana/x/os continue to decolonize knowledge and power within the U.S.

Much of the early work on Mexican American or Chicanx music at U.S. universities and schools comes at a time before the creation of Chicana/x/o Studies programs; therefore, scholars had to find ways to fit their music studies in white-dominated fields in academia. Scholars of Chicana/x/o and Mexican American music have pushed in various ways against coloniality and their work provides routes to examine how the study, teaching, and performance of Chicana/x/o music has decolonial possibilities. Paredes, Limón (1992) and Saldívar (2006) have shown how the corrido has been used to resist U.S. white occupation, while instilling a sense of pride and community. Manuel Peña (1985) and Juan Tejeda and Avelardo Valdez (2001) have expanded on the working-class history and aesthetics of Texas conjunto in society. Maria Herrera-Sobek (1990) and Yolanda Broyles-González (2017) have shown how Mexican American women transcended gender barriers and used music as a tool to resist patriarchy and a racist anti-Mexican society. Moreover, Michelle Habell-Pallán (2005) and Deborah Vargas (2012) have shown how Chicanas in pop, rock and hip-hop have shaped identity and culture and understandings of contemporary transnational social dynamics. Scholars Anthony Macias (2008), Gaye Johnson (2013), and Tyina Steptoe (2015) have shown how, through music, African American and Chicana/x/o musicians and communities have engaged in political and cultural exchange, solidarity, and connection. These activists/scholars have helped lay groundwork that challenges and works to dismantle coloniality through performance and teaching of Chicana/x/o music. This work aligned with varied performances of Chicana/x/o music can aid in recognizing and challenging colonization within our communities. Furthermore, when examining Chicana/x/o music there is a need to highlight the ways Black scholars, activists and artists have pushed the decolonial process through being and convergences with Chicana/x/o, Mexican, and Indigenous cultures. It is crucial in Chicana/x/o Studies to examine how art, literature, and music within Latinidad takes the shape of what Yomaira C. Figueroa-Vásquez (2020) calls "decolonizing diasporas" which she conceptualizes as "radical Afro-diasporic imaginaries that subvert coloniality and usher in new ways of knowing and being, and interrogate and excavate location and dislocation" (25). As the movement to grow Indigenous, Chicana/x/o, and Mexican American Studies and music programs arises, there is a need for a decolonial praxis to honor and value the spaces and people who produce this scholarship. There are many educators now engaged in the movement, and we seek a framework in developing ways to incorporate Chicana/x/o music to interrogate and educate on decoloniality within sacred spaces.

Decolonizing Music Education

While steps have been taken to combat discrimination in music studies, even some of the most well-intentioned efforts to promote social justice or equity within music education spaces further perpetuate the colonial project through notions of diversity, success, and achievement. These words are rooted in structures that have been maintained through coloniality. When Burke Stanton (2018) describes the hegemonic structures surrounding the study of musicology, he writes, "contemporary hegemonic forms of Eurocentric subjectivity have no imperative toward decolonization," and illustrates the importance of "problematizing the relationship between the field of musicology, its role in education, and the global context in which it exists" (Stanton, p. 6). Margaret Walker (2020) notes the importance of music programs in higher education to "reflect on the role that European colonial power structures and extracted wealth have played in the creation of universities and academic scholarship, and re-examine our pedagogical content and methods, questioning their relationships to this larger context" (p. 2). Modernity has had profound effects on the study of music globally. It is crucial in these times to shift the way we approach music education and the additions of music in other disciplines in ways that decenter, witness and value decolonial epistemologies.

Music educators' centering of whiteness and coloniality continues to reinforce ontological differences that others Black, Indigenous, and Chicanx/a/o students and communities within the hegemonic colonial project. Music programs across the Global North and South continue to employ Eurocentric approaches to music education. It is vital to reach our students/communities in ways that challenge paradigms centered on a default whiteness and critically examine how we read and perform music. The authors contained in the reader present an array of possibilities and spaces in which educators have used

Chicana/x/o music to further undo coloniality surrounding Latina/x/o, Chicana/x/o communities towards a consciousness that values and treasures our past, present, and future. We view this as a starting point to embark in further conversations detailing ways a Chicana/x/o history has been embedded in colonization in ways that are complex. This can be a challenge, given that modernity has shaped much of the ways that scholars in the academy approach education. Yet there are cracks/nuances within Chicana/x/o music that allow for a push towards a decolonial consciousness while empowering community, students, and educators. This will require growing, learning, and action, but with each other, we can work to make our educational spaces more about the land and people who inhabit it, than the clutches of a false, capitalist meritocracy.

Organization of Chapters

We divided the book into three sections, "Transborder Movements," "Decolonizing Within the Walls of Higher Education," and "Reflections on Decolonizing Pedagogies," to offer readers different approaches in which scholar-educator-activist-musicians have engaged in decolonizing pedagogies in their praxis. The authors in Section 1, "Transborder Movements" offer personal accounts on how educators and practitioners use their work to decolonize as a way to transcend the U.S./Mexico border and promote resistance against coloniality.

Chapter 1, "Mujeres del Viento Florido: First Transborder Gathering of Indigenous Women Musicians in Santa María Tlahuitoltepec, Mixe Oaxaca," by ethnomusicologists Xóchitl Chávez and Mercedes Alejandra Payán Ramírez, offers a decolonial feminist and Indigenous analysis of their participation in the first all-female transborder gathering of Indigenous Oaxacan and Chicana/Mexicana brass band musicians, ethnomusicologists, and brand directors from Oaxaca and the U.S. This gathering emerged from the need to generate dialogue between women of Mujeres del Viento Florido and U.S.-based musicians and academics who were committed to preserving Indigenous ways of producing music and recovering women's agency in decision-making; addressing patriarchal norms and colonial logics of hierarchies in Oaxacan brass bands; and sustaining civilizational approaches to music creation rooted in community. Their chapter, which transitions between English and Spanish, contributes to the growing body of "epistemologies of the south" (Santos, 2014) and offers an Indigenous feminist approach to decolonizing how music is created, studied, and written, within and across geopolitical borders and western approaches that reproduce the colonial logic of power, knowing, and being.

In Chapter 2, "Decolonizing, Healing and Evoking Resistance through Music: Crossing Ideological and Colonial Borders Using Transmedia and Experiential Educational Approaches," Iris Rodriguez (2022), artist, media activist, writer, and founder of Xica Media, shares the work of Yacatsol, a transborder music project created by Rodriguez, her husband – who comes from a family of indigenous musicians specializing in millennial Mexican instrumentation and Nahuatl songwriting – and their children. As a musician-digital activist-educator, Rodriguez utilizes digital media and experiential educational approaches rooted in Indigenous perspectives to decolonize western cultural practices, while sustaining Indigenous lifeways, epistemologies, and sonicscapes across borders and into digital space. In the spirit of what she calls "digital resistance," Yacatsol serves as a "border-crossing, multilingual, decolonial, 'cura' music and art project" that heals through song and dance (p. 93). Through trilingual lyrics (Nahuatl, Spanish, and English), and visual performative imagery, Rodriguez and creative collaborators call for healing, unity of all colonized peoples, protection of Earth, and recovery of ancestral ways of being.

Framed within Chicana feminist and Indigenous methodologies, Keli Rosa Cabunoc's (2022) chapter, "El Tallercito de Son SATX: Creando Comunidad a Traves de la Cultura" analyzes how Chicanas/xs/os in San Antonio use son jarocho, its communal culture, and legacy of resistance politics to understand and self-make identities through their participation in El Tallercito de Son SATX. Drawing from son jarocho's legacy of Afro-Indigenous cultural resistance and through testimonio methodology, Cabunoc examines how talleristas come to understand their political and cultural identities, form local and transnational communities, center community in their cultural work, and engage in social justice movements. Writing as a fellow tallerista and co-founder of the group, Cabunoc's (2021) research establishes the importance of revitalizing son jarocho as a tool to decolonize identities in the face of "re(colonization)" – the "process of continued colonization across colonial borders" (p. 68). Her chapter also points to the importance of sustaining music traditions that center community-rooted forms of music creation and affirm community-forms of being.

In Section 2, we hear from authors who apply music in higher education in efforts to decolonize classrooms and institutions. In their chapter, scholar-writer Melissa Castillo Planas and hip-hop artist Audry Funk imagine a decolonial hip-hop feminism which is deeply invested in the intersectional approaches developed by earlier Black and Latinx feminists. They center women and girls of color in their analysis, in light of critical gender approaches that have treated Black and Latinx women as an addendum to both hip-hop and decolonial studies. They consider how the creative, intellectual work of decolonial hip-hop feminism invites new questions about representation, provides additional insights about embodied experience, and offers alternative models for critical engagement. Specifically, they imagine decolonial hip-hop feminism as an articulation of feminist consciousness rooted both in the pioneering work of Latin American feminist hip-hop artists as well as Black and Latinx scholars. The authors, who challenge the possibilities and limitations of the performance of a hip-hop *mexicanidad* in a space like Harvard University, note that decolonization implies fundamental changes in relations of power, worldviews, and relationships with the university system as a business.

In his chapter, "Toward Decolonial Teaching in Ethnomusicology: Learning Elements of the Son Jarocho and Writing Corridos as Participatory Pedagogy," Alexandro Hernández, an ethnomusicologist and Chicana/x/o Studies scholar, reflects on the ways in which he's decolonized his Chicana/x/o Studies music courses through a Freirian (2005) approach that dismantles the colonial teacher-student relationship through participatory teaching with music. In doing so, he establishes a decolonial method to teaching ethnomusicology that is also inclusive, anti-racist and gender critical. He specifically focuses on centering Afro-Cuban rumba guaguancó, Afro-Puerto Rican bomba, son jarocho zapateado, and the composition/performance of corridos in classroom teaching/learning. Through these musical genres he engages students with internalizing the sounds and feeling of experiencing music while developing a decolonial critical race, ethnic and gender analysis to music as culture. He connects these approaches to the ways he navigates settler-colonialism in South Texas where he was raised, and in higher education, as he uncovers the social power of music.

Similarly, Noe Ramirez, a professor of social work, also creates spaces in his classroom to center Chicana/x/o histories through Chicano music. In his chapter, "Chicano Movement Derived-Music: An Instructional Approach to Decolonization," Ramirez presents the utilization of musical performance as a pedagogical approach to promote and build student awareness of South Texas Chicana/x/o activism in response to conditions stemming from colonization of Mexican-Americans in this area. To do this, Ramirez draws from music that he composed, referencing the Chicano Movement in South Texas – a four-county area situated in the southernmost part of the state, adjacent to Mexico, also referred as the Rio Grande Valley, or the "Valley" ("El Valle"). His chapter outlines his journey in decolonizing two social work courses – Social Work Practice with Latinos and Social Work Practice with Diverse Populations – and the ways in which music inspired by the Chicano movement can become a part of a social work decolonial curriculum to create greater consciousness around liberation struggles in the region, while connecting to contemporary struggles today.

Section 3, "Reflections on the Path to Decolonial Pedagogies" includes three chapters by teacher-scholars who document and reflect on their experiences towards a decolonial consciousness and praxis in their teaching. In her chapter, "Reconstructing Music Education: One Chicana's Journey," Rachel Cruz, a Mexican American studies professor and music scholar, reflects on her experiences as a Chicana music student and the ways in which her family complimented her formal music education with Mexican music like mariachi and boleros, sustaining her ethnic identity within Euro-centric music and education programs in her K-12 education. Cruz, who continued to pursue music in her undergraduate, graduate, and doctoral education, also reflects on the racial microaggressions she experienced in higher education as a Chicana in a white dominated field and documents her accomplishments as a Chicana professor, including the establishment of the very first Bachelor of Arts degree in Music with all-level teacher certification and a specialization in Mariachi Performance and Pedagogy. As a Chicana musician and scholar trained in Western musical arts, she reflects on the process of decolonizing music education by deconstructing, decolonizing, and re-constructing a culturally diverse, inclusive model music program that allows educators to center Mexican American music in academia and K-12 classrooms.

As teacher educators, Sean D. Hernández Adkins, Lucía I. Mock Muñoz de Luna, Tania Vargas, and Bylasan Ahmad explore how people in various colonial settings use music to heal and imagine "inconceivable futures." Their chapter, "Unsettling Social Justice Teacher Education: An Intergenerational Exploration of Music as Healing, Survivance, and Pedagogy," presents three distinct but interrelated stories that form a transnational connection predicated on a critical reading of music as a tool for unsettling praxis. This work involves the analysis of Latinx/Chicanx music in connection to the struggles of Syrian and Palestinian youth to engage an analysis of music as healing (Anzaldúa, 2015), transformative, and as a tool for survivance that can be used across contexts.

Informed by the decolonial thinking of Indigenous scholars and Chicana feminist writers like Gloria Anzaldúa, in her chapter, "'Haz Algo': Reading and Writing in a Chicanx Punk Pedagogy," Chicana punk/scholar Olivia Jean Hernandez draws from the lyrics and activism of Chicanx punk musicians to articulate her Chicana punk composition pedagogy in the classroom.

As a Chicana punk pedagogue, Hernandez engages her composition students to develop a political consciousness around social justice issues like immigrant's rights, livable wages, antiracism, feminism, and queer recognition, and explores possibilities for decolonial praxis in and beyond the classroom through punk music and punk culture's DIY zine making. Her goal as a college instructor of first-generation Latinx students is for them to envision new futurities outside of the oppressive colonial structures that have marginalized Black and Brown people for centuries. In her words, "Punk artist-activists provide rhetorical models for readers and students to enact anti-colonial action in their own expression and to create community connections that unite students in activism and thinking that can resist and perhaps even dismantle colonial structures in the classroom and beyond it" (p. 13).

Future Directions in Decolonizing Education

The chapters above offer starting points for continued pushes to decolonize education in our communities, and we hope that this reader will expand conversations of how to best use music as a form to decolonize education. Some of the chapters in the reader show how performances allow for an exchange that pushes towards a decolonial shift. Playing percussion, drums, strings, Djing, and rapping present ways our communities have expressed and shared expressions that call for decoloniality. By continuing to tap into these expressions, we can find ways that extend our soul in ways that disrupt domination.

We are at a crucial point in time where pedagogical approaches can make significant changes in how we view and practice education. It is imperative that we shift our teaching to transform the oppressive systems attached to the long horrific legacies of colonization and its ties to occupation, miseducation, cultural removal, theft, slavery, and genocide. While much of this work needs to be done at home and in our communities, the shift in how institutions of power relate to our communities is much needed. There are countless activists, educators, and artists who continue to work tirelessly to change how we engage in education towards change and liberation.

We are still living in a time where colonization still has a detrimental effect on both sides of the U.S.-Mexico border and feeds into false notions of citizenship and belonging. The U.S. colonial project continues to treat lives as expendable while normalizing the imprisonment and separation of families in the name of citizenship and nationalism. Our lands have been contaminated for capital gain and our communities poisoned for the benefit of large corporations. Music is one of the ways to build an awareness of the ways coloniality continues to work against Black, Indigenous, and Chicana/x/o communities.

The readings in this book should be of interest to K-12 teachers, particularly teachers who are building curricula in Mexican American Studies, Latina/x/o Studies, and Ethnic Studies, and music education scholars, Chicana/x/o Studies scholars, ethnomusicologists, and professors in higher education who integrate music in their pedagogy and curricula. While this volume does not include contributions by K-12 educators, we recognize that this is not because of the lack of interest. As MAS activist scholars in the movement for MAS in K-12 schools, we see the powerful work of MAS educators who center borderlands genres like corridos to create spaces for critical inquiry around gender oppression, white supremacy, anti-Mexican violence, and cultural imperialism. We also recognize the work of MAS professors at community colleges who center music in their pedagogy. Music can help us make these connections and shift how we value and honor music as a form of knowledge, healing, and tool for social change. We continue to undo layers of colonization in the spaces that we live in. Whether it's through teaching students about the decolonial roots of our cultural music forms, performing in a community event, organizing community groups, or sharing reflections on how music makes you feel, music offers possibilities to affirm our humanity.

Note

1 In an interview with Xica Nation, Rodriguez writes that the key to building Raza Studies/MAS in Arizona, California, and Texas was/is creation-resistance: "Not one or the other, but in combination and if anything, leaning towards the creation aspect. Because if one only resists, that means you only react to others. And if one only creates independent of one's political reality, then one either becomes irrelevant, detached or oblivious. So we had to do both and I think that is an awesome way to be. Creating and resisting and creating. Really I think the creation part is awesome, especially in a state such as Arizona." https://xicanation.com/tlahtolli-interview-with-roberto-dr-cintli-rodriguez/

References

Aldama, A. J., & Quiñonez, N. (2002). *Decolonial voices: Chicana and Chicano cultural studies in the 21st century*. Indiana University Press.
Anzaldúa, G. (1999). *Borderlands/La frontera: The new mestiza*. Aunt Lute Books.
Anzaldúa, G. (2015). *Light in the dark/Luz en lo oscuro: Rewriting identity, spirituality, reality* (Ed. AnaLouise Keating). Duke University Press.
Arce, M. S. (2016). Xicana/o indigenous epistemologies: Toward a liberatory and decolonizing education for Xicana/o youth. In D. Sandoval, A. Ratcliff, T. Buenavista,

& J. R. Marín (Eds.), *Whitewashing American education: The new culture wars in ethnic studies* (Vol. 1, pp. 11–42). Praeger.

Broyles-González, Y. (2017). *Lydia Mendoza's life in music/La historia de Lydia Mendoza: Norteño Tejano legacies.* Oxford University Press.

Cabunoc, K. R. (2022). El Tallercito de Son SATX: Creando Comunidad A Través de la Cultura. In M. Cervantes & L. Saldaña (Eds.), *Entre El Sur y el Norte: Decolonizing education through critical readings of Chicana/x/o, Mexican, and indigenous music* (pp. 67–91). Peter Lang.

Calvo, L., & Esquibel, C. R. (2015). *Decolonize your diet: Plant-based Mexican-American recipes for health and healing.* Arsenal Pulp Press.

Dominguez, M. (2017). "Se Hace Puentes al Andar" decolonial teacher education as a needed bridge to culturally sustaining and revitalizing pedagogies. In D. Paris & H. S. Alim (Eds.), *Culturally sustaining pedagogies: Teaching and learning for justice in a changing world* (pp. 225–245). Teachers College Press.

Figueroa-Vásquez, Y. C. (2020). *Decolonizing diasporas: Radical mappings of Afro-Atlantic literature.* Northwestern University Press.

Gonzalez, M. (2018). Decolonizing Chican@ studies to Rehumanize Xican@ Youth through indigenous pedagogies. In F. López (Ed.), *Asset pedagogies in Latino youth identity and achievement: Nurturing confianza* (pp. 121–134). Routledge.

Gonzalez, M. (2020). *Chican@ Artivistas: Music, community, and transborder tactics in East Los Angeles.* University of Texas Press.

Grosfuguel, R. (2010). The epistemic decolonial turn: Beyond political-economy paradigms. In W. D. Mignolo & A. Escobar (Eds.), *Globalization and the decolonial option* (pp. 65-77). Routledge.

Habell-Pallán, M. (2005). *Loca motion the travels of Chicana and Latina popular culture.* New York University Press.

Hernández, O.J. (2022). "Has Algo": Reading and writing in a Chicanx Punk pedagogy. In M. Cervantes & L. Saldaña (Eds.), *Entre El Sur y el Norte: Decolonizing education through critical readings of Chicana/x/o, Mexican, and indigenous music* (pp. 199-221). Peter Lang.

Herrera-Sobek, M. (1990). *The Mexican corrido: A feminist analysis.* Indiana University Press.

Johnson, G. (2013). *Spaces of conflict, sounds of solidarity music, race, and spatial entitlement in Los Angeles.* University of California Press.

Limón, J. E. (1992). *Mexican Ballads, Chicano poems history and influence in Mexican-American social poetry.* University of California Press.

Macias, A. (2008). *Mexican American Mojo popular music, dance, and urban culture in Los Angeles, 1935–1968.* Duke University Press.

Maldonado-Torres, N. (2011). Thinking through the decolonial turn: Post-continental interventions in theory, philosophy, and critique—an introduction. *Transmodernity: Journal of Peripheral Cultural Production of the Luso-Hispanic World, 1*(2).

Mignolo, W. D. (2011). *The darker side of western modernity: Global futures, decolonial options.* Duke University Press.

Mignolo, W. D., & Escobar, A. (Eds.). (2010). *Globalization and the decolonial option.* Routledge.

Paredes, A. (1958). *With his pistol in his hand: A border ballad and its hero.* University of Texas Press.

Paris, D., & Alim, H. S. (Eds.). (2017). *Culturally sustaining pedagogies: Teaching and learning for justice in a changing world.* Teachers College Press.

Peña, M. (1985). *The Texas-Mexican Conjunto: History of a working-class music.* University of Texas Press.

Pérez, E. (1999). *Decolonial imaginary: Writing Chicanas into history.* Indiana University Press.

Quijano, A. (2000). Coloniality of power, Eurocentrism, and Latin America. *Nepantla: Views from South, 1*(3), 533–580.

Rodriguez, I. (2022). Decolonizing, healing and evoking resistance through music: Crossing ideological and colonial borders using transmedia and experiential educational approaches. In M. Cervantes & L. Saldaña (Eds.), *Entre El Sur y el Norte: Decolonizing education through critical readings of Chicana/x/o, Mexican, and Indigenous music* (pp. 93-111). Peter Lang.

Rodriguez, R. C. (2014). *Our sacred maíz is our mother: Indigeneity and belonging in the Americas.* University of Arizona Press.

Saldívar, J. D. (2010). Unsettling race, coloniality, and caste: Anzaldúa's *Borderlands/La Frontera*, Martinez's *Parrot in the Oven*, and Roy's *The God of small things*. In W. D. Mignolo & A. Escobar (Eds.), *Globalization and the decolonial option* (pp. 193-221). Routledge.

Saldívar, R. (2006). *The borderlands of culture: Américo Paredes and the transnational imaginary.* Duke University Press.

Sandoval, C. (2000). *Methodology of the oppressed.* University of Minnesota Press.

Santos, B. S. (2014). *Epistemologies of the south: Justice against epistemicide.* Routledge.

Smith, L. T. (2012). *Decolonizing methodologies: Research and indigenous peoples* (2nd ed.). Chicago, IL: Zed Books.

Stanton, B. (2018). Musicking in the borders toward decolonizing methodologies. *Philosophy of Music Education Review, 26*(1), 4–23.

Steptoe, T. (2015). *Houston bound culture and color in a Jim Crow City.* University of California Press.

Tejeda, J., & Valdez, A. (Eds.). (2001). *¡Puro Conjunto! An album in words and pictures.* University of Texas Press.

Tuck, Y., & Yang, K. W. (2012). Decolonization is not a metaphor. *Decolonization: Indigeneity, Education & Society, 1*(1), 1–40.

Vargas, D. (2012). *Dissonant Divas in Chicana music: The limits of La Onda.* University of Minnesota Press.

Walker, M. E. (2020). Towards a decolonized music history curriculum. *Journal of Music History Pedagogy, 10*(1), 1–19.

Zavala, M. (2018). *Raza struggle and the movement for ethnic studies: Decolonial pedagogies, literacies, and methodologies.* Peter Lang.

Transborder Movements

Mujeres Del Viento Florido: First Transborder Gathering of Indigenous Women Musicians in Santa María Tlahuitoltepec, Mixe Oaxaca

Xóchitl Chávez and Mercedes Alejandra Payán Ramírez

This essay uses a combination of decolonizing frameworks developed by Indigenous and Chicana/Mexicana scholars in Mexico and Greater Mexico. Decolonizing is "a long-term process involving the bureaucratic, cultural, linguistic and psychological divesting of colonial power" (Smith [1999] 2008: 98). In this collaborative transborder gathering and analysis, we utilize the frameworks of *Comunalidad* (Martínez, 2003; Díaz, 2004; Aquino, 2013), *Sincere Collaborative Intention* (Chávez, forthcoming), and *Collective Songwriting* (Gonzalez, 2014), as a methodology and lens of analysis that speaks to the process of how the First Transborder Gathering of Indigenous Women Musicians in Santa María Tlahuitoltepec Mixe, Oaxaca took place in August of 2018. We take up the call of decolonizing ethnomusicology and music education through a collaboration between Indigenous band directors and academics from the Mexican state of Oaxaca, Mexico City, and in California.

Esta colaboración fue creada para restablecer los vínculos entre las mujeres integrantes de la banda, para que se reconocieran como pares y crear espacios de identificación entre ellas, pues de esa forma tendrán las herramientas necesarias para darle continuidad a la banda femenil. As co-authors, we have also decided to make this article bilingual, where we linguistically code switch, para abrir el acceso a nuestras colaboradoras a conocer el resultado del encuentro en términos de la producción académica. Additionally, by including both languages, our paper also becomes an act of resistance against English being the hegemonic language in academia (Anzaldúa, 1987; García, 1993;

Perissinoto, 2003; Poblete, 2003; Chavez, 2012; Zentella, 2017; Holguín Mendoza, in press).

The aim of the collaboration among Indigenous female brass band musicians and activist scholars who employ a feminist decolonial Indigenous approach in Oaxaca, México and Los Angeles, California is threefold: (1) it acknowledges women musicians in traditionally male dominated Oaxacan bass brands; (2) challenges a colonial logics by documenting these decolonial efforts and discussions during a three-day retreat among Indigenous women from Oaxaca; and (3) engages Indigenous worldviews and everyday practices. Lastly, the chapter closes by addressing how Indigenous women musicians have continued to maintain these networks and collaborative efforts across international borders. Before proceeding to the theoretical conversation, it is imperative to first present the women musicians and collaborators that organized the First Transborder Gathering of Indigenous Women Musicians in Santa María Tlahuitoltepec Mixe, Oaxaca.

Quiénes son las Mujeres del Viento Florido?

Directora y Maestra Leticia Gallardo es la directora y fundadora de la banda filarmónica Mujeres del Viento Florido. Es oriunda de Santa María Tlahuitoltepec Mixe, Oaxaca y su formación musical comenzó desde temprana edad motivada por su padre, quien también fue músico. Apoyada por su familia, realizó sus estudios musicales de clarinete en el Centro de Capacitación Musical y Desarrollo de la Cultura Mixe[1] y posteriormente de violoncello en la Escuela de Música Vida y Movimiento del Centro Cultural Ollin Yoliztli de la Ciudad de México. En 2016 concluyó la Licenciatura en Artes en el Instituto Multidisciplinario de Especialización en la Ciudad de Oaxaca, demostrando su interés por la formación continua en lo que toca a su educación artística. Cuenta con más de treinta años de experiencia en la música. Realizó también estudios para ser educadora bilingüe de Español y Mixe a nivel preescolar y tiene una larga trayectoria en el ámbito de la educación. Es además madre soltera de dos hijos adolescentes[2], una mujer y un hombre, quienes siguen sus pasos en el ámbito de la formación musical profesional. Como directora ha participado en diversos encuentros y diálogos con otros directores de banda, en su totalidad hombres, de distintas partes de la Sierra Norte de Oaxaca para discutir en torno al rumbo de las bandas filarmónicas de esa región, así como para sistematizar sus estrategias de enseñanza y aprendizaje en el contexto de los pueblos que conservan un gobierno regido por el proyecto civilizatorio comunal.

En 2006, Leticia Gallardo fundó la banda filarmónica Mujeres del Viento Florido con integrantes de Santa María Tlahuitoltepec Mixe y alcanzó reconocimiento a nivel municipal en el 2009. Poco a poco esta banda comenzó a integrar a mujeres músicos de diversos pueblos de la Sierra Juárez de Oaxaca, del lado Zapoteco, y de esta forma empezó a convertirse en una banda intercultural y multilingüe. En diciembre de 2013 realizó su primera producción discográfica con la Banda Filarmónica Femenil "Mujeres del Viento Florido," posicionando a la banda femenil en el ámbito de los músicos que han dejado registro de su trabajo como agrupación[3].

La directora y maestra Leticia Gallardo es quien realizó la convocatoria para el First Transborder Gathering of Indigenous Women Musician in Santa María Tlahuitoltepec Mixe, Oaxaca, construyendo un vínculo entre las mujeres músicos y académicas Mexico-Americanas Directora Jessica Hernández y la Doctora Xóchitl Chávez, y las mujeres músicos indígenas de Oaxaca y la Maestra Mercedes Payán desde la Ciudad de México.

Maestras y Participantes

Las maestras que asistieron al First Transborder Gathering of Indigenous Women Musicians in Santa María Tlahuitoltepec Mixe, Oaxaca son Alejandra Allende y Belén Vázquez de Villa Hidalgo Yalálag, ubicado en la parte Zapoteca de la Sierra Juárez de Oaxaca; Nataly Luis de San Antonio Cuajimoloyas también Zapoteca; Flor Chávez y Alba Martínez de San Pedro y San Pablo Ayutla Mixe y Verónica Bautista de Santa María Tlahuitoltepec Mixe, estas tres últimas en la Sierra Norte. Una de ellas se ha desarrollado como compositora, otra funge como directora de banda filarmónica, otras son maestras de instrumento y otras tantas se desempeñan como maestras de lenguaje musical y solfeo, además de integrar la banda Mujeres del Viento Florido.

Respecto a las participantes del encuentro, asistieron las estudiantes de las distintas maestras antes mencionadas originarias de los Valles Centrales del estado de Oaxaca, de Santiago Juxtlahuaca, en la Sierra Juárez de Oaxaca en la parte Zapoteca, de Santa María Tlahuitoltepec y San Pedro y San Pablo Ayutla, ubicados en la Sierra Norte, en la región Mixe. Sus edades varían de los 10 a los 30 años de edad y todas son parte de bandas municipales en sus lugares de origen además de ser integrantes de la banda filarmónica Mujeres del Viento Florido.

Directora y Maestra Jessica Hernández

Director Jessica Hernández was born in Los Angeles County and raised during the first generation of Oaxacan brass bands (1990s) in southern California. By the age of 10, Jessica began learning music in the public school system. In 2001, she, along with other second-generation youth, began taking *solfeo* (music theory) lessons from her uncle Moises Hernández and father Porfirio Hernández as the community prepared to debut the youth band between the ages of 5–14, *Banda Nueva Dinastía de Zoochila*. The purpose of forming this band was twofold: to keep the youth away from street violence in local neighborhoods and to teach them about the music and culture of their native pueblo in Oaxaca. After three years of learning music, Banda Nueva Dinastía de Zoochila made its grand debut on May 22, 2004. Director Jessica continued to pursue music seriously as a clarinetist and earned an undergraduate degree from the Department of Music at the University of California, Riverside, with a specialization in directing. During her undergraduate studies, she became the director of Banda Nueva Dinastía de Zoochila. Throughout the past decade, Jessica has traveled to Oaxaca to work and collaborate with numerous recognized music directors from Oaxaca.

Director Jessica holds three significant accolades as she is the first female and youngest Oaxacan band director born in the United States, as well as the first person (male or female) of Oaxacan heritage to hold a degree in music from a university in California (UC Riverside, 2010)[4]. The band is often called the soul of the *pueblo* (village) by one of its co-founders as they provide a special joy and energy in the celebrations they attend. Under the Hernández family leadership and with community support, Banda Nueva Dinastía de Zoochila recorded their first album in 2011 titled "Zoochila Vive en mi Corazón" and have returned to Santiago Zoochila, Oaxaca, on three occasions to participate in the cooperative efforts towards the community's patron saint celebration and play alongside other neighboring Zapotec community bands.

Our Positioning as Norteña Scholars Collaborators

The heart of this work deals with processes, practices and notions of power relations, self-definition, hierarchies, status, homogenization, and classification. "We," as co-authors, exercised great care and cultural humility of our voices throughout the writing process of the essay (and during the production of the First Transborder Gathering of Indigenous Women Musicians in

Santa María Tlahuitoltepec Mixe, Oaxaca). As musicians and scholar activists, Mercedes Payán has closely collaborated with two bands in the Mixe communities in the Sierra Norte region, while Xóchitl Chávez has collaborated in a transborder manner with three Zapotec bands from the Sierra Juárez region in Oaxaca and the corresponding migrant organized bands in Los Angeles, California[5]. In order to carry out this research and gathering, we practiced a methodology of "sincere collaborative intention" (Chávez, forthcoming) where each author has fostered a longstanding accompaniment[6] with Indigenous philharmonic community-based bands since 2014. Sincere Collaborative Intention is substantially more than participant observation. We draw from principles in Chicana Feminist Theory such as Trinidad Galvan's concept of *convivencia* (2018, p. 12) and Critical Race Feminista Methodology by Delgado Bernal, Pérez Huber, and Malagón (2018), where collaborators build social relations that are based on living, working, and learning from one another. Additionally, in this context, traditional research power dynamics are broken down. Through our own lived experiences, we add a commitment to the practice of being present, staying attuned to cultural and community protocols, actively showing up, sincere listening, respectfully assisting with community needs, and witnessing everyday life in México and in their new locations of residency. Throughout this work, we practiced an awareness of the process of how knowledge is produced and represented within community and academia. As decolonial ethnomusicologists, we resisted speaking as an authority for a community.

We acknowledge our positionality and the power relations that exist as both authors had the privilege of obtaining advanced degrees from universities in the United States and México. At this moment, we as *Norteñas*, women with northern Mexican roots from the state of Chihuahua, believe it is important to note how we positioned ourselves and how we approached this research as we did before leading workshops in Oaxaca. We write this to reflect our own subjectivity about the why and how of our own participation in this research. Following Andrea Olivera's call to "experience field work as an encounter where new unexpected questions arise about [our] ideas about [our] practices, about [oneself], that allows [one] to build reflection tools" (Olivera, 2014, p. 139) we offer our stories.

Xóchitl's Story

As I embrace my own complex social location within academia, I make it certain to introduce myself as a Rocky Mountain Chicana who grew up in a bilingual and bicultural home where my family and I attended Native American

Pow-Wows across Colorado and New Mexico with my maternal family members and traveled to the sierra village in Chihuahua, Mexico, where my father was born to participate in *fiestas* and *jaripeos*. In driving to these community celebrations, each parent would take turns to recount historical facts, share stories of the social circumstances about the people in the region, and at times share cautionary tales of brujas or other unexplainable occurrences. Little did I know, that at a young age, I would also join in this conversation of cultural storytelling through performance as a Mexican folk dancer and playing the alto saxophone. Never knowing what type of impact my story may have within academic and public settings, I reinforce the fact that community members are also theorists and should always have a place at the table in creating bodies of knowledge and archives where they may articulate how they understand their social location and express their processes of cultural identity. Women's contribution to music has historically been overshadowed or simply omitted in academic text and popular narrative. Taking seriously Sherrie Tucker's notion for "engaged listening" of women musicians, I focus on Zapotec migrant women's experiences as musicians to address the formation of brass bands and the ways they negotiate the challenges they encounter in brass bands. It is through their localized articulations, voiced or played, that women establish a dialogue across the region of Oaxacalifornia (Chávez, 2017). Our deep listening practice breaks these silences and omissions inviting Indigenous musicians to voice their stories and be part of the contemporary processes of documentation.

Mercedes' Story

Mis intereses en los ensambles de bandas de viento se remontan a mi niñez, en la que yo misma fui parte de una banda en mi ciudad natal Chihuahua, Chihuahua, México. Las memorias más importantes de esta etapa de mi vida son las que se relacionan con ensayos, presentaciones, viajes y encuentros nacionales para niños y jóvenes miembros de este tipo de agrupaciones, acompañada de amigos y de mi hermano. Más tarde, comencé a prepararme profesionalmente como flautista en distintas instituciones como la Universidad Autónoma de Chihuahua, la Universidad Veracruzana y la Universidad Nacional Autónoma de México, finalizando estudios de licenciatura educación musical en la Universidad Veracruzana y licenciatura de flauta y de maestría en etnomusicología en la Universidad Nacional Autónoma de México. Estos son mis referentes personales y las lentes mediante las cuales observo en primera instancia el fenómeno musical. Considero importante mencionarlo porque mi análisis, colaboración y participación en esta investigación está fuertemente influido por mis experiencias personales en el campo de la música y el entrenamiento educativo que he recibido. He atestiguado de cerca, desde mi iniciación hasta mi profesionalización como flautista, educadora y etnomusicóloga, algunas realidades en torno a las ocasiones musicales, clases, el trabajo en ensambles, la oralidad y la lectoescritura musical, repertorios, así como las experiencias de otras personas en relación con la mía dentro de estas actividades. Es desde esta posición que trato de deconstruir mis ideas y prácticas para trabajar colaborativamente con las Mujeres del Viento Florido, para reconocernos en nuestras diferencias y encontrarnos en las vivencias en común.

En mi trabajo como etnomusicóloga incorporo las ideas de la decolonialidad como una perspectiva teórica y también como una manera de colaborar con las personas con las que he trabajado. Al reflexionar sobre mi propia posición como investigadora me he encontrado con la necesidad de transitar un camino de deconstrucción de las prácticas académicas tradicionales, donde los conocimientos y saberes tanto de quienes investigamos como de las personas con las que trabajamos pueden ser jerárquicas. Ese camino me ha llevado a renunciar a esa jerarquía y poner en su lugar el diálogo y la negociación, evitando la imposición que puede emanar de mi formación profesional como música, docente y académica.

We have tried to collaborate and interpret the texts and ethnographic data, including conversations with people whom we engaged with in the workshops with the women members of the Mujeres del Viento Florido and our observations of musical occasions. We have tried to continuously confront our own understanding of music, wind band ensembles, the complex reality of Indigenous women in Mexico, the importance of collectivity, music education and society. Additionally, adhering to the decolonial thinking that Olivera (2014) uses, and because we can see that the construction of knowledge in any investigation about processes of socialization of musical knowledge from our position could be tremendously hegemonic and asymmetric, we have tried to deconstruct our own ideas about what being a musician, music educator, academic, ethnomusicologist and woman is, thus letting the "ecology of knowledge" of Boaventura de Sousa Santos (2010) resonate in our work. El concepto de "ecología de saberes" es una propuesta teórica que acepta y demanda la necesidad de coexistencia de conocimientos de distintos orígenes geopolíticos y sus estratos sociales, de modo que el conocimiento científico occidental no se coloque por encima de otras fuentes de ser y saber el mundo. Afirma que la relación entre todo tipo de conocimiento debe ser de diálogo e intercambio epistemológico e intercultural, para que puedan reforzarse mutuamente y no pongan en peligro su existencia, llevándolos al epistemicidio masivo y la pérdida de la valiosa diversidad que hay en materia de habitar y conocer el mundo.

The Emergence of a Transborder Collaboration

In March of 2015, a delegation of eight Oaxacan band directors representing various Indigenous philharmonic bands traveled to Los Angeles, California for a week-long music exchange with first and second generation Oaxacan migrant community bands. The gathering was coordinated by the Los Angeles County Mexican Consulate and the hometown association, Oaxaca Regional Organization. Traditionally, Oaxacan philharmonic bands are male dominant. However, out of this delegation of band directors, one Indigenous woman director was invited, Maestra Leticia Gallardo Martínez (Mixe). Among the invited advanced youth musicians and directors, Maestra Jessica Hernández (Zapotec) and Maestra Yulissa Maqueos (Zapotec) were two of the second-generation women encouraged to participate in this historic musical exchange.

Figure 2.1: SEQ Fotografía*ARABIC 1 Directora y Maestra Leticia Gallardo en su viaje a Los Ángeles, California en el 2015. Source: Xóchitl Chávez

Dr. Xóchitl Chávez, who has a long-standing relationship with the California Oaxacan migrant community, was invited to attend as an observer of the workshops. Noting the gendered dynamics and hierarchies placed by the coordinating entities, the three Maestras Leticia, Jessica, Yulissa, and I quickly gravitated to each other during the short breaks to chat and share reflections about the music workshops. Recognizing the need for a safe place for the women to speak openly, Xóchitl invited the Maestras to dinner after our third day of the workshop meetings. Excited by the idea of having a women musicians' dinner, Yulissa quickly suggested her favorite restaurant, a Korean barbeque location in the heart of what has become known as "Oaxacatown" (Koreatown) for the first *convivio*, informal gathering of women musicians. Over the sizzling sound and smells of vegetables and meat, a dialogue began among the women musicians about the need to create networks of support, even despite geopolitical borders and migratory status, and how they could begin to avoid duplicating hierarchical practices and power dynamics within their respective community bands. The outcome of this dinner meeting was an agreement to organize an all-woman masterclass retreat in Oaxaca and foster a bond of peer mentorship where we collectively maintained almost monthly check-ins via cellular calls and, when possible, with the Los Angeles based women, meetings to break bread and touch base with one another.

Exactly three years later, in March of 2018, Maestra Leticia wrote to Xóchitl:

ML: "*Buenos días* Xóchitl, we have to continue to create the conditions so in the near future young Oaxacan female musicians like Maestras Jessica and Yulissa can share their experiences in some sort of workshop and musical exchange with other Indigenous women musicians."

XCH: "*Maestra Leticia, habla Xóchitl*. I was able to secure funding for a summer research trip to Mexico and will be able to bring along two women ethnomusicologist graduate students to help! Maestra Jessica Hernández will be in Oaxaca as well for her community's patron saint festival."

ML: "This is perfect timing – come to Tlahuitoltepec. Our band, *Mujeres del Viento Florido*, will be playing at one of the opening concerts under the famous Laurel Tree for the Guelaguetza festival in Oaxaca City. After the concert, we will travel together on the bus to the sierra Mixe and have the first Indigenous woman three-day retreat at *Centro de Capacitación Musical y Desarrollo de la Cultura Mixe*."

Held from on July 30 to August 1st, the *Primer Encuentro de Mujeres Músicos del Estado de Oaxaca*, was the first three-day master class workshop of Indigenous women musicians in the State of Oaxaca organized through the transborder collaboration of Director Leticia Gallardo-Martinez, Dr. Xóchitl C. Chávez (UC Riverside Music Professor), Maestra Jessica Hernandez (Los Angeles' first Zapotec female director), and Maestra Mercedes Payán (Music Educator)[7]. In total, forty Indigenous women primarily Zapotec and Mixe representing ten ethnolinguistic communities across Oaxaca gathered to participate in workshops. This gathering was based on the need to address patriarchal norms and colonial logics of hierarchies and toxic competition among women observed by Maestra Leticia Gallardo. The transborder collaboration in creating the thematic workshop took into consideration these suggestions and collectively created the workshops by women musicians and for women musicians and for women musicians. This encounter illustrates the origin story of our transborder collaboration among Indigenous female brass band musicians and activist scholars in Oaxaca and Los Angeles, California. A continuación, hablaremos del marco teórico a partir del cual analizamos y dialogamos con las prácticas decoloniales que estas mujeres activaron durante el *Primer Encuentro de Mujeres Músicos del Estado de Oaxaca*.

Music and Decoloniality

In this research, we have examined the work of Latin American decolonial scholars from the fields of anthropology and music to center their arguments and give coherence to our work which has generated a dialogue between the women of Mujeres Del Viento Florido, their ways of producing knowledge and *musicking*, and our academic peers who share their geography and research about the colonial process in music. Hemos retomado algunos conceptos de estos académicos de México, Costa Rica, Colombia y Argentina para mantener un intercambio de conocimientos en torno a lo decolonial de manera transfronteriza y para sumarnos al bloque académico del "sur colonizado" frente al "norte colonizador". En este sentido, la inflexión decolonial persigue no sólo problematizar la colonialidad del saber occidental y sus narrativas, sino también hace visibles los diálogos entre la diversidad de conocimientos originados desde la diferencia colonial, para hacer un contrapeso a los diseños universalizantes producidos desde una supuesta globalidad epistemológica, que en realidad consiste en darle crédito únicamente a las ontologías y epistemologías de Europa occidental (Maldonado-Torres, 2007; Mignolo, 2007; Quijano, 2014).

El primer concepto que nos ayuda a pensar las dinámicas en torno a las que se organizan las Mujeres del Viento Florido es el de la comunalidad o las comunalidades. Las comunalidades son la diversidad de formas de socialidad que se rigen bajo un proyecto civilizatorio comunal en oposición a un proyecto civilizatorio moderno-capitalista, entendiendo que éste pertenece a la lógica colonial. Las comunalidades tienen su origen en las comunidades indígenas oaxaqueñas y su teorización y conceptualización se enuncia en la década de 1980 entre los intelectuales orgánicos Floriberto Díaz (2004), mixe de Santa María Tlahuitoltepec, y Jaime Martínez (2003), zapoteco de Guelatao. Estos autores elaboran su teoría basados en los análisis y reflexiones alrededor de las maneras en que sus pueblos se organizan, en términos de sus propias formas de gobierno y de reproducción de la vida, que han emergido por lo menos desde la conquista como una forma de resistir al estado colonial, y que conforman sus propias redes y formas de interacción interna. Por otra parte, esta propuesta se planta como una forma de autodeterminación y autogobierno que responde a las políticas neoliberales que el estado mexicano ejerce sobre este tipo de sociedades.

Las discusiones sobre la comunalidad por parte de sus autores llevan consigo procesos de descubrimiento y sistematización del conocimiento que los pueblos indígenas tienen sobre sí mismos, así como el reconocimiento de las relaciones coloniales y neocoloniales que se han mantenido desde la llegada de los europeos a las Américas y posteriormente con el sostenimiento de la dominación por parte del estado mexicano. En este sentido, y siguiendo a Alejandra Aquino (2013), se puede observar a las comunalidades en su potencia de Epistemologías del Sur, donde se reposiciona el pensamiento y ser de las sociedades indígenas y con ello se recupera la agencia que estos pueblos tienen en relación con la toma de decisiones dentro de su mundo y fuera de él, así como la permanencia y adecuación de las prácticas y saberes que requieren para dar continuidad a su existencia comunal.

Las Mujeres del Viento Florido pertenecen a este contexto socio-político. Las integrantes de la banda viven en este tipo de pueblos donde el proyecto civilizatorio comunal se ha desarrollado como forma de combatir la colonialidad y, por lo tanto, participan de él. Las prácticas y saberes de la comunalidad que implican con mayor énfasis a las bandas filarmónicas, y donde participan las Mujeres del Viento Florido, son las del tequio[8], correspondencia o ayuda comunal y la de la fiesta o el goce comunal (Díaz, 2004). En la primera se demanda un servicio gratuito que cada miembro de las comunidades regidas por este Sistema Normativo Interno y que, en el caso de los integrantes de una banda, consiste en tocar en los eventos tanto civiles como religiosos en los que es requerida la música en vivo. En la segunda el papel de la banda es fundamental, pues no hay fiesta sin música de banda, de modo que a nivel interno de cada pueblo es fundamental contar con una agrupación que cumpla esta función. Una tarea extendida y combinada del tequio, correspondencia o ayuda comunal y del ámbito de la fiesta o el goce comunal es el circuito de "préstamo" de bandas, donde a nivel interregional las bandas cumplen la función de tocar en las fiestas de los pueblos vecinos, a cambio de que cuando ellos mismos tengan su fiesta les será "prestada" una banda vecina para acompañarla (Payán, 2017).

En un contexto en el que estas agrupaciones han sido conformadas, dirigidas y cuyo repertorio es compuesto principalmente por hombres, las mujeres músicos revierten el orden establecido y comienzan a tomar roles antes negados para ellas, pues esta situación da "cuenta de una situación de cambio, un ʽmomento de contestación՚ en el que entra en conflicto en el orden representacional" (Alegre, 2015, p. 133) al que han estado sometidas en la colonialidad y patriarcado local. Estas mujeres no sólo han asumido la tarea de consolidar de una banda femenil, sino que también han fungido como semillero de otras bandas de mujeres y, si bien, siguen enfrentando desafíos para legitimarse en un ambiente masculino, han logrado tejer una red de apoyo y trabajo para continuar participando en el universo musical de sus comunidades y representando a nivel regional la presencia femenina a través de la banda Mujeres Del Viento Florido.

Durante los talleres pudimos observar que esta banda agrupa a directoras de distintas bandas, maestras de instrumento y lenguaje musical, así como compositoras de nuevo repertorio que pertenecen a distintas partes del estado de Oaxaca. Respecto a este tema, percibimos que consiste en una confrontación que estas mujeres hacen a la lógica colonial (Mignolo, 2010), entendida esta como una forma en que la colonialidad comprende los Estados-nación, el conocimiento, las narrativas, las ontologías y el poder desde de la totalidad y la homogeneidad (Rosabal-Coto, 2013 y 2016), impidiendo ver una realidad social diversa y llena de interrelaciones. La banda Mujeres del Viento Florido se conforma de una multiplicidad de identidades etnolingüísticas y su consolidación abona al contraflujo respecto a la narrativa totalitaria y la ontología homogeneizante de la colonialidad.

A manera de resolver simbólicamente el conflicto de la hegemonía del repertorio (Hernández, 2007) y del modelo educativo de Europa occidental (Holguín, 2017), las bandas filarmónicas como la de las Mujeres del Viento Florido incluyen en su repertorio tanto piezas musicales de la tradición académica europea como de su propia tradición regional. El balance de la aparición de las distintas piezas en las ocasiones musicales que protagonizan estos ensambles es considerable y se podría decir que mantienen un diálogo intercultural horizontal. El repertorio tradicional que tocan las bandas de la región mixe y zapoteca se puede clasificar por el grado de dificultad, de lo simple a lo complejo, por contexto en lo relativo a lo humano, lo divino y las audiciones y según las ocasiones musicales a las que correspondan los distintos tipos de formas musicales que se interpretan. Como formas musicales dominantes, el son y jarabe tienen una presencia enorme en las ocasiones musicales. Es importante decir que estos géneros musicales se aprenden, enseñan y producen desde la oralidad a la hora de ser aprendidos de "oído" e interpretados de memoria. Respecto a su ejecución en público y el orden en el que aparecen los distintos sones y jarabes, esto dependerá de la cantidad de instrumentistas que asistan a las presentaciones de la banda, así como de las decisiones que se tomen durante las ocasiones musicales.

En una suerte de diálogo entre las tradiciones orales y las de la lectoescritura musical, Payán (2017) anota que:

> El repertorio que corresponde a danzas, valses, boleros, marchas animadas, pasodobles, chotises, polcas, fantasías clásicas, oberturas, fragmentos sinfónicos, piezas para *big band* de *jazz* y *fox-trot* está fuertemente ligado a la lectoescritura musical (...). Por otra parte, estos géneros aparecen únicamente en las ocasiones musicales que consisten en audiciones de concierto y competencias. Normalmente son arreglos especiales de música escrita originalmente para orquesta sinfónica y que se adaptan a la instrumentación de la banda de música. La mayoría son escritos por compositores europeos, aunque en lo que respecta a las marchas, pasodobles y fox-trot también son escritos no sólo por compositores mexicanos, sino músicos mixes (p. 77–78).

Aquí nos gustaría apuntar que, a diferencia de lo que se puede pensar desde las visiones esencialistas, la música indígena en el estado de Oaxaca no se limita a las dotaciones instrumentales de pito y tambor de supuesta raigambre prehispánica. Los complejos procesos de colonización han hecho que estos pueblos incorporen a sus prácticas rituales y festivas distintos tipos de dotaciones instrumentales resignificándolos, entre estos se encuentra la banda de viento.

Sergio Navarrete (2013) documenta la transición de las capillas de viento del siglo XVIII a las bandas de viento en un cuerpo filarmónico actuales. A través de las descripciones y hallazgos en los archivos de las capillas en Oaxaca de este autor, se puede percibir la relevancia que la enseñanza y aprendizaje de la música ha ocupado en la sociedad oaxaqueña desde esa época hasta nuestros días. Donde una organización principalmente gestionada y ostentada en un inicio "en manos de la iglesia por la incapacidad misma del Estado para proporcionar servicios educativos a la población rural" (Navarrete, 2013, p. 209) pasa a las manos de los distintos grupos indígenas que mantienen económicamente la estructura de la escoleta[9], la adquisición de instrumentos musicales y la contratación de maestros que enseñen lectura e interpretación musical. Si hacemos dialogar estas reflexiones con la *comunalidad* de los pueblos indígenas, encontraremos que:

El hecho de que en algunos pueblos se haya mantenido la corporatividad de la tierra comunal y esta se refleje en diferentes aspectos de su vida en comunidad permite lo que ahora se puede observar en el desarrollo de la música. Aunado a esto, "La enseñanza y la ejecución musical como parte de las obligaciones del músico con su pueblo han sostenido la tradición de las bandas hasta el presente en Oaxaca" (Navarrete, 2013, p. 331), dando continuidad a las prácticas mediante la asignación de cargos, ya que son músicos formados dentro de la escoleta los que eventualmente también la administran como Autoridades religiosas en la figura del Capillo, o bien, fungen como directores de la banda (Payán, 2017, p. 90–91).

Esto da testimonio de que una herramienta musical de apariencia colonial puede ser reapropiada y resignificada en un complejo entramado político, social y religioso. Asimismo, la lógica comunal de su modelo de aprendizaje rebasa las fronteras del aprendizaje basado en el modelo colonial, pues incorpora las actividades del servicio gratuito (tequio), el aprendizaje colaborativo y grupal y la lógica de la participación en los contextos festivos por encima de la competencia. Sin embargo, en el caso de las Mujeres del Viento Florido debido a su identidad etnolingüística y al hecho de ser mujeres, así como a los imaginarios creados en torno a los repertorios de sus pueblos que "obligan a las músicas tradicionales a debatirse entre la inclusión y la exclusión, el deseo y el rechazo" (Hernández, 2007, p. 56), se encuentran en la disputa para salir de la subalternidad en la que la colonialidad patriarcal las mantiene sumidas. De igual manera sostienen la batalla contra la hegemonía del modelo universitario de educación musical y sus estrategias, valores y categorías, pues no son inmunes a estas y son vulnerables a ser sometidas a la lógica colonial en tres aspectos fundamentales: el poder, el conocer y el ser (Castro-Gómez, 2007) como seres humanos y músicos.

El caso de las Mujeres del Viento Florido nos interesa en lo que toca a la educación musical porque pertenecen a un modelo en el que el aprendizaje ocurre en el marco de lo comunal y lo festivo (Gonnet, 2015), según las propias lógicas del proyecto civilizatorio al que se adhieren desde los distintos pueblos a los que pertenecen. Además, en su proceso de construcción de redes de trabajo y aprendizaje y en su capacidad organizativa a través de la enseñanza de mujeres para mujeres comienzan a establecer una pedagogía y genealogía de lo femenino en el contexto de las bandas filarmónicas en Oaxaca. Somos sensibles a lo que Sergio Navarrete Pellicer (2015) propone sobre un programa de educación musical profesional intercultural en Oaxaca que parta del análisis de las condiciones sociales que han hecho posible la sustentabilidad de la música tradicional en ese territorio y la potencia que tendrían al incorporarse en una relación de diálogo intercultural al interior de una institución universitaria. Este autor argumenta que la comunalidad (Díaz, 2001, 2004 y 2007), como concepto nacido desde la reflexión de los intelectuales orgánicos de los pueblos indígenas de Oaxaca y la sistematización de su organización comunal, sugiere la posibilidad de una educación decolonial que está en sintonía con los postulados de la ecología de saberes y las Epistemologías del Sur (Sousa, 2011), reflexión con la que estamos de acuerdo.

Hemos tratado de hacer dialogar los conceptos de algunos colegas que han estudiado la música a la luz de las reflexiones en torno a la comunalidad y a la decolonialidad con las formas en que las Mujeres del Viento Florido han llevado a cabo la integración de la banda femenil para entender el contexto de nuestra colaboración. Comprendemos la realidad de estas mujeres desde su identidad de mujeres músicos indígenas oaxaqueñas, compositoras, directoras y maestras en sus comunidades que se enfrentan a la colonialidad y los patriarcados locales en la ardua tarea de encontrar su propio lugar de locus enunciativo y de producción musical.

Queremos añadir a lo anterior nuestras reflexiones sobre el feminismo decolonial (Lugones, 2010) en diálogo con la situación de las Mujeres del Viento Florido, pues debido al caso que nos compete no podemos dejar de mencionar la necesidad de usar la lente teórica del feminismo para trabajar nuestro tema. Se puede afirmar que tradicionalmente las bandas han sido dirigidas e integradas por hombres y las Mujeres del Viento Florido son un ejemplo de la forma paulatina en que las mujeres han comenzado a entrar a esos espacios, para incluso conformar una banda integrada en su totalidad por mujeres. Tenemos que agregar que este fenómeno no ha estado exento de producir una serie de tensiones en sus diversos contextos por romper con los roles tradicionalmente asignados a su género. Los conflictos originados de esta situación son:

1. La disputa de las posiciones jerárquicas y formativas. A saber, los roles de director y directora, así como la posición de maestra o maestro de solfeo e instrumento. Donde pudimos conocer casos de hostigamiento, desplazamiento y desacreditación hacia el trabajo de las mujeres.
2. El menosprecio por el trabajo creativo de las mujeres en su rol de compositoras. Durante el trabajo de campo fuimos testigos de al menos un testimonio donde la desaprobación y menosprecio por el trabajo de una mujer como compositora llegó incluso a la censura, impidiendo que sus obras fueran tocadas por la banda a la que ella pertenece.
3. La competencia como intérpretes entre hombres y mujeres. En este caso la capacidad de la fuerza física de los hombres es la medida de

toda ejecución correcta de la música, por lo que las mujeres son tildadas de ser capaces de tocar al nivel de velocidad e intensidad que los hombres consiguen, o bien, se les acusa de no resistir las jornadas musicales que pueden durar hasta doce horas seguidas y extenderse desde tres a cinco días en los servicios e intercambios musicales de las bandas.
4. La competencia entre las mismas mujeres como pares. En este terreno nos fue externada la preocupación por la disputa de la que son parte las mujeres por los pocos espacios que han conseguido, así como la necesidad de construir lazos de sororidad para reconocerse como agentes que combaten la misma discriminación.
5. Conflictos con el rol de madre y músico. Aquí encontramos que muchas mujeres abandonan la música para dedicarse exclusivamente a la reproducción doméstica, pues su marido, su familia o la sociedad tiene mal visto que salgan del espacio doméstico.

Fue tomando en cuenta todos estos conflictos que fuimos convocadas por la Directora y Maestra Leticia Gallardo para colaborar a través de los talleres del First Transborder Gathering of Indigenous Women Musicians in Santa María Tlahuitoltepec Mixe, Oaxaca, y tratar de revertir la imagen que estas mujeres han tenido de sí mismas por tanto tiempo, la competencia insana que puede darse entre ellas para ser reemplazada por redes de solidaridad y apoyo entre ellas y, en suma, para reflexionar colectivamente sobre estos temas y buscar soluciones comunes entre todas. En la siguiente sección, describiremos las experiencias de los talleres y su orden de aparición en el First Transborder Gathering of Indigenous Women Musicians in Santa María Tlahuitoltepec Mixe, Oaxaca.

Workshops for the First Transborder Gathering of Indigenous Women Musicians

The drafting of the workshops took place months in advance based on conversations with Maestra Leticia about what were the needs of women musicians in Oaxaca. Likewise, workshop facilitators were consulted as to what type of skill sets and ideas they could share with participants. All workshops were held primarily in Spanish with moments in Mixe when in conversation with local community officials and volunteers. Through this collective assessment the following types of workshops were organized for the gathering of female musicians.

Workshop 1. Identity: Who Are We? How Do We Identify Ourselves in Five Cards?

Con este taller iniciamos el encuentro y consistió en elegir palabras clave con las que podíamos identificarnos. Con la finalidad de reflexionar sobre las identidades de las integrantes de la banda, comenzamos con una lluvia de ideas donde todas fuimos aportando los adjetivos que nos definieran mejor. Seleccionamos aquellos que nos parecían necesarios y los anotamos en un pizarrón colocado frente a la media luna en la que estábamos dispuestas. Las características más importantes con las que nos identificamos fueron: ser mujer, la lengua materna, ser músicos, el instrumento musical que interpretamos, ser madres, ser migrantes, ser interculturales, entre otras. Una vez que reunimos las palabras con las que podíamos describirnos e identificarnos, escogimos únicamente cinco y las anotamos en tarjetas de colores.

El siguiente paso fue reunirnos por equipos y compartir nuestras tarjetas con nuestras compañeras de equipo. Cada una explicó con orgullo por qué se identificaba con las palabras escritas en sus tarjetas y cuáles experiencias le habían llevado a escoger esas palabras para describirse. Después de eso, la Dra. Xóchitl Chávez nos pidió que rompiéramos una por una nuestras tarjetas hasta quedarnos con una sola que consideráramos la más importante en el presente. Todas nos sentimos interpeladas por este proceso pues simbólicamente estábamos desmembrando nuestra identidad. Durante el proceso, cada una iba socializando las razones por las cuales eliminaban las menos importantes, haciendo un ejercicio reflexivo de priorizar sus características, necesidades y emociones más importantes en ese momento. Compartir estas reflexiones nos permitió conectarnos entre nosotras y visibilizar los testimonios (Moraga y Anzaldúa, 2015) mujeres que normalmente están silenciados, una herramienta con la que podrían escucharse a sí mismas y que podría ayudarlas a inscribirse en una conversación más amplia sobre su práctica musical y la importancia que tiene en sus comunidades.

El proceso causó muchas emociones, algunas incluso se resistieron a romper sus tarjetas, en lugar de eso les arrancaban apenas una esquina y las iban guardando en sus cuadernos, como una forma de conservar esa característica de su identidad. Al final, se discutió grupalmente lo que habíamos sentido todas con el ejercicio y se expresó el por qué habíamos dejado el último papelito para definirnos. Esta actividad nos ayudó a tender un primer puente de comunicación y empatía, nos permitió establecer un espacio seguro para compartir nuestras experiencias y, lo más importante, nos orientó sobre cómo se perciben a sí mismas este grupo de mujeres.

Figure 2.2: SEQ Fotografía*ARABIC 2 Workshop 1. Identity. Source: Xóchitl Chávez

Workshop 2: Collective Song Writing

> A song as a sonic and literary manifestation is life's soundscape, a unique, cathartic memento as well as a powerful political tool. A song can also be an important historical text. A person's testimonio (testimony), life views, triumphs, aphorisms, and struggles can be expressed in song lyrics. In this way, song lyrics can transmit ways of knowing and theorizing about life. It can also be viewed as alternative ways of creating knowledge. When practiced in community, songwriting can be a powerful exercise in consensus building and collective knowledge production (Gonzalez, 2014).

In this gathering of Indigenous women musicians, all of the participants read and played music. However, when asked if anyone had written lyrics for a song individually or with others, silence filled the room. Collective songwriting does not require prior music knowledge. What it does ask is participation of everyone to come together, to share their experiences and concerns, "to build knowledge and empower each other through the production of a song" (Gonzalez, 2014). As one of the workshop activities focused on establishing a bond of solidarity among the women, Dr. Xóchitl Chávez followed the methodology of Collective Songwriting developed by her sister Rosa Marta Zarate in her collaboration with the EZLN, and further employed by Dr. Martha Gonzalez and Quetzal Flores.

The first workshop on identity helped to develop trust among the participants in discussing topics in regard to their experiences as women[10] in their communities and as musicians in traditionally all male bands. These topics generated further conversations where participants across all age groups and various communities began to see commonalities in their struggles as women and as musicians, thus allowing them to identify problematic situations in the group setting instead of holding these dilemmas as an individual. In this verbal creative process participants were able to establish a vocabulary to express themselves and contest patriarchal forms. Although Director Jessica Hernández and Xóchitl Chávez stood in front of the makeshift board helping to facilitate the initial conversation of themes for the song, they shifted to the role as scribes to write down the exact wording given by the participants. The younger women took the initiative in writing the chorus and the first couple of stanzas while the maestras supported the young in conversations to formulate a total of four stanzas.

Tocamos como mujer

A
Nos dijeron que no podemos
Y demostramos que sí
No tenemos que ser perfectas
Siempre daré lo mejor de mí

B
Agradecemos a las que abrieron el paso
Y a las que vendrán después
La ayuda que nos brindamos
Tocando juntas como mujer

Coro:
¿Que hacemos en una banda?
Tocamos como mujer
Tocamos con alegría
Tocamos con muchas ganas
¿Que hacemos en una banda?
Tocamos entre amigas
Tocamos con mucho amor
Con todo el corazón

C
Que nada ni nadie apague
Los sueños que tienes hoy
Que sea tu pista de vuelo
Y no de un mal aterrizaje

Figure 2.3: SEQ Fotografía*ARABIC 3 Proceso de composición colectiva de la letra de la canción "Tocamos como mujer." Source: Mercedes Alejandra Payán Ramírez

> D
> Vamos tejiendo redes
> De apoyo y fortaleza
> Abriendo nuevos caminos
> Repletos de música y letra

Después del trabajo colectivo de hacer la letra de la canción, bajo la iniciativa de las integrantes del taller, las participantes decidieron dividirse entre las que iban a ensayar la letra y la melodía de las que deseaban trabajar con el ritmo y la armonía que iban a llevar sus instrumentos musicales. Este intercambio fue muy interesante pues algunas de las participantes eran compositoras, mientras que otras eran intérpretes de sus instrumentos, y otras más directoras y maestras de lenguaje musical y solfeo, por lo que la composición colectiva se enriqueció con los aportes y habilidades de cada una de ellas.

Finalmente, se hizo un ensayo general de la canción dirigido por la Directora Jessica Hernández, se incorporaron percusiones y algunas maestras y estudiantes comenzaron a hacer pequeños arreglos instrumentales, dejando la tarea de hacer uno más completo posteriormente[11], señal de que estos encuentros tendrían continuidad en el futuro.

Workshop 3. Digital Storytelling and Ethnographic Interview

Durante este taller teórico-práctico impartido por la Dra. Xóchitl Chávez se revisaron dos módulos. El primero consistió en revisar aspectos teóricos y técnicos de las entrevistas etnográficas y su registro en medios digitales y el segundo se concentró en desarrollar las actividades prácticas.

Teoría y aspectos técnicos

En este módulo se hizo referencia a investigaciones en las que los propios sujetos de investigación llevan a cabo las entrevistas según sus propios intereses y necesidades. Asimismo, se realizó la muestra del equipo que las participantes podían usar para registrar foto, video y audio, que no fue más que el empleo de sus propios celulares y cámaras portátiles para tales propósitos. También se revisaron algunos aspectos técnicos sobre cómo tomar fotos y video tomando en cuenta el encuadre más favorecedor para tal tarea. Finalmente, se les animó a participar en este taller basado en la necesidad de que las mujeres cuenten y protagonicen sus propias historias, documentando sus experiencias con las herramientas que tengan a la mano.

Práctica

Después del módulo teórico comenzamos las actividades prácticas. Se dispuso de los equipos de celular de las participantes para que fueran las mismas estudiantes quienes hicieran las entrevistas a sus maestras. Para lograr las entrevistas, las participantes crearon un guion colectivo con seis preguntas centrales acerca de las trayectorias personales de las maestras como músicos, docentes y directoras de banda, así como los desafíos a los que se habían enfrentado por ser mujeres. Una vez terminado el guión, se dispusieron en siete equipos para entrevistar a las siete directoras y maestras que participaron en el encuentro y se distribuyeron por el espacio para hacer sus entrevistas sin ser interrumpidas por las demás. Algunas incorporaron instrumentos musicales a sus imágenes para que sus maestras tuvieran un elemento de identidad como mujeres músicos. Llegado el momento de grabar y ser entrevistadas se mostraron divertidas, simulando que estaban en una entrevista de noticiero televisivo, incorporando así el elemento lúdico que les permitiera participar con mayor fluidez.

Finalmente, reunimos todo el material para compartirlo entre todas y poder hacer una base de datos de modo que ellas tuvieran el control y el registro de sus colaboraciones. Percibimos este ejercicio como una forma en la que ellas pueden participar activamente en sus propios procesos y hacer de la documentación un trabajo compartido, en lugar de convertir el registro en un archivo exclusivo de las académicas.

Figure 2.4: SEQ Fotografía*ARABIC 4 Workshop 4. Conducting a band tips.
Source: Mercedes Alejandra Payán Ramírez

Workshop 4. Conducting a Band Tips

El taller teórico-práctico de dirección de banda fue impartido por la directora Jessica Hernández y fue dividido en dos momentos uno teórico y el otro práctico. Esta actividad consistió en ofrecer una serie de consejos y técnicas personales para la dirección de una banda filarmónica.

Teórico
Los principales puntos de la parte teórica consistieron en compartir la filosofía, teoría y las concepciones alrededor de la dirección de una banda por parte de la directora Jessica Hernández. También se mostraron algunas estrategias de preparación de la directora antes de llegar a trabajar con la banda, así como la técnica corporal para independizar las manos y lograr hacer las indicaciones de tiempo, matices y velocidades, así como para manejar los distintos tipos de compases de la música escrita.

Una sección fundamental de esta parte teórica consistió en los comentarios que añadió la directora Jessica Hernández sobre su propia experiencia en cuanto a la seguridad con la que recomienda enfrentarse a la dirección, así como el gran universo de estilos que pueden existir para dirigir según la persona que los desarrolle.

Práctico
En esta sección algunas participantes pasaron al frente para practicar y ser observadas por la directora Jessica Hernández, de manera que pudiera hacerles señalamientos y comentarios más individualizados. Para cumplir este objetivo la maestra llevó batutas para practicar y les dio recomendaciones para comprar su propia batuta. Les sugirió distintas actitudes que les ayudarían a desarrollar su estilo y seguridad, para enfrentarse tanto a la banda como al público y a sus colegas directores.

Closing: Collective Conversation – Reflection of the Workshop
Finalmente, el encuentro cerró con un convivio en el que compartimos algo de pan y jugo que llevamos entre la directora y maestra Leticia Gallardo y nosotras como talleristas. Se hicieron comentarios y reflexiones colectivas sobre las actividades, los sentimientos que despertaron los distintos momentos vividos y se expresó la intención de darle seguimiento a este encuentro en el futuro. Fue un espacio para que la emotividad se presentara y pudiéramos despedirnos.

Al abandonar el lugar que nos acogió durante todo el encuentro, recogimos las sillas, las mesas y todo el material que la Directora y Maestra Leticia Gallardo llevó para que se pudiera llevar a cabo el encuentro y lo trasladamos

Figure 2.5: SEQ Fotografía*ARABIC 5 Despedida del First Transborder Gathering of Indigenous Women Musician in Santa María Tlahuitoltepec Mixe, Oaxaca. Source: Miguel Angel Santiago Martinez

a su casa entre todas. Después de esto terminamos nuestro encuentro de la misma manera en que lo comenzamos, dialogando y compartiendo perspectivas sobre la necesidad de darle continuidad a estos encuentros e imaginando las maneras en que podríamos seguir trabajando juntas considerando las fronteras y distancias que nos separan y haciendo el compromiso de mantenernos en contacto a través de las redes sociales a las que tenemos acceso todas. Para ello creamos un espacio privado en Facebook donde hemos mantenido los vínculos e intercambiado reflexiones en torno a los múltiples procesos que se detonaron dentro del encuentro. En esta página continuamos afirmando y dando ánimo a sus logros musicales y actividades cotidianas.

Conclusiones: Reflexiones Finales

A la luz del marco teórico que integramos a la experiencia del First Transborder Gathering of Indigenous Women Musicians in Santa María Tlahuitoltepec Mixe, Oaxaca, interpretamos que este grupo de mujeres indígenas, a pesar de todos los obstáculos a los que se han enfrentado, han logrado construir un espacio para producir conocimiento de contestación a la colonialidad y a la lógica patriarcal entre sus pares desde las siguientes acciones: (1) al integrar una banda femenil, (2) cuando gestionan su participación como directoras, maestras y músicos en las bandas filarmónicas de las localidades a las que pertenecen, (3) al buscar posicionarse en distintos eventos musicales dentro de su región, (4) por formar parte del circuito de intercambio comunal de servicios musicales con los pueblos vecinos, y (5) al buscar alternativas para edificar formas otras para relacionarse entre mujeres y fortalecer su identidad y actividades musicales. Muestra de esto es lo que ocurrió en el First Transborder Gathering of Indigenous Women Musicians in Santa María Tlahuitoltepec Mixe, Oaxaca que fue organizado y provocado por la Directora y Maestra Leticia Gallardo, quien mediante su invitación a colaborar nos reunió a todas en torno a la discusión sobre cómo se vinculan las mujeres músicos de la banda y cuáles son sus aspiraciones y desafíos.

La reproducción que hacen de un sistema organizativo no centrado en una lógica capitalista, sino comunal, en el sentido de que siguen dándole continuidad al circuito de intercambio comunitario a través de la banda femenil, es uno de los aspectos más importantes en el que sostienen la resistencia ante la colonialidad. Asimismo, la interpretación de un repertorio equilibrado entre su tradición local y otras tradiciones musicales pone en práctica hasta cierto punto la ecología de saberes, al colocarlas en un mismo nivel de valor y en diálogo intercultural.

Así pues, encontramos que a través de los distintos talleres se pusieron sobre la mesa cuestiones que ellas ya llevan a la práctica y se lograron verbalizar y captar las experiencias que han tenido como mujeres en la música, las maneras que han encontrado de autodefinirse, así como expresar sus deseos y objetivos profesionales y musicales. Algo fundamental fue la búsqueda de puntos en común para despertar la empatía y la solidaridad entre ellas mismas, pues expresaron que se dieron cuenta de que tienen que hacer frente de manera colectiva a las dificultades con las que se encuentran como mujeres. La posibilidad de ver la coincidencia de sus narrativas como mujeres y el ejercicio de nombrar las emociones y relaciones sociales que dichas experiencias han producido, hizo evidente la necesidad y el compromiso de buscar una ruta de trabajo en común para darle solución a los obstáculos que se les presentan, tarea con la que finalmente despedimos el encuentro y ellas se comprometieron a consolidar.

Respecto a nuestra experiencia como académicas activistas y colaboradoras, hemos tratado de replantear y decolonizar nuestras propias prácticas académicas y nuestra visión sobre el lugar de los pueblos indígenas en el mundo contemporáneo a través de la colaboración entre mujeres. Atendimos a una lógica de Sincere Collaborative Intention y acompañamiento, pues el encuentro se llevó a cabo por petición de la Directora y Maestra Leticia Gallardo. Fue bajo sus sugerencias que surgieron los temas a trabajar, según las necesidades que ella había observado entre las integrantes de la banda. La elaboración del diseño de las actividades de los talleres fue en colaboración con la Directora Jessica Hernández, para asegurar la pertinencia en el contexto de las mujeres músicos indígenas. La formulación de la escritura académica estuvo basada en las consultas que hicimos con la Directora Jessica Hernández para realizar un contraste de nuestras impresiones con las de ella como participante activa del encuentro y balancear la voz que se escucha a través de este relato escrito. Finalmente, consideramos que el uso de referentes académicos desde el Sur geopolítico es central para abonar a la discusión con conocimiento y prácticas emanadas desde los mismos países que han padecido la colonialidad del poder, del saber y del ser.

Sobre la continuidad que se le ha dado y se le seguirá dando a estas actividades planeadas por mujeres para mujeres en un contexto transfronterizo, y a pesar del conflicto político actual entre México y Estados Unidos, tenemos que durante agosto y septiembre de 2018 la Doctora Xóchitl Chávez y la Maestra Mercedes Payán realizamos varias entrevistas en el contexto del trabajo de campo en la Ciudad de México en la Facultad de Música para rastrear las trayectorias migrantes y con fines de profesionalización en la música de diversas mujeres oaxaqueñas, como Diana Gallardo, hija de la Directora y Maestra Leticia Gallardo y otras mujeres indígenas de Oaxaca. Aunado a esto, hemos mantenido comunicación por redes sociales con las participantes del First Transborder Gathering of Indigenous Women Musicians in Santa María Tlahuitoltepec Mixe, Oaxaca para ver la posibilidad de un segundo encuentro en 2019 en Oaxaca, México, así como un encuentro en 2020 en Los Ángeles, USA.

Por otra parte, en noviembre de 2018 la Comisión Nacional para el Desarrollo de los Pueblos Indígenas (ahora Instituto Nacional de los Pueblos Indígenas) organizó el 11vo Concierto Monumental de Bandas de Viento Infantiles y Juveniles, donde la presencia de las mujeres directoras se hizo notar contando a 13 de ellas a cargo de dirigir la banda integrada por alrededor de 1,350 niñas y niños de múltiples localidades[12]. Dentro de este evento la Directora y Maestra Leticia Gallardo invitó a la Directora Jessica Hernández a participar, colaboración que mantiene lazos y redes de trabajo más allá de las fronteras. Asimismo, está en curso la grabación de la canción que se compuso colectivamente en el taller para incluirla en la segunda producción discográfica de las Mujeres del Viento Florido, consolidando a la banda además en el universo de la música registrada en un formato físico y digital.

Todo este trabajo entre mujeres oaxaqueñas que viven en Oaxaca y sus intercambios con la Directora Jessica Hernández, así como el plan para extender a dos encuentros más, uno en México y el otro en USA, nos permitiría reunirnos con más mujeres oaxaqueñas migrantes, para consolidar una propuesta de trabajo transnacional permanente. Esta colaboración sigue una línea decolonial porque posibilita un intercambio sobre las lógicas de sus pueblos, ya sea en territorio oaxaqueño o estadounidense. Nos concebimos como académicas que trabajan desde una perspectiva decolonial al hacer investigación etnomusicológica transfronteriza para documentar y analizar los modos en que estas mujeres músicos han sostenido estas colaboraciones, aún a pesar de las fronteras geopolíticas tan rígidas que se sostienen en estos tiempos, sin embargo, dejamos esta discusión para trabajos futuros. Finalmente, en nuestro papel de académicas, el compromiso con la escritura de textos sobre el encuentro y posteriores acciones del trabajo colaborativo para su publicación pretende ser un dispositivo más donde podamos compartir con ellas estas reflexiones, en una tónica bilingüe y respetuosa del trabajo en conjunto.

Notes

1 Para más información consultar el sitio en línea del CECAM: http://www.cecam.org.mx

2. Entrevista realizada a la directora y maestra Leticia Gallardo por un periódico local: https://pagina3.mx/2015/02/la-banda-femenil-mujeres-del-viento-florido-combate-el-machismo-con-musica/
3. Nota de dicada a la banda Mujeres del Viento Florido en el portal de la Secretaría de las Culturas y Artes de Oaxaca: http://www.culturasyartes.oaxaca.gob.mx/llegan-desde-tlahuitoltepec-las-mujeres-del-viento-florido/
4. For further discussion on women musicians in Oaxacan philharmonic bands in California refer to Chávez, X. (2017). Booming bandas of Los Angeles: Gender and the practice of transnational Zapotec philharmonic brass bands. In J. Kun (Ed.), *The tide was always high: The music of Latin America in Los Angeles*. University of California Press
5. Xóchitl C. Chávez has carried out transborder collaboration and research with Zapotec communities located in Santa Cruz and Los Angeles, California and their communities of origin since 2005. To refer to Dr. Chávez earlier work see: Forthcoming book, *The Guelaguetza: Performative crossroads, ethnicity, and greater Oaxaca*
6. Tomlinson and Lipsitz (2013)
7. The use of Director, Maestra, and Dr. is utilized throughout the text as an acknowledgment of the scarcity of these titles associated with women with intersectional backgrounds (Indigenous, migrant, first generation, bilingual, and working class) within the field of Philharmonic and academic spheres
8. Palabra en náhuatl que denomina el trabajo no remunerado que los miembros de una sociedad con proyecto civilizatorio comunal deben prestar para garantizar su membresía a la comunidad
9. La escoleta es "el espacio dentro del cual se realizan las prácticas de la Banda Filarmónica (...) la escoleta trasciende su dimensión material para configurarse como un espacio complejo, que posibilita un entramado de relaciones humanas y prácticas que hacen que forme parte del complejo sistema de pensamiento comunal y prácticas comunales, además de constituirse en un espacio de aprendizaje musical" (Payán, 2017: 86)
10. Respecto a otras configuraciones de género y sexualidad (Lugones, 2011) no encontramos pertinente apropiarnos de la discusión sobre otras configuraciones genéricas pues durante nuestro trabajo con las Mujeres del Viento Florido no se hicieron explícitas otras vinculaciones sexuales ni identificaciones de género que no se correspondieran con las del modelo binario de hombre y mujer heterosexuales. Entonces estaríamos hablando de una serie de disputas sobre el orden de reproducción de dicho modelo sin encontrar aún divergencias notables con otras teorías sobre género y sexualidad
11. La encargada de los arreglos musicales finales para la grabación de esta canción colectiva fue Diana Gallardo, hija de la Directora y Maestra Leticia Gallardo, que resultó en una cumbia tocada y cantada por las Mujeres del Viento Florido
12. Nota en periodística sobre el evento que destaca el papel de las mujeres directoras: https://oaxaca.eluniversal.com.mx/sociedad/09-11-2018/se-imponen-mujeres-en-concierto-monumental-de-bandas#imagen-1

References

Alegre, L. (2015). *Etnomusicología y decolonialidad. Saber hablar: el caso de la danza de inditas de la huasteca.* Tesis de Doctorado en Música – Etnomusicología. Facultad de Música de la Universidad Nacional Autónoma de México. México. Sin publicar.

Anzaldúa, G. E. (1987). *Borderlands/La Frontera: The New Mestiza.* San Francisco: Spinsters/AuntLute.

Aquino, A. (2013). La comunalidad como Epistemología del Sur. *Cuadernos de Sur: Revista de ciencias sociales. Año, 18*(34), 7–19.

Castro-Gómez, S. (2007). Decolonizar la universidad. La hybris del punto cero y el diálogo de saberes. en S. Castro y R. Grosfoguel (Eds.), *El giro decolonial. Reflexiones para una diversidad epistémica más allá del capitalismo global* (pp. 79–91). Siglo del Hombre.

Chavez, V. (2012). Cultural humility in community-based participatory research & education. Video https://www.youtube.com/watch?v=9cEXqNDOHqM

Chávez, X. (2017). Booming bandas of Los Angeles: Gender and the practice of transnational Zapotec Philharmonic brass bands. In J. Kun (Ed.), *The tide was always high: The music of Latin America in Los Angeles* (pp. 260–266). University of California Press.

——— (forthcoming). "La Sierra Juárez en Riverside: The Inaugural Oaxacan Philharmonic Bands Audition on a university campus." In *Critical folkloristics: Critical and ethical approaches for the 21st century.* University of Indiana Press.

De Sousa Santos, B. (2010). *Descolonizar el saber, reinventar el poder.* Montevideo, Uruguay: Ediciones Trilce-Extensión Universitaria.

De Sousa Santos, B. (2011). Introducción: Las Epistemologías del Sur. In *Formas-Otras: Saber, nombrar, narrar, hacer.* Colección Monografías (pp. 11-22). Editorial CIDOB.

——— (2004). Comunidad y comunalidad, en *Lecturas del Seminario Diálogos en la Acción, segunda etapa.* Consejo Nacional para la Cultura y las Artes. México: Dirección General de Culturas Populares e Indígenas.

———(2007). *Escrito: comunalidad, energía viva del pensamiento mixe = Ayuujktsënää´yën–ayuujkwënmää´ny – ayuujk mëk´äjtën.* México: Dirección General de Publicaciones y Fomento Editorial Universidad Nacional Autónoma de México.

Delgado Bernal, D., Pérez Huber, L., & Malagón, M. C. (2018). Bridging theories to name and claim a critical race feminista methodology. In J. T. DeCuir-Gunby et al. (Eds.), *Understanding critical race research methods and methodologies: Lessons from the field* (pp. 109-121). Routledge. ProQuest Ebook Central.

Díaz, F. (2001). Comunidad y Comunalidad, en *Jornada Semanal* [En línea] | 11 de marzo del 2001, consultado el 29 de agosto 2015. URL: http://www.jornada.unam.mx/2001/03/11/sem-comunidad.html

García, O. (1993). From Goya portraits to Goya beans: Elite traditions and popular streams in U.S. Spanish language policy. *Southwest Journal of Linguistics, 2,* 69–86.

Gonnet, D. (2015). Aprendiendo música en el encuentro. La construcción de conocimientos musicales a través de la práctica comunitaria y situada. Tesis de Maestría en Psicología Cognitiva y Aprendizaje. Facultad Latinoamericana de Ciencias Sociales y Universidad Autónoma de Madrid. España. Sin publicar.

Gonzalez, M. (2014). Mixing in the kitchen: Entre mujeres feminine translocal composition. In A. E. Kinser, K. Freehling-Burton, & T. Hawkes (Eds.), *Performing motherhood: Artistic, activist and everyday enactments* (pp. 69–88). Demeter Press.

Grosfoguel, R. (2006). La descolonización de la economía política y los estudios postcoloniales: Transmodernidad, pensamiento fronterizo y colonialidad global. *Tabula Rasa, 4*, 17–46.

Grosfoguel, R. (2011). La descolonización del conocimiento: Diálogo crítico entre la visión descolonial de Frantz Fanon y la sociología descolonial de Boaventura de Sousa Santos en *Formas-Otras: Saber, nombrar, narrar, hacer*. Colección Monografías (pp. 97–108). Editorial CIDOB.

Hernández, O. (2007). Marimba de chonta y poscolonialidad musical en *Nómadas (Col)* (núm. 26, pp. 56–69). Universidad Central.

Holguín Mendoza, C. (2022). Beyond registers of formality and other categories of stigmatization: Style, awareness and agency in SHL. In M. A. Bowles (Ed.), *Outcomes of university Spanish heritage language instruction in the United States* (pp. 149-168). Georgetown University Press.

Holguín, P. (2017). La música desde el Punto Cero. La colonialidad de la teoría y el análisis musical en la Universidad. *Revista Internacional de Educación Musical, 4*, 149–156.

Lugones, M. (2010). Toward a decolonial feminism. *Hypatia, 25*(4), 742–759. https://doi.org/10.1111/j.1527-2001.2010.01137.x.

Lugones, M. (2011). Methodological notes toward a decolonial feminism. In A. M. Isasi-Daz & E. Mendieta (Eds.), *Decolonizing epistemologies: Latina/o theology and philosophy* (pp. 68-86). Retrieved from http://ebookcentral.proquest.com

Madrid, A. L. (2011). *Transnational encounters: Music and performance at the U.S.-Mexico border*. New York: Oxford University Press.

Maldonado-Torres, N. (2007). La colonialidad del ser: Contribuciones al desarrollo de un concepto en *El giro decolonial: Reflexiones para una diversidad epistémica más allá del capitalismo global* (pp. 127-167). Lesco-Pensar-Siglo del Hombre Editores.

Martínez, J. (2003). Comunalidad y desarrollo. Dirección General de Culturas Populares e Indígenas. Centro de Apoyo al Movimiento Popular Oaxaqueño. CONACULTA. México.

Mignolo, W. (2007). La idea de América Latina: La herida colonial y la opción decolonial. (pp. 46-93). Editorial Gedisa.

Mignolo, W. (2010). La colonialidad: la cara oculta de la modernidad en *Desobediencia epistémica; Retórica de la modernidad, lógica de la colonialidad y gramática de la descolonialidad*. Buenos Aires, Argentina: Ediciones del Signo.

Moraga, C., & Anzaldúa, G. E. (Eds.), (2015). *This bridge called my back: Writings by radical women of color* (4th ed.). State University of New York Press.

Navarrete, S. (2013). Comunidad y ciudadanía: La transición de capillas de viento a cuerpos filarmónicos durante el siglo XIX en Oaxaca, en *Ritual sonoro en catedral y parroquias* (pp. 301-333). Centro de Investigaciones y Estudios Superiores en Antropología Social.

Navarrete Pellicer, S. J. (2013). Etnografía de las culturas musicales en Oaxaca. *Diversidad y educación musical sustentables*. México: CONACYT-Gobierno del Estado de Oaxaca.

Navarrete Pellicer, S. J. (2015). Educación musical intercultural a tercer nivel en Oaxaca, México en *Ponencia para la I Conferencia Internacional sobre México, Centroamérica y el Caribe, junio 18-22 de 2015*. Sin publicar y citado con permiso del autor.

Olivera, A. (2014). Etnografía decolonial con colectivos charrúas: Reflexionando sobre interconocimientos. In S. Romero (Ed.), *Anuario antropología social y cultural en Uruguay*. Departamento de Antropología Social. Instituto de Antropología FHCE UdelaR (pp. 139–153). Editorial Nordan-Comunidad.

Paredes, A. (1977). On ethnographic work among minority groups: A folklorist's perspective. *New Scholar*, 6(1), 32.

Payán, M. (2017). Prácticas comunales en la escoleta de la banda de viento de Tamazulápam del Espíritu Santo Mixe, Oaxaca. Tesis de Maestría en Música – Etnomusicología. Facultad de Música de la Universidad Nacional Autónoma de México. México. Sin publicar.

Perissinoto, G. (2003). Linguistic constraints, programmatic fit, and political correctness: The case of Spanish in the United States. In J. Poblete (Ed.), *Critical Latin American and Latino studies* (pp. 171–187). Minneapolis, MN: University of Minnesota Press.

Poblete, J. (2003). *Critical Latin American and Latino studies*. Minneapolis, MN: University of Minnesota Press.

Quijano, A. (2014). *Des/colonialidad y bien vivir: Un nuevo debate en América Latina*. Universidad Ricardo Palma, Perù: Editorial Universitaria.

Rosabal-Coto, G. (2013). La herida colonial en los orígenes de la educación musical escolar costarricense. *Revista estudios*, 27. San José, Costa Rica: Universidad de Costa Rica.

Rosabal-Coto, G. (2016). Music learning in Costa Rica: A postcolonial institutional ethnography. *The Sibelius Academy of the University of the Arts Helsinki*. San José, Costa Rica: Editorial EDinexo.

Small, C. (1998). *Musicking: The meanings of performing and listening*. University Press of New England.

Stanton, B. (2018). Musicking in the borders: Toward decolonizing methodologies. *Philosophy of Music Education Review*, 26(1), 4–23. Bloomington, IN: Indiana University Press. Stable URL: https://www.jstor.org/stable/10.2979/philmusieducrevi.26.1.02

Tervalon, M., & Murray-Garcia, J. (1998). Cultural humility versus cultural competence: A critical distinction in defining physician training outcomes in multicultural education. *Journal of Health Care for the Poor and Underserved*, 9(2), 117–125.

Tomlinson, B., & Lipsitz, G. (2013). American studies as accompaniment. *American Quarterly*, 65(1), 1–30.

Tucker, S. (2000). *Swing shift: "All-Girl" bands of the 1940s.* Duke University Press.

Zentella, A. C. (2017). Limpia, fija y da esplendor: Challenging the symbolic biolence of the Royal Spanish Academy. *Chiricú Journal: Latina/o literatures, arts, and cultures*, 1(2), 21–42.

El Tallercito de Son SATX: Creando Comunidad a Través de la Cultura

KELI ROSA CABUNOC

As Chicana/x/o identities and communities in the U.S. grow, change, and evolve, documentation is needed by Chicanas/xs/os, for the Chicana/x/o community to tell their stories—through Chicana/x/o eyes, in our voices. Over the last 500 years, people of color have been colonized and (re)colonized through research and documentation by outsiders replicating colonial notions of the "other" (Tuhiwai Smith, 2012). Couched within Chicana feminism (Anzaldúa, 1987) and Indigenous methodologies (Tuhiwai Smith, 2012), this chapter documents and analyzes how Chicanas/xs/os today use son jarocho and its cultura to reexamine and reshape identity. Through the use of storytelling in the form of testimonios (Delgado Bernal, 1998), this chapter describes the powerful ways in which members of El Tallercito de Son use the musical and cultural tradition that is son jarocho to understand and self-realize identities; form local and transnational communities; decolonize how music is practiced within comunidad; and engage in social justice projects—all while representing a transformational decolonial praxis that creates spaces for decolonial ways of knowing and being in the world for Chicanas/xs/os in the U.S.

Growing up in Califas with a Filipino Hawaiian father, and a Chicana mother, I was always surrounded by cultura and familia. I ate lumpia and adobo with my Filipino aunties on Saturday, and tamales and pozole with my Mexican tías on Sunday. From the early age of 3, I began learning how to dance traditional Hula—my father wanted me to learn about his familia through the traditions of ancient Hula. By age 5, I was dancing Ballet Folklórico—dancing my way through the history of México. I spent every Saturday well past high school learning Ballet Folklórico, the bailes, trajes, and cultura instilled in me a love for traditional Mexican music and dance.

It was through Ballet Folklórico that I had my first encounter with live traditional son jarocho (Cabunoc Romero, 2017). Although my ancestral roots in México are in Jalisco, with the Wixáritati, los huicholes, I have found deep ancestral and spiritual connections to México in the music, dance, and cultura of son jarocho. The conocimiento that I have learned from the elders I have met while studying son jarocho in their communities continues to shape and inform my desire to create comunidad through cultura.

(Re)Colonization: Five-Hundred Years of Colonization by Spain, Mexico, and the U.S.

During the colonial era, Indigenous, mestizos, and Africanos were subjected to colonial rule and were forced to convert to the Catholic religion, assimilate to the Spanish language, and leave their rituals, traditions, and cultura behind. Even after New Spain (Mexico) declared its independence from Spain, a process of (re)colonization continued in Mexico.

Nearly 500 years later, Chicanas/xs/os—and other Latinas/xs/os—in what is now the U.S. are continuously colonized in their everyday lives; I call this process of continued colonization across colonial borders (re)colonization. In the U.S., Chicanas/xs/os experience this process of (re)colonization when the work place skips over qualified Chicanas/xs/os for promotions in favor of white employees, when the educational system says "English Only" in schools denying young Chicanitas/xs/os their language, when police officers across the country racially profile young Chicanas/xs/os, arresting them because they are brown.

Chicanas/xs/os are (re)colonized today, when ethnic studies classes are not offered at their schools, when they are forced to learn Eurocentric curricula that erase their history and narratives. Chicanas/xs/os are (re)colonized when the state of Arizona banned books by Chicana/x/o authors. Chicanito young boys are (re)colonized in schools today when they are sent home for having trenzas—braids that fall down their backs, upsetting the white aesthetic. Chicanos/as/xs are (re)colonized in the university when professors tell them that their research is too radical—that no one will publish something so extreme. Best to whiten it up a bit.

In the face of hundreds of years of (re)colonization, Chicanas/xs/os have found ways to survive and thrive. Within the context of U.S. colonialism, Chicanas/xs/os across generations have resisted (re)colonization through cultura. My abuela fought (re)colonization by refusing to learn English, even after being in the U.S. for over 40 years. My mother's generation fought back against (re)colonization through teatro and poetry during the Chicano movimiento of the 1960s. Within my generation, I fight (re)colonization with my fellow talleristas[1] by using El Tallercito de Son as a vehicle to decolonize identity, cultura, and even how music is taught, learned, and shared within a community space.

It's important to note that my positionality as a researcher intersects with my positionality as a tallerista and founding member of this collective. When I moved to San Antonio's Westside in 2014 to attend graduate school at UTSA, I brought with me two decades of learning and practicing son jarocho in different comunidades in México and in the U.S., where I helped start son jarocho collectives across several states (Cabunoc Romero, 2017). Shortly after moving, I found others who wanted to learn and share son jarocho with the comunidad. Together, we founded El Tallercito de Son SATX, and I began teaching the weekly talleres. This chapter pulls from a larger ethnographic study on Chicana/x/o identity through son jarocho (Cabunoc Romero, 2017).

Testimonio: A Methodology to Heal, Reclaim Identity, and Bring Change

It is important to research and document lived experience with methodologies and frameworks that hold space for the complexities and intersections of Chicana/x/o identities. Drawing from Chicana feminist epistemology (Delgado Bernal, 1998) and decolonizing methodologies (Tuhiwai Smith, 2012) this chapter investigates the ways in which members of El Tallercito de Son use the cultura and música of son jarocho to decolonize their identities. Moreover, this chapter examines the ways in which El Tallercito formed transnational communities and relationships with son jarocho communities in México, challenging the coloniality of the U.S.-Mexico border. Finally, this chapter examines El Tallercito as a vehicle for decolonizing how music is created in community and for community in the face of assimilationist colonial practices that erase community-rooted forms of knowledge creation and community-forms of being—the ways in which one relates to the world, to others.

To examine this, I conducted focus groups or pláticas—informal conversations to share stories about specific ideas or topics—as we called them (Delgado Bernal, 1998). These pláticas included five to ten talleristas and lasted about an hour each. Three members of the colectivo also shared their testimonio with me in individual one-on-one conversations. Both pláticas and testimonios offered spaces to document the lives of El Tallercito members and analyze the decolonial praxis of this grass-roots Chicana/x/o collective.

By collecting testimonios, or counter-stories, talleristas articulate the injustices they have faced as Chicanas/xs/os in the U.S. These testimonios also document how El Tallercito de Son has come to play a role in the decolonial identity of a group of Chicanas/xs/os, as well as how son jarocho has become a space to decolonize historical narratives on race, community music, gender roles, and how they intersect with cultura through collective knowledge. Delgado Bernal, Burciaga, and Flores Carmona (2012) write that:

> Testimonio is and continues to be an approach that incorporates political, social, historical and cultural histories that accompany one's life experiences as a means to bring about social change through consciousness-raising ... these testimonios demonstrate the possibility of social change and transformation of self and society (p. 364).

Documenting the testimonios of talleristas through a Chicana feminist epistemology, this chapter places their stories and voices at the center. Chicana feminist epistemology "maintains connections to Indigenous roots by embracing dualities that are necessary and complementary qualities, and by challenging dichotomies that offer opposition without reconciliation" (Delgado Bernal, 1998, p. 4). Moreover, Delgado Bernal (1998) shares that a Chicana feminist epistemology "arises out of unique social and cultural history, and demonstrates that our experiences as Mexican women are legitimate, appropriate, and effective in designing, conducting, and analyzing research" (p. 6). As talleristas share and document their testimonios they not only heal themselves from years of (re)colonization, but also contribute to the documentation of how son jarocho and reclaiming musical traditions through El Tallercito have become vehicles for social change, as well as sites of decolonial transformation (Tuhiwai Smith, 2012).

El Tallercito de Son: Son Jarocho as a Decolonial Intervention

I turn to the work of Maori scholar, Linda Tuhiwai Smith, best known for her groundbreaking book, *Decolonizing Methodologies* (1999) where she puts forth a vision for how research can be used as a decolonial practice. Tuhiwai Smith (2012) identifies "research as a significant site of struggle between the interests and ways of knowing of the West and the interests and ways of resisting of the Other" (p. 2). Tuhiwai Smith (2012) introduces the Indigenous research agenda where Indigenous people and their narratives are central to research methodologies and practices.

Similar to Chicana feminist Dolores Delgado-Bernal's testimonio approach, Tuhiwai Smith (2012) emphasizes the power behind individual and shared storytelling. She writes that through these perspectives "truth is being revealed ... Indigenous testimonies are a way of talking about an extremely painful event or series of events" (p. 145). For Tuhiwai Smith (2012), these stories become a "narrative of collective memory ... a method for making sense of histories, of voices and representation and of the political narrative of oppression" (p. 145). The testimonios of the talleristas become a narrative of collective memory on identity and the role that cultura—in this case, son jarocho—plays in decolonizing identity.

I also draw from what Tuhiwai Smith (2012) calls claiming. Colonialism has invalidated Indigenous people's language, cultural practices, and ancestral knowledge. By researching Chicana/x/o stories, and writing our stories for our community, we are able to claim and reclaim who we are. (Tuhiwai Smith, 2012, p. 144). By collecting testimonios from talleristas, which serve as counter-narratives, this research provides a space for claiming and reclaiming where healing, decolonization, transformation, and mobilization can occur through Indigenous research practices.

Through testimonios with talleristas of El Tallercito, I gained a more profound understanding of how son jarocho is a decolonial practice where talleristas are able to reclaim, examine, and define their identities in community. The testimonios provided invaluable insight into how son jarocho has shaped the identity of talleristas. These testimonios—whether in a one-on-one interview or in a group plática—became a place of sharing, empowerment, affirmation, and healing. Several of my compañeras/xs/as discussed that "aja" moment—that guiding moment that helps transform perceptions of reality—what Anzaldúa (2002) refers to as conocimiento. To that end, this study and the testimonios shared by the talleristas documents the ways in which Chicanas/xs/os in San Antonio, TX participate in the construction of knowledge and research that is dedicated to achieving social justice for Chicanas/xs/os everywhere while at the same time creating a space to learn about our ancestors, heal from the pain of colonization, and create community through cultura (Delgado Bernal, 1998; Tuhiwai Smith, 2012).

El Tallercito de Son SATX

El Tallercito de Son SATX is an intergenerational colectivo of Chicanas/xs/os, Latinas/xs/os, and inmigrantes, whose mission is to crear comunidad a través de la cultura—create community through culture. The talleristas—the people who make up the collective—participate in free weekly talleres, or workshops, that use a traditional Mexican Afro-mestizo music called son jarocho as a vehicle to reclaim cultural identity, decolonize cultura, and to participate in social justice efforts within the comunidad.

El Tallercito de Son's mission statement reads:

> El Tallercito is a collective of students, teachers, artists, activists, queers, community organizers, and musicians who share son jarocho with the community of San Antonio through FREE community talleres, or workshops. El Tallercito de Son uses son jarocho as a vehicle for social justice and human rights. We are inclusive and everyone is welcome to join us as we learn, share, and live nuestra cultura[2]. For the talleristas de El Tallercito, our ultimate mission is to create community through cultura. El Tallercito creates transnational communities with collectives in Veracruz and throughout México. We are artivistas[3] who bring awareness and raise our voices through music and dance.

To combat racism and oppression in their everyday lives, Chicanas/xs/os seek out spaces where they can come together, share lived experiences, and learn from one another. When Chicanas/xs/os find a space—una comunidad, una casa—where they can explore their true identity, they find that they are home in what Gloria Anzaldúa (1983) calls El Mundo Zurdo, the lefthanded world (p. 196). Anzaldúa (1983) describes El Mundo Zurdo as a place where the "colored, the queer, the poor, the female, the physically challenged" feel at home (p. 196). El Mundo Zurdo becomes a place where Chicanas/xs/os can struggle together and form a vision which "spans from the self-love of our colored skins" (Moraga and Anzaldúa, 1983, p. 196). In a similar way, El Tallercito is a form of Mundo Zurdo; a manifestation of a collective vision of Chicanas/xs/os, struggling together to create a place of our own, where we can decolonize our identity through exploration, finding connections to our roots.

As a founding member of the collective and as a maestra of El Tallercito, I actively work towards a praxis that stays true to the mission statement of creating community. As a scholar and artist with over 20 years in son jarocho, I am intentional of developing a methodology where documentation and research can be done as a collective. As such, this research study turns to Linda Tuhiwai Smith's (2012) Indigenous research agenda, which is conceptualized as "constituting a programme and set of approaches that are situated within decolonization politics" and is focused strategically on the goal of self-determination (Tuhiwai Smith, 2012, p. 120). Research, then, can become more than a case study and/or documentation—it can become a tool for social justice (Tuhiwai Smith, 2012). The Indigenous research agenda "necessarily involves the process of transformation, of decolonization, of healing and of mobilization" (Tuhiwai Smith, 2012, p. 120)—much like El Tallercito's goal of creating decolonized spaces for Chicanas/xs/os where ancestral cultural practices like son jarocho are recovered and reclaimed as social justice interventions.

Over the past 5 years, we have met every Tuesday for approximately two hours. Even during the 2020 global pandemic of COVID 19, we have been able to come together as a comunidad through virtual talleres and have even been able to sustain our transnational comunidad throughout San Antonio and México with teaching artists from Veracruz, Baja California, and Puebla. Everyone is invited and no experience or instrument is needed—that is how we recruit talleristas, letting them know that none of us studied music in a conventional Western sense. In a collective whose members include scholars, community activists, teachers, line-cooks, insurance agents, mothers, students, and construction workers, and whose ages range from a 7-year-old girl scout to few sixty-something abuelas, our space is decolonial. We disrupt the creation of strong held stereotypes or assumptions that have been encouraged by colonial practices and structures by promoting a convivencia among everyone, supporting the natural sharing of ideas and experiences, which in turn validates all individuals across social class, gender, age, profession, language, immigration status, and level of experience in son jarocho.

The talleristas sit in a circle, with new folks on one side of the circle, and those who have been playing son for a while on the other side; this helps with new talleristas being able to follow those who are more advanced across the circle. I make sure to walk around the circle, encouraging each tallerista to challenge themselves within the level at which they are currently at. The most advanced members are able to create music with people who are strumming a jarana for the first time. We always start together, using the knowledge that the talleristas have learned as a tool to share cultura with newcomers. El Tallercito weekly talleres create a safe space where abuelitas who came here from México are able to relate to 1st and 2nd generation Tejanas/xs/os, Chicanas/xs/os, and Latinas/xs/os. Son jarocho provides the common thread that leads to intergenerational discussions about education, cultura, roots, social justice, and local politics—just to name a few. I have witnessed abuelitas share their testimonios about crossing the border with youth who had never been able to put a real face to the border-crossers they know exist. Through decolonial practices revealed through the testimonios of the talleristas, El Tallercito has become a decolonial space where Mexicanas/xs/os, Chicanas/xs/os, Tejanas/xs/os, and Latinas/xs/os use son jarocho as the tool in their journey to self.

In addition to our weekly talleres, at least once, if not twice a year, we host a teaching artist from México. Since El Tallercito began in April 2015, we have hosted teaching artists from México nine different times. Through this intercambio, we create transnational communities across borders. In spite of geopolitical colonial borders, we have created a transnational comunidad spanning across several countries, including México, the United States, Canada, and Spain. Our transnational relationships provide a way to decolonize our reclaiming of cultura in several ways. We have created under-the-radar economies, using our money as an auto-sufficient collective to directly support communities in Veracruz—economically with money, through the donation of supplies, and through the purchase of instruments, textiles, and goods directly from Indigenous and Afro-mestizo communities. Through our transnational work with communities across Veracruz and México, El Tallercito has constructed and cultivated relationships with people that have been separated from us historically by colonization. Son jarocho becomes the vehicle in which we begin to revitalize our ancestral ties to México.

Son Jarocho: Música Que Transforma

The first archival documentation of son jarocho was in a colonial edict in 1776 banning a popular son (a term used for a song played within son jarocho), "El Chuchumbé" for the "lascivious body movements associated with the dancing of 'El Chuchumbé' by communities of 'broken color'" (Díaz-Sánchez & Hernández, 2013, p. 187). Catholic Spanish colonizers during the Holy Inquisition found the lascivious dance movements and poetic lyrics that often mocked religious authority, leading them to order an edict that publicly outlawed "El Chuchumbé" (Díaz-Sánchez & Hernández, 2013). Those who simply played son jarocho, and were a part of la comunidad de son[4], acted against colonial edicts. Thus, they resisted their colonizers and kept their cultura alive by playing this music.

It is public knowledge among the comunidad de son that the third root, the African root, can be found in the instruments used in son jarocho. Over the past two decades, I have learned the history of the instruments of son jarocho from elders throughout Veracruz, México. At the heart of son, is the tarima, a wooden platform that zapateado, traditional tap-like poly-rhythmic dancing is danced upon. The traditional step that elders teach throughout Veracruz is called "café con pan," and the improvised complex poly-rhythms that bailadoras dance on the tarima are the melding together of Indigenous and African rhythms, danced in Spanish colonial heeled shoes. The instrument most commonly played is la jarana, the traditional small guitar-like eight string instrument that is played percussively, like beats on a drum. The jarana is different from the guitar in that traditionally it is carved from one solid piece of wood by a laudero—luthier.

Anunciando el son[5], marking the melody, is the requinto jarocho, a smaller guitar-like instrument made in the small pueblos throughout Veracruz, traditionally and more commonly known as la guitarra de son. The large bass-like instrument is traditionally known as la guitarra grande or la vozarrona, and more recently, as la leona. La quijada de burro o de caballo, the jawbone of a donkey or a horse, is played percussively by hitting the flat side with the side of the fist causing the teeth to rattle, and scraping a wooding stick along the teeth for a güiro-like sound. La quijada came to Veracruz with African slaves and survived colonization through the living traditions of son jarocho. El cajón is a wooden box that was originally made from shipping crates on slave ships. African slaves turned the crate on its side, sat on it, and began beating it like a drum. El pandero, a tambourine-like percussion instrument, is a direct result of outlawed African and Indigenous drums—el pandero became a hand drum that was easy to transport and easily hidden. El marimbol is another percussion instrument that is a large box with a sound hole in the front where small metal keys or tongues are plucked to create a bass-like sound. El marimbol is a direct result of the ingenuity, creativity, and improvisation of African slaves trying to create the kalimba from their homeland.

Jaranero (a male who plays jarana) Patricio Hidalgo—a master at all things son jarocho, whose familia has been playing, dancing and singing son for generations—when interviewed by Chicana/x/o scholars about the effects of the Holy Inquisition on the son jarocho community states: "todo lo que se hacía con las manos, se lo llevaron a la tarima —all rhythms once played by hand were transferred to the tarima" (Díaz-Sánchez & Hernández, 2013, p. 192). Colonization made its way to the música that Chicana/x/o ancestors were playing, outlawing not only certain sones like El Chuchumbé, but also outlawing instruments of African descent. Hidalgo shared that when hand drums and other percussion instruments that slaves brought with them from their native Africa were made illegal, those rhythms were not lost, but rather transformed into percussive dance on the tarima[6] through zapateado[7] (Díaz-Sánchez & Hernández, 2013).

La tarima has become a sacred place, un altar sagrado[8], a place of transformation and empowerment. Bailadora (a woman who dances traditional zapateado to son jarocho music) Martha Vega from la familia Vega—a family who has conserved son jarocho and all of its traditions for generations—stated in a 2006 Mexican American produced documentary, "Fandango, Searching for the White Monkey" (Rodriguez and Braojos, 2006) shares:

> Siento que me transformo. Siento que volví a nacer en la tarima. Con que me sienta mal, yo sé que si me subo a la tarima, se me olvidan los problemas. En la tarima soy otra. Soy otra Martha. [English translation within the documentary]

> I feel transformed. On the tarima I feel that I am born again. When I feel bad, I get on the tarima and I forget my problems. On the tarima I am a different Martha.

Martha shares her personal insight as a bailadora on how powerful the tarima is for her as a mujer[9]. While zapateando—dancing, improvising, creating percussive rhythmic music with her feet—she is transformed, she is free. La bailadora has resisted the colonization of her ancestors, and has resisted (re)colonization by keeping once silenced traditions alive and well.

Son jarocho has survived centuries of (re)colonization; its musical traditions continue to be heard en los pueblos de Veracruz, México[10]. Colonial edicts outlawing son jarocho failed to kill the traditions and culture of son; it thrived as a resistance music played by Indigenous and Afro-Mexicans. When the early Chicano movement started back in the late 1960s and early 1970s, young Chicana/x/o activists found their voice through traditional son jarocho. When the working class Chicano community of Barrio Logan in San Diego, California won their battle for Chicano Park, son jarocho was played in celebration by Chicano activists like Corky Gonzales (Mulford, 1989, 0:52:23). Some 50 years later, en los barrios de los Estados Unidos[11], you can still hear son jarocho, as Chicanas/xs/os of all generations create new spaces where son can continue to flourish. Despite (re)colonization, la comunidad de son jarocho—and the Mexicanas/xs/os y Chicanas/xs/os who live its traditions—has managed to transgress colonial borders and create a transnational community. As a transnational community, these Chicana/x/o artivistas cross borders to ensure that this music flows as easily as the música de un radio[12] floats through the air.

Son Jarocho: Una Música Sin Fronteras

El fandango has played a vital role in the survival of son jarocho. El fandango is the traditional community gathering where jaraneras/xs/os[13] and bailadoras/xs share food and celebrate, sing, and dance around la tarima. The fandango—also known as el huapango—becomes central to son jarocho, and without it, la música would cease to exist. In the documentary "Fandango, Searching for the White Monkey" (Rodriguez and Braojos, 2006) the fandango is described by various native Veracruzanos, the people who take part in son jarocho and all of its tradiciones in their daily lives, as:

> – Esta cosa de los fandangos, es estar toda la noche ... se nutre el espíritu de un modo. [English translation provided by the documentary] This

El Tallercito de Son Satx: Creando Comunidad a Través

thing about the fandango is to be there all night ... it nourishes the spirit.
- Como que te llenas de gusto, de alegría. Es algo que te conmueve, ¿no? It fills you with joyful pleasure. Something moves you.
- Es una forma de amor, ¿no? Pero concentrado. A form of love, but concentrated.
- Es algo que te envuelve, como un remolino. De repente, ya estas envuelta. It wraps you like a tornado. Suddenly you're surrounded.
- En el fandango, hay de todo: convivencia, romance ... el fandango incluye todo, no deja nada afuera. The fandango includes everything: friendship, romance ... nothing is left out.

El fandango becomes a decolonial way to heal from centuries of colonization/(re)colonization. El fandango becomes a safe space to nurture. Jaraneras/xs/os who represent the living, breathing, growing comunidad of son jarocho, overcome geopolitical borders inflicted by colonial immigration policies that control the movement of people. Even when a physical border stands between people, forcing them to be separated, there will be a fandango to bring people together. For example, El Fandango Fronterizo, The Borderland Fandango—organized by son jarocho collectives on both sides of la frontera—exists in spite of the physical border that separates Tijuana, México and San Diego, California, U.S. This is a transnational collaboration between colectivos of Chicanas/xs/os from California y Tejas, and as far as Washington, D.C., and communities in Veracruz, México that takes place yearly in May. Together we share cultura through the thick, layered wire fence that towers over us, reminding us as Chicanas/xs/os and Mexicanas/xs/os we are still being (re)colonized today by colonial borders and policies. Through son jarocho, Chicanas/xs/os have found a way to resist and decolonize through cultura. Moreover, we have found a collective identity, una comunidad, a place to be safe, a place to be Chicana/x/o. Son jarocho has no borders, and cannot be stopped by the physical wall that separates México and los Estados Unidos.

The Talleristas: Our Stories Hold Power

El Tallercito has provided a space where Chicanas/xs/os from San Antonio use son jarocho as a vehicle for discovery. Tuhiwai Smith (2012) writes that to "discover the beauty of our knowledge" is about "discovering our own indigenous knowledge ... and its continued relevance to the way we lead our lives" (p. 161). Son jarocho becomes the beautiful knowledge that talleristas use to reshape and remake identity, and to reclaim cultural traditions and practices.

Three of the 13 talleristas shared their testimonio through one-on-one interviews. These talleristas shared their stories de todo corazón[14] and without fear, revealing intimate details of their lives. The three talleristas who gave their testimonio in one-on-one interviews included Cuauhtli Reyna, Johanna Briones, and José Luis Gonzalez.

Cuauhtli is a founding member of El Tallercito and facilitates requinto talleres. He traces his family roots back to Texas, when it was "still México." Cuauhtli began his journey with son jarocho at the age of 17, when Mono Blanco—renowned traditional son jarocho group from Veracruz, México— visited his hometown during his high school years. He was born in Del Rio, Texas, a small town along the border between Tejas and Coahuila, México. He grew up with a mother who used the words Tejana and Chicana interchangeably, but noted that "Tejano was to explain where we were from, and Chicano was to explain our state of mind." Cuauhtli says of his hometown, "There's a lot of people in Del Rio that were first generation and didn't have a clear identity because their parents were too busy working. Too busy trying to make it. So, they had to find their own identity." Cuauhtli has been a student of son jarocho for roughly 15 years, and spent years living in Veracruz, México, mastering the requinto jarocho. He has spent the last 5 years teaching requinto and son jarocho to talleristas, sharing the ancestral knowledge he has learned from maestros/as in Mexico.

Johanna is a native to San Antonio, who studied Mexican American Studies at San Antonio College. Johanna first heard son jarocho 5 years ago, when she saw El Tallercito perform at the city of San Antonio's Día de Los Muertos celebration, Muertos Fest. She and her daughter fell in love with the music, and El Tallercito has become a family affair for Johanna—she, her husband Ricardo, and her daughter Annabelle attend Tallercito weekly together as a familia. She identifies as a white and Mexican American Chicana who was "raised in a first-generation Mexican immigrant household. My mom was an immigrant from Monterrey, México. She came over, and then I stayed with her the whole time. That's how I grew up, with all my Mexican family."

José Luis was born in Ocotlán, Jalisco, a pueblo southeast of Guadalajara. José Luis came to the United States after his father found work:

> Llegué a los estados unidos a través de mi padre, porque trabajó en el campo. Como era jornalero, se venía y se iba, y ya cuando se decidió quedarse aquí en los estdos unidos, fue los principios del 1986 y ya nos trajó a nosotros en el 1987 ó 1988. Yo tenía como ocho años.[15]

José Luis spent his childhood in Los Angeles, then moved to Ontario, California and stayed there until moving to San Antonio "por el amor," for love, when he married his wife. He first learned about son jarocho and El Tallercito almost five years ago when he saw a Facebook post about some free talleres for kids, so he took his two daughters to the classes. He remembers falling in love with son jarocho at their first taller, "hubo el primer taller de niños, y es cuando me interesó mucho, y empecé a traer a mis niñas, y ya de ahí, me enamoré más yo que ellas."[16]

Chicana/x/o Identity: A Political Coming of Age Story

All the talleristas felt the Chicana/x/o identity is an identity that is realized through a journey. Moreover, they articulated Chicana/x/o identity as one rooted in a political consciousness of being Mexican American. They also described Chicana/x/o identity as one that cultivated a unique aesthetic. During the one-on-one testimonio, Cuauhtli spoke about the struggles that Chicanas/xs/os face with their identity:

> Identifying as a Chicano is not having your identity clearly handed to you ... having to struggle with your parents over who you are. Having to struggle with your family over who you are. They struggled to find their identity and they did it by calling themselves Chicanos ... because lucharon.[17] Chicano is solidarity, a movement, the state of mind. It was like the penacho[18] I put on to go into war, like a coat of arms, like a uniform. The Chicano is the guerrero[19], the person who will take action to give rights to their fellow Mexican-Americans.

Cuauhtli emphasizes the struggle that comes with finding one's Chicana/x/o identity—one that is rooted in a political consciousness and struggle or la lucha. As cultural studies scholar Luis Urrieta (2010) notes: "The understanding of identity ... is one of becoming, not being" (p. 69). José Luis still finds himself in that struggle as well,

> Yo soy entre Chicano y Mexicano porque yo nací en México, entonces soy Mexicano de nacimiento, entonces como ya estoy de este lado del charco, se puede decir pos medio Chicano. Cuando digo 'de este lado del charco' es por el Río Bravo pues porque es lo que divide en dos países lo que es un solo país en mi punto de vista, es un solo país, no hay barreras pero ... si tenemos que brincar el puente como quien dice, por eso yo lo digo.[20]

José Luis finds himself still struggling with his identity; he sees himself as only "sort of" Chicano, "medio Chicano." He is navigating the world of Anzaldúa's (2012) nepantla as he explores the different nuances of his identity, as he grows and transforms as an immigrant in the U.S.

Being Chicana/x/o also means fighting against assimilation. In a society where assimilating to mainstream culture is encouraged, for Johanna, being

Chicana is a way to reclaim her roots, her way to fight against assimilation. Before identifying as a Chicana, Johanna would say that she was "half white, half Mexican" but she noted how strange it felt saying that because "it's not really saying anything. I don't feel white; I don't feel Mexican." Johanna only recently began identifying as a Chicana:

> It wasn't until a couple years ago that I was like I'm Chicana. And I even asked around, like what makes someone a Chicana, and it's a little bit being of Mexican descent living in the United States, but it's also political. A term to reclaim your roots and to have more pride. It comes with a little bit more pride, I think, being Chicana.

By Johanna reclaiming her roots, she is embracing through Chicana feminist epistemology the dualities that are necessary to deconstruct and navigate the complexities of the society we live in today (Delgado Bernal, 1998). Johanna's Chicana identity is also a way for her to reject the dominant ideology's expectation that people of color should assimilate, as she clearly stated when she said:

> Being a Chicana means determined not to assimilate. This is who I am, I'm going to be a Chicana even though you look down on this—which Chicana is a word that used to be looked down on, and we reclaimed it as something that we take pride in. We are OK with being Mexican, and in fact we are proud of it.

Johanna's pride in her Mexican heritage and her Chicana identity grounds her, making it a political stance against society's cries for assimilation.

Celebrating survival is Tuhiwai Smith's (2012) answer to non-Indigenous research being "intent on documenting the demise and cultural assimilation of indigenous peoples. Instead it is possible to celebrate survival" (p. 146). Son jarocho, el fandango, and the community traditions, is a cultural celebration of not only Indigenous culture, but the African legacies that are ignored in Mexican cultura. Through the sharing of son jarocho and its traditions with the community of San Antonio, we can "retain cultural ... values and authenticity in resisting colonialism" (Tuhiwai Smith, 2012, p. 146).

For talleristas who shared their testimonios, Chicana/x/o identity is still very much consciously and critically assumed (Alarcón, 1990). It is a personal journey, riddled with struggle—a struggle in which one of the talleristas still find themselves. Identity is self-made as we search for connections, for truths that have been denied. Through son jarocho talleristas have found the counter narrative in the living traditions of Mexico's Afro-mestizo/a/x legacy. The Chicana/x/o identity is also a political guerrera/x/o[21], Chicanas/xs/os are people who fight assimilation, people who fight for the rights of their community.

Son Jarocho: A Vehicle for Change

For each tallerista, son jarocho has been a vehicle for personal change. Many described son jarocho as a vehicle for examining and exploring their cultura through Indigenous and African legacies in México. For the talleristas, son jarocho has become the gateway to lost rituals and traditions like Día de los Muertos. For some talleristas, son jarocho has changed the way they communicate with others. Son jarocho—the space El Tallercito provides—has changed the way that Chicanas/xs/os build comunidad in San Antonio. Son jarocho has changed the way we communicate with people. The fandango provides much needed convivencia, a word that literally means coexistence, but more than that, it means to be in community with others around you, to truly be present, invested, and share in the spirit of community—decolonizing the way in which we relate to each other, the ways in which our comunidad comes together.

El Tallercito has provided a space where Chicanas/xs/os from San Antonio use son jarocho as a vehicle for discovery. Tuhiwai Smith (2012) writes that to "discover the beauty of our knowledge" is about "discovering our own indigenous knowledge ... and its continued relevance to the way we lead our lives" (p. 161). Son jarocho becomes the beautiful knowledge that talleristas use to reshape and remake identity, and to reclaim cultural traditions and practices.

The community convivencia that son jarocho provides has impacted Cuauhtli's identity: "Son has become part of my identity because it is a community music. It is a way to link with other people." Feeling connected to others is related to not only identity and relationships, but to the well-being of a community as well (Tuhiwai Smith, 2012). Son jarocho becomes the common thread through which Cuauhtli feels connected to people, both as an individual and as an individual who is part of something larger—helping la tradición grow. Sharing son jarocho and la tradición is how Cuauhtli uses collective knowledge that was shared with him to help other Chicanas/xs/os decolonize as they search for roots and ancestral knowledge (Tuhiwai Smith, 2012).

Tallerista Johanna believes that music is a form of communication, "You are able to converse through the music, and even if you're shy, you have something to talk about. The music itself is a form of communication, and everybody feels connected by their roots." Tallerista Jen Negrete agrees sharing, "Music unites people. It touches people. Music is an international language. Tallercito and son jarocho have exposed me to a whole new world. It's amazing how close-knit son jarocho family is." Much like Cuauhtli, Jen feels a connectedness to people through son jarocho, through music. Son jarocho has opened a whole new world for Jen, one filled with music and family.

Several other talleristas mentioned family when discussing their experiences with son jarocho. José Luis shared that "El son es cultura y tradición, y más que nada es familia."[22] Talleristas have found a chosen family in son jarocho, people that they are connected to on several levels through music, dance, cultura, and tradición.

Johanna heard son jarocho for the first time just as she was beginning a journey to find her roots, "I will never forget the first time I heard son jarocho. It was when I was starting to get back into my roots as an adult, and I was starting to recognize, there is more to it." Son jarocho came into Johanna's life at a time when she was journeying through her own version of nepantla (Anzaldúa, 2012)—an in-between space—searching for a way to grow, conocimiento (Anzaldúa and Keating, 2002) guiding her in her search for her roots. Son jarocho provided the space Johanna needed to shape her identity into who she is becoming, El Tallercito became her nepantla (Anzaldúa, 2012).

The traditional fandango and the convivencia that is created through the gathering around a tarima and creating community with music and dance, was present in every testimonio. The fandango has become a place of growth, exploration, and transformation. Tallerista Doña Lupe Segura shared:

> El son jarocho crea comunidad de ésta forma, el fandango. Y en el fandango tu invitas a cualquier subirse a la tarima a bailar como sea y como salga. Entonces eso crea comunidad. En la forma en cómo crear comunidad es a través del fandango que es propio y clásico del son jarocho. Y los fandangos crea comunidad porque todo el mundo wow, se incluye, y se avienta en la tarima y baila, aunque no sepas bailar te avientas a la tarima. So, es una forma de envolver a la gente y crear comunidad.[23]

Doña Lupe stresses the importance of the fandango when creating community. Fandangos become a nepantla (Anzaldúa and Keating, 2002) where the community can grow and develop together.

El Tallercito: Una Comunidad Sin Fronteras

El fandango has become an integral part of how El Tallercito is able to crear transnational comunidades across the geopolitical borders that separate us from comunidades in Veracruz and México. Visiting maestros/as become community musicians alongside talleristas at fandangos in San Antonio, Tejas, and it is gathered around la tarima immersed in música, zapateado, and cultura where deep friendships form. Another tallerista who joined in the first few months of the colectivo's existence—when discussing visiting maestros/as shared:

> Being part of the whole family that nucleates around this thing, that has no borders, is something that is very unique, and something that I've never really seen before in my life. Tallercito really facilitates those types of connections and transfers of knowledge and things like that.

Johanna also values the deep connections she has formed with visiting maestros/as, and the importance that these visits have in her life. When discussing a visiting maestra, Raquel Palacios Vega, a jaranera and bailadora who hails from a long lineage of son jarocho and familia Los Vega, Johanna said, "having the opportunity to meet these maestros, and maintain our friendships and relationships across the border is important to me. Raquel and I nos hicimos muy amigas a través de la distancia."

In addition to bringing teaching artists to San Antonio, Tejas, El Tallercito supports comunidades in Veracruz and México through the purchase of instruments for our comunidad of talleristas, textiles from collectives of women throughout Veracruz, along with other hand crafted and homemade goods from artesanos throughout México. Moreover, COVID 19 has pushed the way we learn into the virtual world and talleristas have adapted and are able to take one-on-one classes on a sliding scale, paying what they can, with maestros/as throughout México. By creating our own transnational communities, El Tallercito is decolonizing the ways in which communities can support one another across borders.

Tallerista Oscar Cantua shared:

> When I joined El Tallercito de Son, I had no idea I would have the opportunity to learn directly from visiting maestros. Getting to know the people who are keeping this culture alive has been the definitive experience of my time in this community, and continuing to learn from them through virtual talleres gives me a vision of the heights we could reach. I am excited to see how these relationships will continue to grow into deeper connections and significant crossnational projects to create an intertwined community through son jarocho.

Joel Cruz Castellano—master musician, community worker, and part of Grammy nominated Los Cojolites—spoke about convivencia and the economic support that El Tallercito has been able to provide for Indigenous and Afro-mestizo comunidades in Santiago, Los Tuxtlas, Veracruz.

> Desde algunos años el son jarocho ha tenido una presencia importante en las comunidades Chicanas de los estados unidos, generando distintos procesos de colaboración con las comunidades soneras en Veracruz, estas redes han favorecido el intercambio y la interacción. El tallercito de Son de San Antonio es un

> grupo de personas que a través de la promotora Keli Rosa Cabunoc Romero han aprendido y cultivado el fandango y la música sonera en San Antonio, Texas han creado comunidades transnacionales con nosotros en el Colectivo Tecalli en Santiago Tuxtla, Veracruz, estos puentes se construido de muy diversas maneras, pero la que es mas evidente es la cooperación económica misma que se ha manifestado en la compra de instrumentos de cuerdas para los talleres, la compra de vestuarios tradicionales y el consumo de bienes culturales: clases onlines, talleres presenciales y conferencias.
>
> El impacto que ha tenido en la vida de las personas beneficiadas en Santiago Tuxtla ha sido significativo en el sentido de que estos pueblos son de escasos recursos y falta de opciones laborales, con esta colaboración sea abre una vía para que los musicos, constructores de instrumentos y manufactura de textiles tengan un mercado al que antes no podían acceder y los bienes adquieran un valor que difícilmente se lograría en Mexico, dignificando así la vida de los creadores.[24]

Several other talleristas who are continuing their son jarocho journey through virtual one-on-one talleres privados have shared similar sentiments. More research is needed to document the impact of these virtual talleres on creating transnational comunidad through son jarocho—in communities on both sides of la frontera.

Across geopolitical colonial borders through transnational comunidades, el fandango creates music and dance through living traditions. Tuhiwai Smith (2012) provides the project of creating to understand the importance that the arts hold in indigenous research: "creating is about transcending the basic survival mode through using a resource or capability that every indigenous community has retained throughout colonization—the ability to create and be creative" (p. 159). Creating through the continued tradition of playing son jarocho at community fandangos with El Tallercito becomes a way of resisting (re)colonization. Tuhiwai Smith (2012) explains that "throughout the period of colonization, indigenous peoples survived because of their imaginative spirit" (p. 160). Son jarocho embodies this creativity and imaginative spirit of the Indigenous and Afro-mestiza/x/o populations of Veracruz.

Social Justice: Son Jarocho y Cultura as Resistance

Son jarocho is community music, it happens in the moment, it is a living, breathing comunidad. Son jarocho creates a space for solidarity between Black and Brown communities who are too often pitted against each other. As Chicanas/xs/os, son jarocho has given us the knowledge that Mexico's roots are deeply connected to Africa—showing that our struggles have been connected for generations. The free nature of versos, means that Chicanas/xs/os at the marchas can use son as a tool of popular education, teaching those around us about important political issues through son, through cultura.

Tallerista Johanna attended her first marcha[25] as part of a social justice movement through El Tallercito:

> Since learning son, and being in Tallercito, I participate more in social justice movements. For a long time, I didn't really care what was going on. But then, being in Tallercito and hearing like 'oh we are going to go to the International Women's Day March' ... Actually, the first march that I have ever been to, was the Women's march with Tallercito. I want to go to all the marchas I can now.

Johanna has found a way to participate in social change through son jarocho and El Tallercito. By marching with El Tallercito, Johanna has found a way to resist:

> As a Chicana playing son at the marchas, I feel like I'm a bigger part of it, because we are making noise. And everybody brings their noise makers, and for us that is our noise, but its more than just noise. It's not just like the beating of a whatever or yelling, it's singing, it's using our cultura as resistance. Culture is resistance. Chicanas are one of the least liked minority groups in the U.S. because we don't assimilate. We won't assimilate.

Johanna uses her voice, her jarana, as her resistance; because for her, cultura is resistance. She has even made the connection between son and punk rock:

> It's resistance music. It's like the original Mexican punk rock—yes, it's punk rock. It's like Indigenous from back in the day, this is the original punk rock. The very nature of the music itself is resistance. That is why when we go to the marches, it means so much to me that we play son jarocho, because of the connection it has to resistance. They weren't allowed to play the music, the African slaves weren't allowed to have instruments. So, the cajón is a wooden box that was on the slave ships, and they used it as an instrument. And that is how they would create these things, and it was resistance. And to me, that is punk rock.

Johanna makes an important connection between son jarocho's beginnings as a resistance music, and Chicanas/xs/os using son jarocho today as a revitalized form of resistance in our comunidad at marchas (Tuhiwai Smith, 2012).

Being present at the marchas is something that is important to talleristas, every testimonio shared included marchas and social justice as a vital part of El Tallercito's mission. Tallerista Dra. Aimee Villarreal expressed how important our participation is:

> We've been very visible at different marches. There are different causes that we have played for, and it has been very diverse. I think we are recognized as being a group that is always supportive of causes for social justice. Because we play,

and we play for free or a small donation, and it always goes back to our taller, and that ethic is important. Because we're not here to make money off of son, we're not here to make a disco[26], or become famous. We're just here to provide the soundtrack for different causes.

Son jarocho becomes a powerful tool that talleristas can use as their voice at marchas and rallies. For Cuauhtli our jaranas, requintos, and other traditional instruments become so much more than just a musical instrument:

> They're not just instruments, they're tools of mass disruption. A lot of times in the Chicano culture, I think especially in California, after the introduction of son into California, it was used in all kinds of marchas and that made it very much like a tool. We like to say armas, but it's not really that it's a weapon. You know, there's things that don't directly translate ... They are your armas, you don't go into battle without them. The end.

For Cuauhtli—and talleristas— instruments become "tools of mass disruption" as he affectionately refers to his requinto; holding true to what Chicana scholar Norma Alarcón (1990) wrote; that the Chicano identity is consciously and critically assumed, serving as a point of redeparture for dismantling—in this case, cultura. Talleristas take their instruments, or as they call them armas—literally translated means weapons, but for the talleristas, it's a nonviolent tool—to marchas where talleristas fight injustices, and for Cuauhtli "you don't go into battle without them. The end."

Tallerista José Luis shares Cuauhtli's sentiments about marchas being a battle ground, and that son jarocho is its rhythm:

> Estaba viendo muchos videos en mis redes sociales, y en cada marcha o en cada lucha social, siempre hay ese requinto, o esa jarana tocando, el ritmo a la lucha. Sentí como, cuando vas a la guerra y están tocando los tambores y así sentía yo el rasgueo de la jarana. Como que, nos está llevando hacia una batalla.[27]

For José Luis, son has become the heart and soul of the marchas:

> Una vez lo comenté, y lo sigo comentando, que el son aquí en San Antonio, el son jarocho, El Tallercito viene siendo el alma, el corazón de la marcha. Porque es alegría, y a la misma vez vamos luchando por la causa que estemos en esa circunstancia, en ese momento. Yo siempre he dicho que el son, es el alma de la marcha.[28]

The beautiful resistance music that son jarocho creates transformed the way that José Luis participates in marchas. Over the past 5 years, I have observed him at several marchas, with his daughters carrying signs, jarana in his hands—the International Women's Day march, the César Chávez march, just to name a few. It is a powerful image of a Chicano father, leading his daughters, his comunidad, into the battle field. It is a truly moving experience, and I feel honored to stand with my fellow talleristas at the marchas, providing the soundtrack, the battle call for Chicanas/xs/os everywhere to come and march, to come and fight.

By revitalizing the traditions and practices of son jarocho through social justice, El Tallercito uses decolonial practices to protect traditions that could be lost through continued (re)colonization. Protecting is a multi-faceted project that is "concerned with protecting peoples, communities, languages, customs and beliefs, art and ideas, natural resources and the things Indigenous peoples produce" (Tuhiwai Smith, 2012, p. 159). Tuhiwai Smith (2012) links the survival of Indigenous peoples with "the need to protect a way of life, a language and the right to make our own history" (p. 149).

The testimonios that talleristas shared show how Chicanas/xs/os in 2017 in San Antonio, Texas, revitalized son jarocho as a tool for social justice (Tuhiwai Smith, 2012). Son jarocho has given them a voice at the marcha, a way to resist through cultura. The requintos and jaranas that the talleristas play have become tools of mass disruption, a way to fight against oppression and racism as Chicanas/xs/os. El Tallercito, and the son jarocho that is played at marchas, has become not only the soundtrack, but the alma y el corazón of the marcha.

Creando Comunidad A Través de La Cultura

Storytelling—cuentos that are passed down from generation to generation—is a powerful source of knowledge, a way to learn stories of our past, our ancestors' way of keeping traditions, rituals, and cultura alive in the face of (re)colonization (Tuhiwai Smith, 2012). Searching for our ancestors, finding out their stories, shapes how we create and self-make identity, so much so, that we often times even go searching for them. Through the testimonios shared by the talleristas as a Chicana/x/o collective and community, we have told our stories through our eyes, told them in our own voices.

Son jarocho becomes a decolonial tool, a way for Chicanas/xs/os searching for roots to find a connection to their antepasados through community music and dance. Son jarocho is the community music that bridges the gap—the generational gap, the gap in cultura which was lost because of colonial erasure in the U.S., the gap caused by the economic and geographical displacement of people in México and throughout the Southwestern U.S. For each talleristas who shared their in-depth testimonio, Día de los Muertos was a transformative ritual that helped them connect to their ancestors (Cabunoc Romero, 2017). Rescatando[29] traditions and rituals through son jarocho is a way for Chicanas/xs/os to decolonize themselves, transforming themselves through the traditions and rituals of their antepasados, using this ancestral knowledge to reshape and reconstruct self-identity (Tuhiwai Smith, 2012).

The fandango provides the cultural space to come together as a comunidad and through convivencia, collectively create music, dance, and song. Tallercito fandangos are a place to grow, explore, transform, and decolonize together as a community; all while discovering the beauty of our ancestral knowledge and celebrating the survival of that knowledge through the living traditions and cultura of son jarocho (Anzaldúa and Keating, 2002; Tuhiwai Smith, 2012). The transnational relationships that talleristas have formed through the intercambios culturales with maestros/as from México—both in person and virtually—have been a way to connect to their past and discover the beauty within our collective knowledge (Tuhiwai Smith, 2012).

El Tallercito provides talleristas with decolonial tools for "mass disruption," as Cuauhtli expressed, at the social justice marchas. They make noise with their versos and with their jaranas, talleristas provide the soundtrack for several social justice causes in our comunidad. The talleristas have become artivistas—activists who use their art as a tool for social justice—their jaranas becoming the battle cry, calling all Chicanas/xs/os to the marchas, inviting them to stand in solidarity as a comunidad. For some talleristas, son jarocho and El Tallercito have become el corazón y el alma of the marchas.

Everything about El Tallercito de Son SATX is homegrown, grassroots, the result of the immense need that Chicanas/xs/os feel for community, comunidad—a place to call home. Together, through son jarocho—sus tradiciones y su cultura—Chicanas/xs/os have created a safe space, a third space. For the entire comunidad of El Tallercito de Son, being presente[30], having a voice that is heard, is a right that will always be fought for. Documenting not only the emergence of spaces like El Tallercito and the important role they play in our communities, but the testimonios of the Chicanas/xs/os who create those spaces is necessary.

Tuhiwai Smith (2012) calls on indigenous research to share as a way of "demystifying knowledge and information and speaking in plain terms to the community" (p. 162). It is my goal through this research to provide accessibility to my comunidad—both in the academy and outside of higher education—about the ways in which Chicanas/xs/os in San Antonio, TX are using son jarocho, its cultura and traditions, to decolonize through the reshaping, remaking, and transforming of identities.

More research is needed on the power that son jarocho has to heal the wounds caused by (re)colonization among the Black and Brown communities. Son jarocho as an Indigenous, African, mestiza/x/o resistance music can become a space where Black and Brown communities can come together to heal through música, through cultura, through resistance of (re)colonization. In the future, I look forward to working with talleristas and El Tallercito using son jarocho—the decolonial community space the fandango creates—to heal the wounds that Black and Brown communities have suffered because of (re)colonization. Further research is also needed on the impact of the transnational communities that have been formed, and continue to form, between comunidades Chicanas in the United States and comunidades in Veracruz and throughout México. What is shared by the talleristas and teaching artists in this chapter on transnational comunidades formed a través del son, needs to be further researched and documented—by us, for us.

El Tallercito as a research site gives Chicanas/xs/os a say in how their work is documented, researched, and applied. Talleristas make sure our work remains accessible to other Chicana/x/o communities—as well as communities of color—as a model to self-empower through researching and documenting their own stories. El Tallercito de Son SATX provides a transformative cultural space where Chicanas/xs/os of all ages, from all walks of life, have decolonized, remade, reshaped, and transformed their personal and social identities through son jarocho, creando comunidad a través de la cultura.

Notes

1. Tallerista: this is the what the members of El Tallercito call themselves. Tallerista means "people who attend the taller"
2. Our culture (all translation provided by the author)
3. Artivista—Someone who is an activist and an artist, and uses art for political actions
4. The community of son jarocho (translation provided by the author)
5. Announcing the song (translation provided by author)
6. A wooden platform used for dancing son jarocho (translation provided by the author)
7. Tap-like percussive dancing (translation provided by the author)
8. A sacred altar (translation provided by the author)
9. Woman (translation provided by author)
10. In the small towns of (translation provided by the author)
11. In the barrios in the United States (translation provided by author)
12. Music of a radio (translation provided by the author)
13. A person who plays the jarana, the traditional string instrument played in son jarocho
14. With all their heart (translation provided by author)
15. I came to the United States because of my father, he worked in the fields. Since he was an unskilled laborer, he would come and go, and when he decided to stay here in the United States, it was the beginning of 1986, and then he brought us in 1987 or 1988. I was about eight (translation provided by the author)

16 There was the first taller for kids, and that is when I became very interested, and I started bringing my girls, and from there, I fell in love more than they did (translation provided by the author)
17 They fought (translation provided by the author)
18 The traditional headdress worn by Indigenous Mexica peoples for war and other types of ceremonies and for ceremonial purposes
19 Warrior (translation provided by the author)
20 I am in between Chicano and Mexicano because I was born in México, so I am Mexican by birth, but since now I am on this side of the puddle, you can say that I am sort of Chicano. When I say "this side of the puddle" it's because of the Rio Grande, well because it is what divides into two countries what is only one in my point of view, it's one country, there are no barriers, but we do have to jump the bridge, as they say, and that is why I say it (translation provided by the author)
21 Warrior, using "x" as a gender neutral ending, allowing all genders to be warriors (translation provided by the author)
22 Son is cultura and tradition, and more than anything, it is family (translation provided by author)
23 Son jarocho creates community in this way, the fandango. And at the fandango, you invite anyone to get on the tarima, and dance, however it comes out. So, that creates community. The way to create community is through the fandango that is unique and classic of son jarocho. And fandangos create community because the whole world, wow, is included and they just go for it on the tarima and dance, even if you don't know how to dance, you just go for it on the tarima. So, that is a way to involve the people and create community (translation provided by author)
24 For a while now, son jarocho has had an important presence in Chicano communities in the US, has generated distinct collaborative processes with communities in Veracruz, and these networks have favored the exchange and interaction between our communities. El Tallercito de Son from San Antonio is a group of people, who through the cultural promotor Keli Rosa Cabunoc Romero, have learned and cultivated el fandango and the son music in San Antonio Texas, have created transnational communities with our collective, Colective Tecalli, in Santiago Tuxtla, Veracruz. These bridges have been built in very diverse ways, but the one that has been the most evident, is the community economic support that has manifested through the purchasing of instruments for the talleres, the purchasing of traditional clothing and textiles, and the financial support from cultural exchanges: online classes, cultural exchanges through in person talleres in San Antonio, and conferences
The impact that this has had on the life of the people who benefit from this transnational community in Santiago Tuxtla has been significant in that these small communities have scarce resources and limited to no options for work. With this collaboration, we have created a way for musicians, instrument makers, and textile manufactures to have a market, one that they couldn't access before, one where their goods can be sold at a cost that would be very difficult to get in México, and in this way, dignifying the life of the creators (translation provided by author)
25 March (translation provided by the author)
26 Disc, as in musical CD (translation provided by the author)
27 I was seeing a lot of videos on my social media accounts, and in every march or in every social justice fight, there is always that requinto, or that jarana playing, the

rhythm of the fight. I felt, like when you go to war, and they are playing the drums, and that is how I felt the strumming of the jarana. Like, it is taking us to a battle (translation provided by author)

28 I once commented this, and I keep saying, that son here in San Antonio, son jarocho, El Tallercito has been the soul, the heart of the march. Because it is joy, and at the same time we are fighting for the cause that we are at in that circumstance, in that moment. I have always said that son, is the soul of the march (translation provided by author)

29 Rescuing (translation provided by author)

30 Present (translation provided by author)

References

Alarcón, N. (1990). Chicana feminism: In the tracks of 'the' native woman. *Cultural Studies, 4*(3), 248–256. https://doi.org/10.1080/09502389000490201

Anzaldúa, G. (1987). *Borderlands/La frontera: The new mestiza* (1st ed.). Spinsters/Aunt Lute.

Anzaldúa, G., & Keating, A. (2002). *This bridge we call home: Radical visions for transformation* (1st ed.). Routledge.

Cabunoc Romero, K. R. (2017). *El Tallercito de son satx: Creando comunidad a través de la cultura* (Publication No. 10686084) [Master's thesis, The University of Texas at San Antonio]. ProQuest Dissertations Publishing.

Delgado Bernal, D. (1998). Using a Chicana feminist epistemology in educational research. *Harvard Educational Review, 68*(4), 555–583.

Delgado Bernal, D., Burciaga, R., & Flores Carmona, J. (2012). Chicana/Latina testimonios: Mapping the methodological, pedagogical, and political. *Equity & Excellence in Education, 45*(3), 363–372. https://doi.org/10.1080/10665684.2012.698149

Díaz-Sánchez, M., & Hernández, A. (2013). The son jarocho as Afro-Mexican resistance music. *The Journal of Pan African Studies, 6*(1), 187–208.

Moraga, C., & Anzaldúa, G. (1983). *This bridge called my back: Writings by radical women of color*. Kitchen Table--Women of Color Press.

Mulford, M. (Director). (1989). *Chicano park* [Motion picture]. Cinema Guild.

Rodriguez, E. (Producer), & Braojos, R. (Director).(2006). *Fandango: Searching for the white monkey* [Motion picture]. United States: Los Cenzontles Mexican Art Center.

Tuhiwai Smith, L. (2012). *Decolonizing methodologies: Research and indigenous peoples* (2nd ed.). Zed Books.

Urrieta, L. (2010). *Working from within: Chicana and chicano activist educators in whitestream schools* (3rd ed.). University of Arizona Press.

Decolonizing, Healing and Evoking Resistance through Music: Crossing Ideological and Colonial Borders Using Transmedia and Experiential Educational Approaches

Iris Rodriguez

Yacatsol is an intergenerational musical ensemble and production house composed by the Borsegui Rodriguez family of Texas and Jalisco. Our group is a border-crossing, multilingual, decolonial, *"cura"* (healing) music and art project by a family of five which includes me (Iris Rodriguez, artivist and founder of Xica Media networks), my husband, musician and producer Ce Acatl Borsegui, (of the musical group *Huehuetl* and its musical offspring *Yetlanezi*) and our children ages 10, 8, and 1.5 years. As detribalized Indigenous peoples from Mexico and the U.S. who are in the process of decolonizing/re-membering ourselves and encouraging our community to do the same, we turn to our Indigenous lifeways and mindset to live, make decisions, and birth our creative work. Our family-based musical production group, *Yacatsol*, is rooted in the fusion of energies and experiences of each member as well as in the land and physical geographies from which it is birthed. We believe this combination has energetically charged and spiritually amplified the power of this project in a way that unites and heals peoples across land, time, space, and medium.

Through utilizing transmedia and experiential educational approaches rooted in Indigenous perspectives, *Yacatsol* crosses the U.S./Mexico border virtually and connects with people directly, in person and online. Whether performing, conducting workshops, or infusing our music into frontline social justice movements and online resistance/awareness campaigns, we understand that we are weavers with threads from the past. Before examining the multi-dimensional approach of our work, it is critical to first analyze the grounds from which the *Yacatsol* project operates, as it directly affects the virtual, geographical and cultural territory it covers. The following section examines the foundations of *Yacatsol* by digging into its soil.

The Soils and Roots from Which the Seeds of Yacatsol *Sprout*

In tipi ceremony, we learn that the intention and root of all things matters – from the way the fire is prepared and taken care of, to the deer meat we eat (of an animal that was hunted in a ceremonial way), to the way in which the peyote medicine was harvested and brought to the fire. It can guide and energetically/spiritually affect the ceremony. Even the way in which we introduce ourselves in front of the fire by evoking the name of our peoples and lands, matters. In this same tradition, the following section introduces the geographical, individual, and virtual soils/roots that form our base as a family and musical group.

Geographical Soils/Roots/Seeds

Our family is descended from both sides of the colonial border – from the sacred forests of Central Texas (the region known as *Yacatsol/Dacate*, near *Yanaguana*) and from *Atemajac/Chimalhuacan* in the Jalisco/Colima region of central western Mexico. We currently produce/birth our creative work from atop the sacred mountain *Xictepetl*, the still-buried *teocalli* pyramid also known as "El Cerro de La Reina" in Tonalá, Jalisco – land where the sun is born. Apart from the lands we carry within us, this project draws its unique energy from these geographies.

The name *Yacatsol* is one of the Indigenous names of the Texas Hill Country of Central Texas which is a Nahuatl-rooted word referring to a region of "noses" and "faces" on the stone. Although the so-called Edwards Plateau sits in the middle of the state, its connection to the mesquite and cactus-laden landscape to its south and east (towards the coastline on the Gulf of Mexico) is inextricable. Having been devastated by European arrival, the trans-Atlantic slave trade, and subjugation by six different nation-states within the past 500 years, the land itself has been usurped by white ownership. Descendants of the land are often detribalized and are labeled as "Mexican" and othered out of historical memory. Currently, the colonization continues and the land and its networks of springs and rivers are under attack by the construction of oil pipelines and the border wall.

My name is Iris and I am the matriarch of the *Yacatsol* musical family. I am a multidisciplinary artist, digital strategist, network producer, and writer from San Antonio, Texas. My peoples are native to so-called Texas and I am of Tonkawa, Karankawa and Coahuiltecan lineage. I consider myself *Nahua Tolteca* in terms of my cultural practices and lifeways as a *danzante*, *peyotera* family/person, and traditional practitioner. Since 2002 my bodies of art and community-based works have addressed social justice issues such as environmental racism/justice, family detention, decolonization, cultural arts, guerrilla media, feminism, and public archives. I am the founder of Xica Media, a Xicana-powered network of independent multimedia channels (that preserve/promote culture, decolonization, and Indigenous resistance) which include Xica Nation, End Family Detention, Xicana Chronicles, and the *Yacatsol* project. Understanding that technological, cultural, linguistic, and age divides are used to our collective detriment, through our work we strive to bridge them through the use of text, audio, video, in-person, and immersive web-based experiences. With a trajectory spanning almost two decades at these critical intersections of frontline resistance, digital resistance, culture, education, and decolonization, my transition into art (as an artist) is relatively new but extends across historical community grounds and relationships with elders and longtime community activists.

Ce Acatl Borsegui, my partner and other adult member of the group, was born into an Indigenous musical family ensemble from Tonalá, Mexico. His musical roots span generations back, as he was raised in the Indigenous musical tradition of Mexico alongside his parents in *Grupo Huehuetl*. For the past three decades he has served as a cultural ambassador of Indigenous Mexican music as a performer, teacher, and artisan specializing in millennial Mexican instrumentation.

The two youngest members of *Yacatsol* are Ameyalli and Sol, our children. Their participation in the music is significant as they have been raised outside of the Western medical and cultural paradigms. Their births were significant and historical for the family, as they were born at home (in ceremony with a midwife, *danza Mexica*, and *curanderas*) and represent a return to home birth after a generation of hospital births with medicalized interventions and no cultural influence or birth ceremony. These children have been raised inside the tipi and the *Danza Mexica*, with preparation and teachings rooted in *Nahua Tolteca* culture. They also remain outside of the American public school system. Born in Central Texas but raised in Jalisco with linguistic roots in English, Spanish and Nahuatl, their presence also represents a living example of what decolonization can look like for Mexican/Xicanx/ detribalized Indigenous peoples – a multilingual future where colonial borders and histories cannot bury our cultural identity; where our children can arrive in ceremony rooted in the earth without the artificial lights and touching/hands of the Western medical system; and grow with the millenary sounds of the *huehuetl* and sacred instruments made from nature along with our traditional songs in our traditional languages.

Virtual Soils/Roots

Yacatsol is grounded in the social justice roots of Xica Media and its trailblazing trajectory within frontline resistance, community news and "digital resistance," a term and concept I created through my trajectory in digital social justice work.

Yacatsol was first promoted and introduced by the Xica Media network and its sister site, Xica Nation. Birthed in the era of corporate media control and digital divides across race/class/age/digital access, Xica Media introduced *Yacatsol* in 2016 to a national audience that had previously referred to the network for news and community perspectives. The audience immediately embraced the idea of adding musical media to complement its longstanding base of written articles, photography, poetry and video interviews. By creating music that touches on current events, frontline resistance movements, culture and decolonial concepts through multiple digital mediums and multimedia approaches, we found that we were able to circumvent the mass media information saturation and emotional fallout of shock doctrine through song and dance.

We fully understand that our community and audience base spans borders and languages that many are not able to cross. Produced by Xica Media, we work to create a comprehensive, multifaceted, multilingual experience by using a transmedia approach that fuses storytelling across multiple digital mediums and languages via video, song, and written text/poetry. We believe that stimulating as many senses as possible is necessary to evoke the most potent point of contact and awakening of genetic information. However, we adjust our approach when creating virtual work and intentionally try to overstimulate as many senses as possible when reaching across technology and the literal glass/plastic of a phone, tablet and computer screen to move hearts to emotional response and action.

Dismantling Coloniality: Educational, Lyrical and Performative/Visual Aspects of Yacatsol

Through the lyrical and performative aspects of our music we strive to dismantle colonialism in ways that are not confrontational, enjoyable, and easy to understand. Whether embedded in trilingual lyrics of belonging and connection to the land, replicating the *tonalli* (Mexica day signs) in masks that student performers wear, or creating culturally-focused educational toolkits that include music and printable PDFs, we strive to connect with our audiences in as many mediums as possible. Our roots in digital resistance work have taught us that people's ability to receive information is affected by their emotional state, thus we use the vehicles of pleasurable sounds and beauty to audibly and visually educate without using trigger words that evoke negative emotions associated with colonial trauma like anger, sadness, or resentment. By making the learning experience pleasing to the senses, we are able to educate and plant seeds of social consciousness, unity, and radical perspective to a more receptive audience who may benefit and heal from the negative effects of colonization in a non-confrontational or healthier, creative way – in person and online through performance and immersive audio/visual websites.

Educational

In our traditional ways as native peoples of this continent, we were engaged with music through song, dance and/or playing instruments. To this day, whether you are in powwow, tipi or *danza*, you interact with instruments and sound and add your own unique energy to the music and the moment. Thus, when performing or participating as teachers in educational settings, we believe that in order to unearth and wake up the genetic information hidden in our cells across generations of genocide, that touching, feeling and playing the music – *becoming* the music – best facilitates the reconnection to culture and reawakens DNA. We believe in conducting immersive, experiential educational circles to promote decolonization, indigenization and healing.

Having been part of the musical heritage of *Grupo Huehuetl*, Ce Acatl Borsegui has engaged with audiences and students of all ages through performances and facilitating musical workshops for people from all backgrounds since birth. Over the course of the past three decades, he has specifically worked with youth from communities in crisis, youth in detention and children of color who come from economically challenged backgrounds in the U.S. as a teacher of Indigenous Mexican music and instrumentation. By rooting his teaching style in Indigenous lifeways and ceremony, he has been able to connect and engage with his students in ways Western teachers cannot. In the United States, workshops and performances have been conducted as part of non-profit cultural and artistic curriculums for youth of color and imprisoned youth. In Mexico, the workshops have been conducted in municipal youth programs as well as public elementary schools as part of a special invitation by community-level school administration.

In our traditional and ceremonial ways, engaging with and directly touching the earth is a common practice. Our hands would touch the earth to pray. Incense like *copal* tree resin or salvia/sage would burn, stimulating our sense of smell. Our food was prepared in a ceremonial way. Our *palabra* was sacred. This combination of elements focused on healing and releasing things that hurt us. We work to re-create this experience in a modern, urban setting and have found our approach successful. Ce Acatl states:

> We burn *copal* as we convene. There is an awakening that occurs when a child beats a drum for the first time or touches the wood of a rattle and feels the *ayoyote* seeds in their fingers. We teach them basic rhythms that are Indigenous to cultures all around the world and introduce them to the touch/feel/sound of the *huehuetl*, *teponaztli* and clay drums. Through their execution of repeating ancient beats and patterns and their experimentation with different earth-based organic instruments, they begin to develop a personal connection to the sounds and the materials before our eyes. They connect with music in a way that is very different than society has programmed them to connect. They are no longer audibly perceiving sound, they are now creating sound, touching sound, and *becoming* the music. At the same time, we teach them to use their tongues and pronounce the names of the instruments in the Indigenous languages from which they are derived from. This stimulates parts of the brain that Western society does not. In particular, when a Xicanx or Mexican-origin student who lives in the barrios of the U.S. begins to play and connect with the music and instruments, we have witnessed a phenomenon, a sort of spark and awakening in their eyes, that occurs. Across the board, it has been our experience that the kids labeled 'troubled' or 'at-risk' are the ones that connect the most with the music. We also see this same phenomenon happen with Black children and kids from other historically-oppressed communities.

We believe that this phenomenon happens due to several factors: (1) genetic connection/stimulation to millenary music and instrumentation that has been suppressed for the past 500 years that is coming back to life; (2) lack of connection to ethnic/cultural identities and traditions, specifically within the context of the U.S. and its emphasis on homogenous, Indigenous-heritage-erasing terms like "Hispanic" and "Latinx"; and (3) intentional lack of arts and cultural programming in public education.

The incorporation of Indigenous instruments and rhythms into our classes make discussions of history and historical perspectives from an Indigenous lens inevitable. Although our expertise is in Mexican-origin Indigenous music and instrumentation, we also reach into African and other Indigenous traditions from around the world through the incorporation of their instrumentation and musical styles, as there are connections and commonalities between all of them. In particular, we include the African *djembe* in our workshops. We create a circular seating arrangement and distribute the instruments around it. As we speak and through the conversations, we incorporate rhythms and encourage the students to play. As we discuss the history and ceremonial meanings behind the instruments, we are able to cover a musical history that spans millennia across the Americas and Africa. Our discussion of history then moves forward through time.

The concept of "divide and conquer" has been used to subjugate peoples of color via colonial borders, diaspora, family separation, separating people from their culture and history, and separating the spirit from animate and inanimate objects/concepts. It is for this reason we find it important to be inclusive when we speak of the past by citing the connections that exist between Indigenous cultures of the world, their ceremonial musical foundations and the similar earth-respecting beliefs they share.

In this generation of buried histories, intergenerational genocide and tech advances, and within the context of an American society that continues to dismantle ethnicity and culture in favor of American empire and caste, we find it appropriate to fuse elements from the old and new to provide a forum for decolonial teaching. We use musical mestizaje (mixing of musical genres and timelines) to bridge from the current day into the past. For example, by introducing our cumbia songs, which incorporate Indigenous instruments, we begin with a genre that is familiar to many of the students who live in *barrios* or low-income areas. Our workshops bridge Indigenous and African histories and connect Black and Brown students with their African roots. We believe it is important to highlight the music of Black and Brown Indigenous cultures because the majority of children we have taught come from these communities. Historically, we have had similar experiences under colonization and (in particular) in the borderlands as part of the Transatlantic Slave Trade.

We believe it is of critical importance to evoke the concept of decolonization and indigenization simultaneously through our work and workshops. It is not enough to, for example, dismantle colonization if it will be replaced with something as dangerous. Indigenization is a critical next step of decolonizing as it provides the spiritual, theoretical, structural, and cultural framework from which to heal, live, and build. In discussing history, it is important to convey the sense that decolonization is not centered around the point of contact/Spanish arrival. It defeats our purpose to speak of our ancestors as being a great people "before" colonization as opposed to stating that we remain a great people presently and come from a long lineage of great people. As the case in ceremony, our *palabras* matter. It is important to evoke the processes of decolonization and indigenization in teaching/learning because they are complimentary processes. We do not believe it is enough to dismantle colonization because it can leave the person feeling baseless in the middle of fracturing their understanding of their place within the colonial mentality and world. Indigenization is a critical part of restoring an individual's self-esteem, power, and understanding of self as well as time, place, and belonging.

Lyrical

Our discography includes albums in three primary languages with no emphasis in a particular one – English, Spanish and Nahuatl. To supplement our educational outreach and also connect with audience members who prefer to read, we publish our lyrics as individual poems in multiple languages along with embedding the MP3 songs to accompany them. The following is a breakdown of our EPs and the languages they contain:

- *La Cultura Nos Cura* – English, Spanish, Nahuatl
- *Cenzontle – Lullabies in English, Spanish and Nahuatl* – English, Spanish, Nahuatl
- *Return to the Red Road* – Estok Gna (Carrizo Comecrudo), Nahuatl, Spanish
- *Canto A La Tierra*[1] – Spanish

The lyrics for *Cenzontle*, *Return to the Red Road* and *Canto A La Tierra* can be considered more traditional and ceremonial, whereas *La Cultura Nos Cura* is a danceable cumbia album with conscious trilingual lyrics that speak to dismantling colonization, unity between historically oppressed communities, and preserving Earth. One of the songs in this album, *Abre la Tierra* written by Laura Ríos Ramírez, an Indigenous *danzante* and community leader, invites listeners to "open the earth with your blade, inside Mother Earth is *the* healing." The lyrics instill the idea that one has the power to plant seeds of change if you work in a loving way with the Earth.

Abre La Tierra *(Lyrics by Laura Ríos Ramírez)*

Abre la tierra con tu cuchillo, en la madre tierra está la sanación
abre la tierra con tu cuchillo, en la madre tierra está la sanación
entre tus manos están las semillas
ponlas en la tierra con mucho amor

Decolonizing, Healing and Evoking Resistance

From one song to other on the album, the concept of personal agency is layered into the message of belonging through lyrics that promote taking direct action towards healing. Whereas *Abre La Tierra* discusses relationship to earth, *Beat Be Too Hot* discusses relationship between a Xicanx and the U.S. government/capitalism and the methods of direct action one can take to realize collective healing. Our Indigenous wisdom teaches us that the well-being of the community depends on the well-being of the individual.

Beat Be Too Hot (Lyrics)

Those in power don't care about hurting us
Their power sits on our backs so let's stand up
They say "pay your taxes" and obey silently
Mechanize your part in their machine

Gotta stay trucha, pon ojo
Families imprisoned, ICE raids, and who knows
They want us scared, like cucuy! cucuy everywhere!
Together let's break through the fear

They want borders, bombs, to eat death and fear
Frack, enslave, oppress, and profiteer
We must join together to survive
Let's take a leap, break them chains, and let's unite

We're all up in the system
It's come down to us versus them
Take the white blindfold off your eyes
Divest, direct action, decolonize

Returning to our earth-based ways is key
For all the colors of humanity
We gotta move, we gotta act, we're out of time
Take my hand, our liberation is intertwined

We're all connected for a reason
Trust your gut, trust your vision
Even if you're deep in the machine
Together (los) tenemos que sacudir

The first stanza to this song is addressed to the working-class community it is a part of and speaks to the silent obedience the U.S. system imposes upon its still-colonized subjects, all of whom pay taxes regardless of citizenship. The lyrics then discuss the systemic use of fear by agents of the law, like ICE and call for people to stay "*trucha*," a word derived from Xicanx code speak that means to be vigilant. The *cucuy* that is cited is a cultural concept within the

Mexican-origin community of a being or monster that evokes fear and brings harm. The third stanza unites the interconnection between capitalism and its inherent violation of the earth and violation of the human body by aligning border, bombs, fracking, enslaving, and profiteering of suffering, separation, and destruction. The song then reminds the audience that the majority of people are facing the same ills and that we can unite to effect change through divesting from harmful capitalist structures, taking direct action on the ground to protest when needed, and decolonizing to re-understand/re-conceptualize our individual and collective power within the operational framework of life within the U.S. capitalist system. Lyrics in the fifth stanza invoke the need to re-indigenize as an effective model to return to as a way of living that is in alignment with respect for all life. The audience is reminded that the public is out of time to act and must take action now. They are also reminded that without the liberation of all others that no one will truly be free. The song then ends with an acknowledgment of the fear listeners may have in taking direct action against the U.S. government (or capitalism) and implies that following intuition is important here (in light of the propaganda or messaging in media inundating them with information that works to numb critical thinking.) It indicates that people need to come together and "shake off" the ills of colonization, not with a light dusting but rather an exaggerated physical exertion of shaking to "force the bad things off."

From *Beat Be Too Hot* to the lyrics of *Children of Anahuac*, which are discussed and analyzed below, remind listeners who are detribalized and looking to reconnect with their culture that they have an ancestral connection to *Anahuac*, a Nahuatl word meaning "land surrounded by water" that is often considered North America or Turtle Island.

Children of Anahuac (Lyrics)

Children of Anahuac:
we carry the medicine inside.
We hear Mother Earth now.
We have removed the wasichu lies.

Labels can't define us,
through our blood to this land we are tied.
Tierra sagrada:
maíz, mesquite, nopal give us life.

Their walls can't confine us.
Millennial caminos will survive.
Wasichu can't blind us.
We've had enough of suffering and lies.

> We remember our place here.
> All that was taken has come back to life.
> Children of Anahuac:
> we carry the medicine inside.
>
> Noyollocuicatl tlazocamati Tonantzin tlalli
> atl ne tlayoli ka'nochi nonemilis

The term *wasichu* in the first and third stanzas is a Lakota-origin word meaning "takers of the fat" which commonly refers to those of Euro-American descent who have historically stolen and taken the land, culture, identity from Black and Brown peoples. The song continues by invoking "*Tierra sagrada: maíz, mesquite, nopal give us life*" which translates to "sacred land: corn, mesquite, and cactus give us life." This line reminds the audience that the borderlands are also considered sacred land by Indigenous peoples and have foods such as corn, mesquite and cactus that are used to eat but can also be made into curative medicines. The concept of having "medicine inside" implies that our healing as detribalized peoples is woven into our DNA – from intergenerational trauma/resilience to the health that can be obtained from eating a diet that is traditional to our genetic makeup. The song ends with a phrase in both "traditional" Nahuatl and the dialect from the *Huasteca* region of central Mexico. It translates to, "*From my heart I sing, thank you Mother Earth, water is life, all my relations.*"

The next song, *La Cultura Nos Cura* (for which the album is also titled) opts for a more direct messaging to drive the point home that decolonizing/re-indigenizing holds the key to our healing and wellness. *La Cultura Nos Cura* was the first song and video of the album, and we felt it was important to enter into our listener's ears with a simple message: that the culture we carry inside us can heal us. As a detribalized peoples whose names have been erased from our memories, and whose land has been taken by six waves of colonizers (aka the "six flags of Texas") many of us are displaced, albeit, even in our own ancestral homelands. Many embark on a journey to find out their DNA to find clues of their tribal identities. This song proposes that the answers actually reside within us:

La Cultura Nos Cura (Lyrics)

> La cultura nos cura
> La cultura nos cura
> La cultura nos cura
> La cultura nos cura

This song is made of a simple phrase, *la cultura nos cura*, which translates to "culture can cure us." The underlying message of this song is that indigenizing our perspective, food, and lifeways can not only feed our mind/body/spirit but also heal the ills of colonization. But healing will not only require a journey inward to our personal physical terrain – we must also heal the actual terrain we walk upon – Mother Earth.

The following song, *Mother Earth Is Calling*, takes the listener from the point of awareness of our interconnection to all life and to the earth in *La Cultura Nos Cura* and then offers a set of specific realizations to (re)connect the listener to their personal geography/earth – their body – by reflecting on the four elements of nature and how they apply to our individual bodies. In our traditions as Indigenous peoples, we understand that the nature that exists outside and around us is also inside us . . . and that Mother Earth herself is speaking to us through that connection:

Mother Earth Is Calling

> Mother Earth is calling us to help her
> and it's come down to now - or never
>
> Earth - land we depend on is sacred
> Air - the air that we breathe is sacred
> Fire - light you carry inside is sacred
> Water - from the womb, earth, and sky is sacred
>
> ----
>
> Madre tierra nos llama a ayudarla
> y es ahora o nunca
>
> Tierra - de cual dependemos es sagrada
> Aire - que respiramos es sagrado
> Fuego - que tenemos adentro es sagrado
> Agua - de tierra, vientre y cielo es sagrado

Mother Earth is Calling reminds us that aside from our relationship to self, we also have a relationship to our environment. What is in the macrocosm exists in the microcosm – we are part of – and also a reflection of – nature. We are also made up of the same four elements. We wanted to promote the idea that 500 years of colonization cannot sever thousands of years of relationship with nature and that Mother Earth is not only still speaking to us, but also calling us to help her survive colonization. By reflecting on the nature inside of us, we can better listen to what Mother Earth is saying as we return to our traditional worldviews and re-connect sacred relationships to the elements that colonization has cut us away from.

While *Mother Earth is Calling* uses Indigenous instrumentation such as the flute, the *teponaztli*, and the *huehuetl*, the beat of the song is based on a basic cumbia rhythm. We attempted to guide the listener's ear from a modern context that borders the sacred as a means to connect in the present. In the following song, *Canto A La Tierra*, which we released as a single and follow-up to the *La Cultura Nos Cura* album, we take the opportunity to finish crossing the bridge from the modern to a ceremonial musical past, where we connect with and sing in honor of Mother Earth herself using rhythms from the *danza Conchero* tradition. The *Concheros* were *danzantes* (ceremonial dancers) who codified the ancestral natural knowledge embedded in the songs and ceremonial dance steps into Catholicism after the invasion and were able to keep elements of our traditional ceremonial *cantos* and *danzas* alive. The lyrics of *Canto A La Tierra* were written by my maestro of *danza*, Juan Axixic Huehuecoyotl, who is credited for maintaining the *danza* tradition in Jalisco outside of the Catholic fusion of the *Conchero* style.

Canto A La Tierra (Lyrics)

> Estamos enlazados por un hilo por la cuerda de la vida y del amor.
> Por la piel y el corazón todos unidos juntos al mismo tronco de un tambor.
>
> Como un huehuetl de tamaño de la tierra pa sonar con el gran eco de su entraña.
> A vibrar para danzar y pa cantar nuestro rezo del ayer, hoy, y mañana.
>
> Alientados por el viento y el aroma del copal y el incienso de la salvia
> Tatemados por el sol y el temazcal y andando de la mano de una sabia.
>
> De una ancestral tradición de nuestro ser, compartiendo lo mejor de cada uno.
> Con la idea de mejorar y trascender, buscando nuestro interior en cada ayuno.
>
> Y girando en espiral todos trenzados no importando el color ni la nación.
> Con las siete direcciones conectadas en el trabajo de alegría y sanación.
>
> Como hermanxs, como amigxs, como un todo festejando la existencia de hoy y aquí.
> Por la siembra de maíz y de más granos, por las frutas y las flores y por ti.

English translation:

> We are bound by a thread on the rope of life and love
> through the skin and the heart all united together to the same trunk of a drum.
>
> Like an earth-sized drum that sounds with the great echo of its entrails,
> we vibrate to dance and sing our prayer of yesterday, today, and tomorrow.
>
> Encouraged by the wind and the scent of copal and salvia incense,
> toasted by the sun and sweat lodge, walking hand in hand with a sage.

From an ancestral tradition of our being, sharing the best of ourselves,
with the idea of improving and transcending, looking for our interior in each fast.

And spiraling, braided together, no matter the color or the nation
with the seven directions connected in the work of joy and healing

as brothers/sisters, as friends, as a whole celebrating the existence of today and here.
For corn crop and the other grains, for the fruits and the flowers and for you.

This song celebrates daily social life by comparing it to an Indigenous ceremony. The reference of people of all nations coming together as a drum evokes a sense of unity and consciousness through each drumbeat/heartbeat. They come together to make a sound the entire earth can hear. The description of specific plant medicines (*copal* and sage) evokes a sense of spiritual cleansing and protection. The reference to the *sabia*/sage is a reference to a woman elder, a grandmother, or the earth as a woman, who is wise, experienced, and willing to teach and help you heal as you go through your life journey. The emphasis on time and the "here and now" is rooted in the *Nahua Tolteca* cosmovision and specifically the *Huey Cuauhxicalli Iixiptla* (Nahuatl), "*Gran jicara del águila diurna: El Sol su representante*" (Spanish), "Great bowl of the diurnal eagle: The Sun, its representative" (English) also known as a "day" in the *Tonalpohualli* or "Mexica/Aztec calendar."

Performative/Visual

As is the case with our workshops, our musical performances emphasize the participation of the audience through singing, dancing and playing of Indigenous instruments. We open our performances with the burning of *copal* and in some cases, give *limpias*. We make small offerings with ancient foods such as *alegrías* made of amaranth/*huautli* and honey (which literally translate into "happiness") or handmade *regalitos* (giveaways) for the audience, as is done in ceremony. We ask our audience to dance with us and invite them to play one of our Indigenous instruments. Our lyrics are trilingual, thus every element of our self-produced songs show a comprehensive learning experience for audience members to push their tongues to speak and reach outside the monolinguistic mindset and linguistic binary of English and Spanish, and into a trilingual framework where they can learn as they sing/dance/play. This also serves to remind people that Spanish is not our mother tongue.

Whether we are addressing loss or reconnection to our traditions and worldview, we use our collective historical experience as a people as a bridge to directly engage with people in our performances and videos. The visual aesthetic of our music does not depend on a storyline that follows a character, but instead uses elements that can be perceived as commonplace, familiar, and relatable. By making the messaging personal, we create a visual aesthetic in our videos (also produced by us) that then takes the listener/viewer by the hand and walks them gently through an intentional dismantling of colonial paradigms. We mix ancestral, ceremonial and modern concepts in a way that breaks down taboos that range from working with peyote, *curanderismo*, radical womyn in the kitchen, the feminine body, among other themes. The following section offers a decolonial analysis of performative/visual imagery in "*La Cultural Nos Cura*" (2016) album. The music video for the single release opens with a scene that depicts Black and Brown kids beating a Donald Trump *piñata*. That scene is original footage of a birthday party in Oakland, California and was filmed well before he won the 2016 presidency. Those who would become the eventual targets of his regime are featured joyously beating a *piñata* of him in a suit. Celebrating. As peoples currently (2020) in and under the thick of the weight of his fascist regime, this particular scene breaks boundaries and allows the mind to enter the space with a future beyond Trump, and by extension, the western paradigm, if not the *wasichu* altogether.

After the opening scene as Indigenous Xicanas from different generations are dancing, a peyote blossoming in a superimposed contrast over the dances evokes a very powerful, feminine sense of a better tomorrow through the divine feminine and the youth, who are intended to represent powerful forces that can dismantle colonization for all. The Indigenous peoples of the Texas borderlands have a unique relationship to the peyote cactus and its medicine. Although criminalized by the U.S. and Mexican governments, it is traditionally used to assist in physiological, emotional, and spiritual ailments and conditions. Its blossoming as a semi-transparent image in the background where Xicanas are dancing in the forefront is a reference to celebrating the culture as well as the divine feminine, connection to earth, *curanderismo*, and our historical relationship with the peyote plant.

In a following scene, Tara Evonne Trudell, daughter of John Trudell and a warrior and social justice activist in her own right, appears in her home kitchen, cooking hand-made flour tortillas. Her placement in her home is a visual reminder that we are in *our* home, our traditional lands. As an Indigenous woman on the frontlines of resistance, she is happily preparing food, akin to the concept of a physical/spiritual nourishment and sustenance provided by the music she is listening to (*La Cultura Nos Cura*.) The imagery of a flour tortilla is a reference to the wheat or mesquite flour tortillas commonly associated as traditional food from the Southwest U.S./Northern Mexico borderlands.

Throughout the videos, we felt it was important to celebrate feminine beauty in all its shapes as a form of resistance to the modern Euro-centric standard of beauty. We also wanted to show womyn wearing jeans with traditional/ceremonial blouses. We wanted to evoke a sense of time and place to the dancing womyn, making it obvious they represent a modern context and have a foot in the Indigenous and Western worlds. It shows womyn dancing in downtown Juarez, Mexico, a site of femicides. The scene of womyn dancing in Juarez in front of a bull evokes a celebration of the divine feminine and a joyful, resistant fearlessness within a capitalist, male-centric social order in a city known for its femicides.

In a following scene I am dancing and doing a *paso* (step) of putting a hole in the ground with my foot and dropping a seed into it, the day signs of the *Tonalpohualli* iconography appear all around me, serving as a visual reminder that Indigenous peoples of the continent had a different concept of time than the one of the current social order, one that relates to interconnectivity with nature as exemplified by the nature-based glyphs of the *Tonalpohualli* "Aztec calendar." It also reminds us that we are a part of nature, in the mix with all these energies.

My presence in the shot shows me as a womyn in exile in Mexico, dancing. By showing me as an Indigenous Xicana woman of Texas who works towards decolonization and indigenization of her community as a means to heal personal and collective systemic wounds, the metaphor of dancing in spite of my criminalization and forced move (to keep my freedom) from my lands (the U.S.) to Mexico evokes a sense of joyful resistance instead of longing, sadness, or anger. My intention of my dance was to represent a sense of positivity, growth, hope, and moving forward. The *paso* (dance step) I was doing of planting seeds was inspired by my maestro de *danza*, Juan Axixic Huehuecoyotl, who also wrote the lyrics to "*Canto A La Tierra.*"

Another important scene is the one we repeat where the hands of adults and youth are sowing seeds of the "three sisters" (corn, beans and squash). This imagery reminds Indigenous borderland peoples of their traditional planting practices, specifically the planting of corn, beans, and squash together to increase crop yield. The agricultural practices were also moon-based and were often the root of numerical foundations and the mode of teaching of mathematical knowledge. In the video, we use the count Nahuatl, "*Ce, ome, yei, nahui,*" to get people to begin verbally speaking aloud the ancient language. We wanted to make the process of indigenizing and re-learning Indigenous culture fun by singing the numbers 1–4 in Nahuatl (audibly) while displaying the numbers on the screen, making it easy to learn for all ages.

Decolonizing, Healing and Evoking Resistance

Another notable paso in the video is one where we wanted to evoke a spiritual resistance. In this dance move, womyn are emulating doing a traditional Indigenous *Nahua Tolteca limpia* on themselves. Given the movement is made into a dance and placed within a modern context, we show that despite the historical demonization of womyn healers as a weapon of colonization and genocide, they still remain ... and are actively healing and protecting themselves. As they do the *limpia*, the flags of the U.S. and Mexico are depicted. We did not plan for this; the clip was submitted by one of our followers. As transborder artivists, we felt it was important to show the current political context of the borderland territory, which in the modern day comprises two countries, the U.S. and Mexico. As the repeated lyrics of the song, "*la cultura nos cura*," conjures a sense of memory and belonging to Xicanx and Indigenous heritage, showing the two flags of our audience (borderland peoples) watching the video who are often forced to identify with one side or the other. Through digital resistance of this decolonial project, this image encourages our borderlands audience to exist and or resist together in the same space, dancing.

It is important to note that the videos were submitted by womyn across the borderlands (San Antonio (TX), El Paso (TX), Ciudad Juarez (Mexico), Tonalá (Mexico), Oakland (CA), and McAllen (TX). In our Indigenous way of thinking, the origins of everything matters: we consider where food is planted, how it is harvested, what intention we have behind an action. We felt that by inviting the participation of womyn from the public across the borderlands that we would be co-creating something of beauty and resistance at the very root of the creative creation process and practice. We felt this would be a blessing to the project.

The album cover for *La Cultural Nos Cura* (2016) album also represents the way in which *Yacatsol* decolonizes ideological and colonial borders through imagery. Featuring a Xicana woman dressed in jeans, a cowboy hat, and glasses that is riding a broomstick, we play with the modern social mythology of the feared Brown witch or *bruja* and evoke a notion of resistance to *machismo*/male supremacy, religious conquest, and white supremacy. In the image I am standing with my broomstick in between my legs as I wear a cowboy hat and sunglasses. By placing native plants of the borderlands in the background, I reference a geographical location in lands along the U.S./Mexico border. My use of a traditional woven broom from Jalisco and a reed-woven cowgirl/Western hat evokes belonging to modern cultures from both sides of the border as well as the Indigenous cultures that live(d) there. My use of glasses and jeans places me in a modern somewhat Western context, while my use of a traditional Mexican skirt for young girls as a shirt reflects

Figure 4.1: Yacatsol. Source: Iris Rodriguez

a mixture of tradition and culture in a new way that is beautiful and also practical.

In sum, all the music videos emphasize Indigenous culture, womyn, youth iconography, Indigenous sites of resistance, Indigenous plants, and Indigenous culture/lifeways. Whether the song is in the genre of a medicine song/canto or a cumbia, the audiovisual experience is one of cultural resilience.

Conclusion

Our intention with *Yacatsol* was to create a multidimensional musical project that is able to cross borders physically and musically while working to decolonize and indigenize our peoples as a form of resistance to ongoing occupation and destruction of the Earth. Over the years as we have worked with people in educational spaces as well as in digital and physical frontline resistance movements, we have found an effective way to resist coloniality and heal inner/collective wounds – through music and arts that unites and recognizes Indigenous peoples and our relationship to earth in a positive way. Through direct language and verbal/visual metaphor we have found that music education and production have the power to combat the division and erasure of communities of color within capitalism and living within the U.S.

Whether our projects take us to work physically or virtually, in the U.S. or Mexico, we feel responsible for doing our best to walk in a sacred way. We humbly understand the power of our ability to virtually cross the borders and how we are witnesses to the power of our ancestral music to students and audiences, in person and online. We feel blessed to have the tools to stimulate the senses with creating and participating in works that fuse video, film, audio, and bits of media to document, digitize, and disseminate a possibility of a better world for us all. We see ourselves as amplifiers of resistance on the ground and digital resistance warriors as we work to dismantle coloniality by healing through music and speaking out against colonial injustices that divide people and erase identities. We are aware that we hold a great power in our hands as a digital generation. We also know that we walk with our ancestors – even in the modern digital highways.

Rooted in prayer and manifested based on the dreams and visions we receive, *Yacatsol* represents far more than a musical group or a simple musical workshop. We strive to be living bridges that connect the past with the present into a future where the generations can coexist. Rooted in our Indigenous traditions and in stimulating the senses as was done ceremonially for over a thousand years, *Yacatsol* has found a way to cross the border and reach across generational, linguistic, digital divides in all directions through transmedia and immersive experiences. Our vision and prayer moving forward is that these seeds of the past continue to grow across time, space and the physical/digital worlds for our children and our people.

Note

1 Select Lyrics (by Iris Rodriguez, unless otherwise noted)

Decolonization Within the Walls Higher Education

Towards a Decolonial Feminist Hip-Hop

MELISSA CASTILLO PLANAS AND AUDRY FUNK

On March 4, 2018 Mexican rapper Audry Funk, alongside her husband Bestia BX and Salvadoran DJ Loup Rouge, traveled from the Bronx to Cambridge, Massachusetts to give a lecture and perform at "A Day of Hope & Resistance," part of a semester-long discussion at Harvard University around immigration policy. Audry Funk is no stranger to educational spaces, having given numerous workshops and lectures in both high schools and universities in Mexico, as well as performing in national and international venues including Chile, Bolivia, El Salvador, the Dominican Republic, Ecuador, and New York. Thus, moving into educational spaces in the United States was an opportunity to spread her narrative of a feminist Mexican immigrant hip-hop artist to new audiences. Nevertheless, speaking and performing in a majority white space was disconcerting. Quickly, the dream of having made it to the hallowed halls of Harvard dissipated. Being in Harvard was a uniquely odd experience. She felt that this place did not belong to her, not only for obvious reasons, but it was so far from her people that she was very powerfully affected. She saw no people of color walking the streets of the university, she felt entirely unrepresented on campus, and there was a moment when she and her partner asked themselves: will there be Latinx people here, will they take in our message, or is it that we were only working for them? Just a moment before their talk, however, they met a young Mexican woman who studied education. Audry was proud to see her there resisting, especially as the young woman recounted the nullity of people of color at Harvard and how she met few people who were interested in issues of gender and diversity.

Audry's personal musical style is a unique mix of hip-hop with reggae, soul and funk, using rap to explore the nuances of life as a Mexican woman, with themes from love to discrimination to defying expectations. She has a specific critique of Mexican standards of female beauty, and wants to dignify the beauty of all women. Audry is not a skinny girl—as she says of herself, she's a "big sexy mama." Is that something she is supposed to feel bad about? Mexican television—much like Harvard yard—is full of skinny blonde girls. Yet in Mexico women are not all blonde and not all skinny, nor are they in the U.S. So why do the systems tell us we should look like WASPY Americans, and feel bad about our accents, our size, our skin color, and the color of our eyes?

As then a first-year Mexican American postdoctoral fellow at Harvard, I understood this sentiment completely. At the time of Audry Funk's visit, I was teaching a course on Latinx Music History in a university with few Latinx tenure-track professors and few Latinx students, most of whom seemed to be in my class. I was also a tangential collaborator on this series, and had been asked by a white male full professor to be the Master of Ceremonies for that evening's concert.

For both of us, our experiences at Harvard led us to the realization in a very symbolic way that we were not completely welcome in that institution, but that perhaps it was important for us nonetheless to put ourselves front and center in that space. But for whom?

For myself, growing up Mexican American in upstate New York, hip-hop was not part of my culture. And while the sounds of 1990s gangsta rap followed by the commercial rap of the 2000s played in the background, it was not a music that I identified with or sought out. The mainstream late 1990s hip-hop I had been exposed to was masculine and Black [and Latinx] and did not relate to my experience, and reggaetón was machista and sexist and often made me uncomfortable as a young Latina. I preferred "Latin Alternative," a genre whose very premise was non-conformity to a specific musical style or tradition, with a blend of rock, salsa, pop, electronica, cumbia and anything else (including rap), that resonated with my hyphenated existence. I never considered hip-hop mine until 2010 when a co-worker at a Lower East Side restaurant who also happened to be a member of the Mexican New York hip-hop group Hispanos Causando Paniko (HCP) shared their track "Recession," with me. Blending lyrics about the Mexican community in Queens, immigration issues and daily struggles in the city, with a clean, classic New York sound, the music spoke to me in a different way. To the backdrop of the now destroyed 5 Pointz, Mexican migrants live painted graffiti in a localized form of hip-hop expression that was also something I could both sonically and lyrically relate to. At a time when the Mexican community in New York though substantial, was largely invisible—even to myself—HCP's music represented a statement, a presence, I desperately needed. In the years that followed, the

Mexican hip-hop scene in New York would become both my community and main area of research.

Thus, in a similar way, it was this lack of both Mexican and Latinx presence at Harvard that drove my activities over my postdoctoral year at Harvard, which included inviting Audry Funk to participate in the concert and DACA seminar. Collectively we began to question both the possibilities and limitations of our performance of a hip-hop *mexicanidad* in a space like Harvard. Independently we wondered, "Is it possible for an institution of knowledge like Harvard that is rooted in the settler-colonial state to function as an agent of decolonization?" Here, decolonization implies fundamental changes in relations of power, worldviews, our roles as scholars and performers, and our relationships to the university system as a business. Both of us found ourselves independently doubting our presence at Harvard. What was my (Melissa) role and responsibility as a poet and a contingent sort-of faculty? What was Audry's role as a mestiza Mexican immigrant woman rapper invited to perform at one of oldest and most prestigious institutions of settler colonialism and white supremacy in higher education? Was it an opportunity for hip-hop and *mexicanidad* to serve as a site of resistance, or were we just there, each in our different ways, to put on a show? How could Audry Funk's work as a hip-hop artist and Melissa Castillo Planas' as a scholar and teacher of hip-hop and other Latinx music act as a decolonizing agent in higher education?

Decolonial Hip-Hop Amongst the Ivy Walls

Neither of us were supposed to be at Harvard. I was amongst the post-doctoral applicants rejected from the Charles Warren Center for Studies in American History and then given a spot when a fellow left the two-year program early, opening up funding for a year. I was at the edge of academia, thrown a one-year lifeline and forced to immediately move to Boston from New York City while immediately preparing myself to get back into the tenure-track job ring. Audry Funk was brought into perform at the DACA seminar solely upon my suggestion and backing, for a performance that did pay expenses but did not offer an honorarium. I, of course, was led to believe there would be an honorarium and immediately felt embarrassed and disempowered. In my own organizing activities on campus—which included the first Latinx Poetry Reading and Workshop Series—I was told I didn't need to pay the poets, because "people just came to Harvard." I paid them anyway, not wanting to be a part of an elitist culture that had doled out plenty of money to white speakers and performers every week, but seemingly did not have money for people of color.

Founded in 1636, Harvard University is the United States' oldest institution of higher education. Since its founding, it has been intricately linked to systems of power: eight of the past presidents are Harvard graduates; 21 Supreme court justices have attended Harvard: both represent more than any other university. It was only in 2016 that past Harvard president Drew Faust – the first woman in that role – acknowledged that the University was "directly complicit in America's system of racial bondage" (Krantz, 2016). We could go on and on about Harvard's connections to political and business worlds but the conclusion would be the same; no institution of higher education is more closely tied to America's political present nor its Anglo-Saxon settler colonial past (and present) and its investment in racial capitalism. For legal scholar Nancy Leong, racial capitalism is not just a system of economic injustice or marginalization but also a measure of value. According to Leong (2014), racial capitalism is "the way that white people and predominately white institutions derive value from nonwhiteness" (2154). In other words, racial capitalism captures the way nonwhiteness is commodified and monetized whether as laboring bodies or as the goods produced from that labor and circulated in shipping containers around the world. Of course, the practice "of using nonwhiteness as a justification for the commodification of nonwhite individuals is older than America itself," as the history of slavery brutally demonstrates (Leong, 2014: 2155). In the much smaller context of "A Day of Hope & Resistance," both the authors of this article were problematically inserted into this dynamic: a day celebrating nonwhiteness and hope out of 364 days of despair. At the same time, both of us were expected to volunteer our time for the emotional and mental labor of educating the Harvard elite.

As an extreme contrast, the history of hip-hop and its emergence in the late 1970s and early 1980s in the South Bronx represents a story completely devoid of powerful connections. Rather it reflects a reaction against racialized systems of power. As Navarro (2015) has written, the 1970s in the United States saw a direct reaction against the Civil Rights movements and their gains in racial equality. The election of Richard Nixon was illustrative of this white backlash, marking a return to publicly privileging white supremacy in the United States, albeit in racially coded terms. For example, Ian Haney López notes that in his November 1969 address, Nixon appealed to the "great silent majority" in order to be elected. His appeal called out to the many white people in the U.S. who felt "displaced" or "silenced" by the Civil Rights movements of the time (2014: 23), paralleling the appeals our former

President Trump made to his white political base, albeit in a less coded and more overt way.

Meanwhile in the South Bronx, from the Forrest Houses in Morrasania, to 1520 Sedwick Avenue in Morris Heights, a diverse group of Black, Latinx, and immigrant men and women created a hip-hop arts culture that spread around the world and forever changed the course of music history. Significantly, this explosion of creativity emerged in the late 1960s and 1970s, when African American and Latinx youths were trapped in decaying neighborhoods devastated by economic recession and an influx of drugs amidst disinvestment and government neglect. As young people in the Bronx found themselves increasingly disfranchised from not just educational and work opportunities, but the arts as well, they invented a new music that fused verbal improvisation, scratching, and back beats with fragments of previous musical genres into a jarring, densely rhythmic, compulsively danceable mix.

Over the past 40 years, hip-hop has grown into a multilingual, multiethnic, intergenerational, global yet localized and regional collection of cultural expressions. Descendants of Latin American migrants in the United States were instrumental in the foundations of hip-hop's four elements (MC, DJ, breakdance, graffiti) on both the East and West coasts, adapting some of the cultural traditions of their ancestors' homelands to a different environment and time. On the East Coast, those early stages of development took place primarily within the Puerto Rican and African American communities of the South Bronx, while on the West Coast, artists like Mellow Man Ace and Kid Frost opened doors by infusing Spanish into their lyrics. From the earliest days, hip-hop has been not just about music, but about community and exchange, in which Latinxs have been extremely instrumental and influential.

Although it has prospered as a commercialized industry in recent decades,[1] nevertheless hip-hop has also continued to flourish among those whose working-class backgrounds do not provide an opportunity for formal training in music or dance. That cultural exchange has expanded by traveling to Latin America and back as visual artists, music producers, MCs, vocalists, and dancers from across the western hemisphere create localized art combining their surrounding culture with influences from north of the U.S. border. In this respect, activist hip-hop has the task of making our cultures visible, where the basic and essential thinking is to decolonize our actions, discourses and processes in order to better understand our present. At the same time hip-hop has the ability to reflect on what was taken from us, what was silenced and for women, to reconnect to ourselves as inhabitants of female bodies. Through hip-hop we recognize each other as transplanted persons of color and know that these historical circumstances have made wounds that we collectively work to heal.

One way of describing the project of decoloniality is as a political and epistemic project to delink from modern colonial designs, whether political systems (like democracy or communism), neo-liberal policies, or Western epistemology (Mignolo, 2011), and to create alternatives or "decolonial turns" that reflect material and epistemic changes to the colonial matrix of power (Maldonado- Torres, 2011). Decoloniality seeks to dismantle modern colonial relations of power and create alternatives to the colonial matrix that has systematically denied the existence and knowledge of people of color. Particular to this effort are critical texts such as Linda Tuhiwai Smith's (2012) *Decolonizing Methodologies*, which has used decolonial theory to pry Indigenous studies from the grasp of anthropology and create a space in which Indigenous ways of being, knowing and doing are more than mere curiosities or stylistic gestures; they are embodied practices and protocols in our work both within and beyond the institution.

Mignolo and Maldonado-Torres are important and highly recognized figures in the western academy, and the scholarly form their analysis takes has advantages for certain audiences particularly within an academic realm, where value is linked to institutional markers of prestige and use of elaborately allusive language. At the same time, we want to argue here that hip-hop's history as well as its accessible characteristics make it an important educational structure and decolonizing agent in Latin America as well as amongst U.S. Latinx populations in the U.S. with a broad reach. For activist artists like Audry Funk, Rebeca Lane and Bocafloja, hip-hop is radical movement. It is a cultural expression that bridges divides of anti-blackness and internalized colonialism that are present in the embodied experiences of colonized peoples. While we cannot deny the way coloniality has used hip-hop to further its own goals, the very existence of hip-hop in its varied forms and innovations refutes this essentializing narrative. As such, we believe hip-hop serves as a way to express a decolonial identity, specifically a woman of color feminist identity which has been largely invisible since colonization.

Significantly, Latin American and Latinx rap includes quite a few artists who have taken decolonial thought as a central tenet, celebrating the original peoples who are present in our cultures, but extremely marginalized and racialized, highlighting the demand for an identity that is constructed from an autochthonous understanding, and from the clarity to be able to see things in different ways from the imposed western gaze. This rap is meant to make the listener reflect on their circumstances, to think and learn about the past, and present, so as to create a stronger, more unified future. For mestizas like us, it both recalls our own indigenous makeup as well as Mexico's indigenous present. Nevertheless, with the term "mestizo/a," we also recognize the European roots of its meaning often used to police racial identifications up and through the thinking of Jose Vasconcelos' "raza cósmica" which problematically was based in eugenics. Still, we find utility in the word as was adopted by Gloria Anzaldúa to both embrace indigenous heritage and to situate oneself as a colonial subject in relationship to the United States.

Thus, decolonial hip-hop lyrics remind us that mestizo identity is built *from* the acceptance of all our constructions, and also *for* those who have been denied and confined to the shadows by the hegemonic mandate. According to Audry Funk, mestiza is her identity which reflects the reality that she is Indigenous, Black, Spanish and who knows what else. Significantly, her identity as mestiza is also a direct product of colonization. Thus, mixed musical forms like Audry Funk's hip-hop provide ways to critically explore and engage in decolonial practices that break silences, disrupt dominant narratives, and create a transformative consciousness among our students, particularly around issues of race, migration, feminism.[2] Because of this, we are intentional about our argument that the use of hip-hop can be a decolonizing agent towards current structures of power, more generally, and higher education more particularly. We are intentional in our choice that this paper must be collaborative and co-written amongst two mestizas from both sides of the border, whether from the U.S.-Mexico *frontera* or academia's various walls.

Through hip-hop's space-claiming power we open an avenue for a different reality of an Indigenous, mestiza and Black identity that does not prioritize a European standard. Hip-hop as an avenue is important because it comes from an oppositional non-white, Afro-diasporic perspective, and does not speak in the language of the white colonizer, nor that of conventional academic theory. When Sheffield (2011) highlights the power of hip-hop as a sonic archive in her writing about hip-hop and healing, she argues, "The *power of hip-hop* (indeed any music) as a form of political expression is the speed with which it travels across audiences and the sheer simplicity of the medium" (99). The issue of *simplicity* without *simplification* is a goal that both authors of this article strongly advocate.

Today, hip-hop's decolonial possibilities are increased through the speed by which we transcommunicate knowledge, a speed which accelerated through the use of new technologies. In this way, cultural producers around the world are able to engage with one another's content, processing it, and often times remixing it, all while transgressing spaces like established borders. The narratives told through remix culture move the violence of coloniality from the margins to center, repositioning our understanding and experiences as the foundation for knowledge and cultivating spaces of remembrance and healing.

In this respect, to talk about the decolonial, we have to talk about the traumas which the colony has brought us, traumas that we are still trying to heal, and the different trenches from which we continue to fight. This includes the continuing problem of colorism, the denial of indigenous identity, the prevalence of binary systems, the valuation of capital over land and well-being, the denial of any kind of spirituality that is not of white origin, and the submission of a gender for "natural" causes. For example, in her song "Alma Mestiza" Rebeca Lane Tzk`at teaches us:

> *conciencia cósmica de herencia mágica*
> *buscando en las sombras los rastros de mi alma*
> *aprendiendo a convertirme en un jaguar como un nahual,*
> *.... mi lenguaje es ancestral, viajo en un espiral entre mundo y fronteras*
> *Cuestionando lo real, el bien y el mal*
> *lo desigual, lo heredado y lo impuesto por igual*

> Cosmic consciousness of magical heritage
> looking in the shadows for the traces of my soul
> learning to become a jaguar like a nahual,
> .... my language is ancestral, I travel in a spiral between world and borders
> Questioning the real, good and evil
> the unequal, the inherited and the equally imposed

One of the first Guatemalan rappers to gain international recognition, Lane's album of the same title, *Alma Mestiza* is both a record about her indigenous heritage and an indictment of racism within the Latinx community. Here, in the title track, she reaches back to her Indigenous roots and spirituality but in a way that rejects western linear bordered thinking. Torn between cultures, her identity becomes one of constant questioning amidst centuries of taught racist colonial thinking, leading to the song's conclusion that her Indigenous heritage must be protected. Moreover, the song begins with Indigenous chants while the accompanying music video begins with an Indigenous woman, centering not just indigeneity in her hip-hop, but womanhood, both sonically and visually.

In a similar way, our own experiences in both Mexico and the U.S., have demonstrated the consequences of a lack of ancestral history which also denies us the right to see our communities as aspirational models or reasons for pride. A decolonial hip-hop serves as a reminder that our nations derived their riches from stolen resources (an unresolved historical debt), and are shaped by the work of people of color in every realm, from thought to physical labor. It rewrites history to remember that without us the dominant culture would not be who they are. Instead, we reclaim our people for visibility, for history, bringing forward the contributions of people who, apart from having been plundered, have also been forgotten in all possible symbolic ways. Thus, in "City of Color," Rebecca Lane raps:

> *Voy a pintarles un cuadro con palabras*
> *Esta primera mancha que algunos llaman patria*
> *Es la fachada que pusieron los criollos*
> *Para que defiendan sus monopolios,*
> *Expoliaron nuestras tierras, nos metieron en reservas*
> *Fueron las manos morenas las que hicieron sus riquezas*
>
> I'm going to paint a picture with words
> This first stain that some call homeland
> It is the facade that the criollos put
> To defend their monopolies,
> They ransacked our land, they put us in reservations
> It was the brown hands who made their wealth

Here Rebecca Lane tells the story of the plunders of racial capitalism from an Indigenous perspective. While this quote is in Spanish, like Lane, other Indigenous hip-hop artists throughout the Americas are currently challenging cultural genocide and contemporary post-racial discourse by utilizing ancestral languages in hip-hop cultural production.

While the effects of settler colonialism and white supremacy have been far-reaching genocidal projects throughout the Americas, one primary site of resistance has been language. Artists such as Tall Paul (Leech Lake Band of Ojibwe), Tolteka (Mexica), and Los Nin (Quecha), who rap in Ojibwe, Nahuatl, and Kichwa respectively, trouble the pervasive structure of European-language cultural imperialism that persists throughout the Americas. As a result, Indigenous hip-hop is a medium to engage the process of decolonization by (1) disseminating a conscious pan-indigeneity through lyricism and alliance building, (2) retaining and teaching Indigenous languages in their songs, and (3) implementing a radical orality in their verses that revitalizes both Indigenous oral traditions/storytelling and the early message rap of the 1970s and 1980s (Navarro, 2015).

For Latinx people, as Pancho McFarland (2017) has discussed, "Hip hop can and has been a site for decolonial aesthetics" which seek to recognize options for liberating the senses (p. 17). The revolutionary potential of hip-hop lies in its ability to challenge colonial ideology. In *Toward a Chican@ Hip Hop Anti-colonialism*, he examines a set of Chicanx hip-hop texts for evidence of anti-authoritarian, anti-colonial, alterNative politics. Through a synthesis of anti-colonial Indigenous thought, anarchism, and transnational decolonial feminism he proposes a framework by which to assess the degree to which Chicanx hip-hop texts can serve an emancipatory agenda. Part of its power is its lack of borders:

> Hip hop was birthed and nurtured at the dawning of the new millennium (McFarland 2008, 2013; Peláez Rodríguez 2016). Perhaps, it was the love child of late capitalism and the resistance to it. Or maybe it developed in order to chronicle the tensions resulting from the clash of capitalist colonialism against the global working class and the indigenous. What is certain is that it has united many across racial and geographic lines (1).

It is what Emma Perez (1999) has termed a "decolonial imaginary" in that it "embodies the buried desires of the unconscious, living and breathing in between that which is colonialist and that which is colonized. Within that interstitial space, desire rubs against colonial repressions to construct resistant, oppositional, transformative, diasporic subjectivities that erupt and move into decolonial desires" (p. 110). The decolonial imaginary, according to Emma Pérez, is the ruptural timespace between the colonial and postcolonial, piercing through dominant narratives of history. Inherently oppositional, the decolonial imaginary is also generative, energizing other histories and occluded forms of knowledge.

Moreover, hip-hop allows for an opportunity for Latinx to rethink African diasporic histories. By applying an African diasporic reading to Mexican culture, for example, we can examine the importance of Blackness within Mexico's history (Banks, 2006; Hernández-Cuevas, 2004; Vinson & Vaughn, 2004), as well as explore Black and Latinx historical, cultural, and political fusions (Johnson, 2013; Mariscal, 2005; Menchaca, 2002) that can improve Black and Brown relations, while making for an overall more thorough education for individuals of all colors and ethnicities (Cervantes, 2015). One excellent example of this is Mexican poet, rap artist, scholar, cultural ambassador, and founder of the Quilomboarte Collective, Bocafloja. One of the most revered icons in Spanish-speaking hip-hop communities, Bocafloja travels widely and collaborates with numerous U.S. Latinx artists, encouraging and spreading his redefined version of hip-hop's four elements, "Decolonize, self- manage, transgress, emancipate" (8).

Significantly, his hip-hop collective is named "Quilomboarte" to recognize the quilombos, which during the colonial period on the American continent, specifically Brazil, were communities established by fugitive Black slaves (also known as maroons and cimarrones in other countries), Indigenous peoples, and others who rejected colonialism's domination, who preferred to live as free people in communal form.

Lastly, in a similar way, for Mexican migrants to New York City hip-hop serves as a space of educational empowerment, creative expression, and community building. In spite of a highly racialized climate of fear and immigrant criminalization, we find a rich and ever evolving movement toward creative responses through hip-hop in forms of both individual and collaborative expression. Through hip-hop, members of the Mexican population form social networks to cope with this modern-day form of "social death" (Lisa Cacho, 2012).

Decolonial Feminism: Layers of Exclusion

Feminism and hip-hop don't always figure in the same equation as the decolonial struggle, yet we believe that this line of questioning helps us to develop new hip-hop paradigms and to question our environments in order to understand and improve them. For MCs like Lane and Funk, this questioning is a result of their experience of the ways in which women are excluded from canons, from history, and from the stories of our society, including hip-hop.

For Audry Funk, feminism has been taking shape little by little, a constant question in her life that she sees as partly related to having been born in a country as machista as Mexico—obviously a strong incentive to adopt the feminist struggle. At the same time, she also recognizes privileges she has enjoyed in her country of origin that more than half of the population cannot have: to have earned a university degree, to have access to learning new languages, to have the ability to choose what and how she wants her future, things that maybe on the U.S. side of the border are taken as universal rights. However, in Mexico more than half of women have no right to the most elementary aspects of decision making, that is, to decide what they want for themselves. The coloniality of gender is still with us; it is what lies at the intersection of gender/class/race as central constructs of the capitalist world system of power. Moreover, this gender binary is itself one of the legacies of colonialism.

Something was taken away during the colonial process: the way in which our ancestors looked at the world as quite fluid, not stuck in the duality of good and evil, white and dark, male and female. Coatlicue, the Aztec "mother of gods," for example, is represented with male and female aspects. Thus, we posit a decolonial feminist hip-hop as a way to connect the feminist and LGBTQ movements with these aboriginal concepts of gender as a way to understand our bodies in this world where they have been forced to follow only two systems of existence. In this respect, we argue with María Lugones that the concept of gender as introduced by Western colonizers became a tool for domination by designating two binary oppositions and hierarchical social categories. Here, women not only became defined by their subordinate relation to men, colonization created the concepts of race and gender; the imposition of race accompanied the marginalization of the indigenous and the imposition of gender accompanied the marginalization of Indigenous women. As such, decolonial feminism deconstructs Western gender concepts that have become normalized, and seeks to recover Indigenous worldviews of gender and incorporate them into feminist discourse. Thus, in a hip-hop context, we ask the question: Why do many men of color, colonized, and/ or enslaved men treat women of color as subordinated and/or with violence?

We believe hip-hop is a form of pedagogy of and for the oppressed (to use Paulo Freire's (1972) famous concept) that reminds us that there is not just one form of oppression, but that there is also oppression within the genre of hip-hop itself, which in its commercial form is often associated with powerfully masculinist voices. At the same time, women have been active since hip-hop's origin, and feminism provides a roadmap in how to decolonize these and other male dominated spaces, whether in politics, hip-hop, or higher education, as women of color. It is from this visibly outsider status that we claim our territory. As Durham, Cooper, and Morris (2013) have theorized, over the past ten years, hip-hop feminist studies have demonstrated the centrality of hip-hop's aesthetics and epistemologies in the everyday, lived experiences of young women:

> we use "hip-hop feminism" as an umbrella term to encompass creative, intellectual work regarding girls and women in hip-hop culture and/or as part of the hip-hop generation. Drawing from Joan Morgan (2006) and Patricia Hill Collins, Aisha Durham (2007) [this study] defines hip-hop feminism as a cultural, intellectual, and political movement grounded in the situated knowledge of women of color from the post–civil rights or hip-hop generation who recognize culture as a pivotal site for political intervention to challenge, resist, and mobilize collectives to dismantle systems of exploitation (p. 721)

Thus, hip-hop feminism sees itself as an intervention at both the personal and community level in sites of gender marginalization ranging from all male street rap battles to white male dominated Ivy leagues. It is a way, as Rebeca Lane posits, to break down the borders that seek to trap us in unfulfilled identities.

María Lugones argues that Aníbal Quijano's understanding of sex/gender in his well-regarded analysis of decoloniality is defined by patriarchal and heterosexual contestations over "sexual access"—a paradoxically Eurocentered understanding of gender. She, therefore, sees Quijano's framework as a further means through which the subjection and disempowerment of colonized women has been be obscured. According to Lugones, coloniality permeates all aspects of social existence and gives rise to new social and geo-cultural identities, thereby creating gendered identities, as well as racial identities. She acknowledges Quijano's historical understanding, and adds:

> Quijano's analysis provides us with a historical understanding of the inseparability of racialization and capitalist exploitation as constitutive of the capitalist system of power as anchored in the colonization of the Americas. In thinking of the coloniality of gender, I complicate his understanding of the capitalist global system of power, but I also critique his own understanding of gender as only in terms of sexual access to women. In using the term coloniality I mean to name not just a classification of people in terms of the coloniality of power and gender but also the process of active reduction of people, the dehumanization that fits them for the classification, the process of subjectification, the attempt to turn the colonized into less than human beings (p. 745).

This is why hip-hop feminism must focus on everyday lives. We believe that feminism and colonialism are not superimposed, that a decolonial feminism will decolonize machista social interactions. Thus, the first step for feminism to work in a decolonial manner is to decolonize our own feminism. We need to fully understand that intersectionality is primordial and that many women do not aspire to the presumed universality of a white man. We need to foster dialogue among all women. We must understand that the aspirations of a woman from India may not be the same as a woman from Manhattan, but this does not mean that the two are wrong, or that they don't both have a feminist truth. The relationship with the truth and with the goals that we desire as inhabitants of female bodies will only be achieved with the full freedom to decide about ourselves, and this will only be achieved if the chains of colonialism are broken.

Crucially, as Carlos Bouza (2015) outlines, hip-hop did not just arrive to Latin America, but did so in a time and context that makes female participation even more significant. As he describes:

> Al igual que en EEUU, el rap latino funcionaba como un amplificador de realidades sociales concretas, por lo que no es extraño que fuese permeable a las heridas históricas (regímenes militares, feminicidio, profundas brechas económicas) que el mapa latinoamericano arrastraba durante un largo tiempo. De esta forma, junto a las expresiones más lúdicas del género, se desarrolló un foco de resistencia desde el que se devolvía al rap su condición de herramienta de combate. Es en estos márgenes donde se gesta lo que hoy identificamos como un boom de las rimas feministas, en el que cientos de femcees descubren su poder y deciden pasar a la acción, reclamando su papel de sujetos activos dentro de una cultura que las había desplazado durante años (para.5)[3]

As such, hip-hop not only magnified the realities in Latin America of social inequality, racism, and indigenous erasure but also of femicide and women's marginalization. Here, the experience of Audry Funk illuminates this link, over a period of 15 years dedicated to the struggle in her community and for gender equity. This process taught her to understand many different forms of using hip-hop, to give voice to those of us who are voiceless is essential, to highlight the challenges we face as migrant women and women of color, to really know that even if one is born in this country, many of our fellow women continue to suffer the violence caused by patriarchy. Here is where social transformation begins, where we no longer remain silent, where we try to demonstrate the path to emancipation brought about by community-based and intersectional feminism to other women who do not think there are any alternatives, thus breaking down barriers within and beyond our communities.

The extreme violence of Latin America's social realities has meant that hip-hop continues to exist as an important youth expression of social realities. Outside of reggaeton, which is commercially popular but mainly a Caribbean based music,[4] hip-hop remains an underground sub-culture of anti-establishment expression. This does not mean, however, that the male dominated aspects of the genre, nor machista aspects of Latin American culture do not combine to marginalize women in hip-hop as well. Rather this is what binds the women together both as femcees (female MCs) and as women in the region. Hip-hop developed in Latin America as a common youth language of societal ills; women in Latin America adapted that language to develop regional feminism and form new female networks (Álvarez)[5].

As Carmen Díez Salvatierra outlines, very little research exists on the topic of Latin American femcees. Research is mainly limited to pieces on U.S. Black feminist rap (p. 41). Still, twenty years of U.S. hip-hop feminist studies have developed alternative methods of critical engagement to address questions of representation, forms of feminist consciousness, embodied experience, creative aesthetics, and more generally the political prerogatives of hip-hop culture (Durham et al., 2013, p. 722). The context of hip-hop is critical to answering these questions about the perceived absence of women; however, the analysis has almost entirely been one concerned "with the ways the conservative backlash of the 1980s and 1990s, deindustrialization, the slashing of the welfare state, and the attendant gutting of social programs and affirmative action, along the increasing racial wealth gap, have affected the life worlds and worldviews of the hip-hop generation" (Durham et al., 2013, p. 722–3) .[6] While indebted to this body of hip-hop feminist scholarship, we hope to broaden the field to be more inclusive of voices south of the border, using the experiences of both femcees and hip-hop aficionados.

Towards a Decolonial Feminist Hip-Hop: Successes and Spaces to Grow

Over the past 20 years, hip-hop feminism has effectively made space for itself in the broader fields of Black and women-of-color feminisms. During a similar period, many women of color in the United States have theorized racial and gender oppression from within a resistant relationality with people of color without necessarily using the term "decolonial" (Lugones, 2010 2010, 2012; Pérez, 1999; Sandoval, 1991, 2000). We imagine a decolonial hip-hop feminism which is deeply invested in the intersectional approaches developed by earlier Black and Latinx feminists. We insist that women and girls of color remain central to our analyses, particularly in light of critical gender approaches that have treated Black and Latinx women as an addendum to both hip-hop and decolonial studies. Within both hip-hop feminist studies, and decolonial feminist studies, hip-hop, decoloniality, and feminism act as discrete but constitutive categories that share a dialogic relationship. In both cases, rather than treating feminism as a lens, we consider how the creative, intellectual work of decolonial hip hop feminism invites new questions about representation, provides additional insights about embodied experience, and offers alternative models for critical engagement. Specifically, we imagine decolonial hip-hop feminism as an articulation of feminist consciousness rooted both in the pioneering work of Latin American feminist hip-hop artists as well as Black and Latinx scholars. In this way, it is equally concerned with hip-hop's aesthetics as it is with the lived experiences of young women.

Historically, we remember that it is also through colonization that the disappearance of the non-binary systems of our ancestors occurred. Feminism is a modern day construct necessary to address these losses. In her song, "Puro Estereotipo," Ecuadorian rapper Caye Cayejera addresses this issue:

> *ciudadanos alienados como soldados,*
> *Dos tipos de cuerpo rígidamente controlados*
> *Nada nuevo somos esclavos*
> *La norma moldeando cuerpos pal mercado...*
> *Géneros rígidos perfecto mecanismo*

> citizens alienated as soldiers,
> Two body types rigidly controlled
> Nothing new we are slaves
> The norms shaping bodies for the market ...

Rigid genres/genders perfect mechanism

Audry Funk has frequently spoken about the prison of stereotypes, especially relating to a feminine white appearance in her songs. As a result of coloniality, women have been separated and encouraged into competition rather than solidarity. But in fact, as Audry Funk posits, re-cooperating solidarity is an important decolonial feminist act. As she raps:

> *En reuniones secretas uníamos fuerzas,*
> *enseñanza abuelas somos sus nietas*
> *Trabajamos por el bien, la magia está en este tren*
> *Donde no solo es ella y el sin género también*
>
> In secret meetings we joined forces,
> teachings of grandmothers we are their granddaughters
> We work for good, the magic is in this train
> Where it's not only her and the genderless too

We recognize the long history of female solidarity, especially among women of color, and the way certain forms of social interaction have been downplayed and ignored, especially in the classroom. The great waves of feminism have been from a white perspective, and for a white perspective. For example, in the first wave feminism in the United States, white women aspired to be like white men, while in the second wave, women of color aspired to be the white woman, who in turn aspired to be like white men. Instead, the decolonial hip-hop feminism we imagine builds off reflections such as community feminism and decolonial feminism, recognizing ourselves as inhabitants of dark bodies, but also heirs of cultures that have been silenced and demonized for years, where the non-binary systems were excluded from official culture.

Hip-hop collectives like Somos Mujeres Somos Hip-Hop and Mujeres Trabajando see one woman's success as essential to advancing all femcees. Audry Funk is also a member of Somos Guerreras (We are Warriors), a feminist hip-hop tour organized by another Somos Mujeres Somos Hip-Hop MC, Rebeca Lane. This group includes women who practice everything from break dance, graffiti, visual arts, photography, and other media forms in addition to rapping. This type of project is important not just to promote women in hip-hop but to support them in their personal lives as wives, mothers, daughters, and border crossers so that they can continue to be hip-hoppers as well. With members now from all over Mexico from Puebla to Juárez, they continue to put on shows while expanding into other areas such as a clothing line called Funky Beast.[7] As such, "Mujeres Trabajando" makes an important statement about valuing the labor of women in hip-hop, but also helping to support all the other labor women must shoulder due to gender roles and

Towards a Decolonial Feminist Hip-Hop

expectations so that they may continue to do hip-hop. This song by Rebeca Lane Tzk`at speaks to a community-based feminism, as well as the need to return to our roots:

> *Con la energía vital de las ancestras,*
> *de las mujeres que caminan con mujeres*
> *Las sanadoras que usan sus poderes,*
> *De las que tejen con su energía de selva,*
> *La que convocan libertad con su palabra,*
> *Las que convocan la defensa de los cuerpos . . .*
> *. . . la sabiduría, la red de la vida la energía que transforma*
> *El odio en alegría la energía de mujeres combativas . . .*

> With the vital energy of the ancestors,
> of women who walk with women
> The healers who use their powers,
> Of those who weave with their jungle energy,
> The one that summons freedom with its word,
> Those that call for the defense of bodies . . .
> . . . wisdom, the web of life the energy that transforms
> Hate into joy the energy of combative women . . .

Lane asserts that these women, these healers, are also part of our cultures, where Indigenous women use the herbs and fruits of Mother Earth to heal illness. The maintenance of these practices is also synonymous to resistance against capitalist pharmaceutical companies. To be able to feed our bodies with what nature has provided is important, not just as a healthy form of life, but also as a spiritual practice, and to see it from that perspective is also able to decolonize our minds. This song by Nakury, a rapper from Costa Rica, "Rima" illuminates this point:

> *la música es mi machete medicina campesina*
> *Raíz subterránea se prepara en la cocina*
> *Pura substancia como recuerdo de infancia . . .*
> *Cultiva conciencia, sin semilla no hay planta,*
> *Se agradece la herencia, esencia criolla*
> *Producto local en la olla.*

> Music is my peasant medicine machete
> Underground root is prepared in the kitchen
> Pure substance as a memory of childhood . . .
> Cultivate awareness, without a seed there is no plant,
> The heritage is appreciated, Indigenous essence
> Local product in the pot.
> Likewise, "Ave" takes on a similar theme:
> *Siempre un té de hierbas que calma mis angustias*
> *Recetas de la abuela que me dan la cura*

> *Piedras de la madre tierra*
> *Se dicen fortuna, es la flor de muerto y el nopal lo que*
> *Nautre cultura . . .*
>
> Herbal tea always calms my anxieties
> Grandmother's recipes give me the cure
> Stones of mother earth
> It say luck, it is deadman's flower and cactus that
> Nurtures culture.

Many of the women who are working in the hip-hop music scene try to decolonize their lyrics. It is important to clarify that, even when not specifically addressed in the lyrics, the patriarchal system traverses us all. It is of utmost importance, then, to recognize this is not just entertainment for the public, but rather we are engaged in a project of education and critical reflection for our communities. Marginalization is not only in an economic situation, it is also a moral imperative, and thinking about these issues reminds us to be alert and determined to change the situation to benefit all human beings and not just a few.

The song "Máscaras," in *Latinoamérica Unida* defies listeners' expectations. It describes the cages of societal views that limit women. And while domestic violence is one aspect of this cage, gender violence runs much deeper, with roots that extend and oppress in many ways. The final track both encourages female strength and unity as well as pointing out systems of gender oppression:

> *Y nos juntamos todas las guerreras*
> *Disolvemos fronteras*
> *Quisieron separarnos*
> *Acusarnos de hechiceras*
> *Consignar en el olvido*
> *A las que dan vida a la esfera*
>
> And we unite all the (female) warriors
> Dissolving borders
> They wanted to separate us
> They accuse us of being witches
> To consign to oblivion
> Those that give life to the planet

Guerreras is an important way of conceptualizing this form of feminism. Not only is the female warrior a recognizable symbol of female power, it is one that does not diminish women's importance as the gender that also literally carries and gives life to the future. It is one that reaffirms women's place as mothers while also questioning gender roles that diminish women as weak followers rather than strong leaders.

Back in the (Harvard) Classroom

It was a powerful program, a mix of people from many backgrounds, with tremendous talent, and there among the group of rappers was Audry Funk, with her brown skin, her unconventional beauty, her native language, her anger, her sadness, her lyrics decolonizing the minds of her sisters. The lyrics were hers, but the pain was shared collectively, as was the trauma, and the fury against those who say you can't because you were born a woman, poor, and brown, and Mexican. At that moment it didn't really matter if the members of the audience spoke Spanish or not. The road is hard and full of challenges, but the audience were all moved by the show, and learned something from these voices, these bodies.

For the Latinx students in my (Melissa's) Latinx music history class, attending the day long events, culminating with Audry Funk's performance was a powerful experience. As one described:

> I went to the concert at around 7pm on Monday, and had the privilege of listening to Audry Funk, with help from Dj Loup and Bestia BX on the keys and production. Audry makes an intoxicating concoction of reggae, hip-hop, and dancehall-based music that is inimitably groovy. When I first came in the audience were sitting down in the pews, listening to the necessary introductions for Audry and her band; by the time I left, people were dancing in the aisles. At first the beats and energy coming out of the booming dub sound system seemed to contrast awkwardly with the cavernous aura of Memorial Church, but after people embraced the music there was a jubilant atmosphere, as though we were all being lifted up to the caverns above. This uplifting atmosphere was fuelled not just by Audry's music, but by her words. She would talk in between songs about how she was in a space where she felt liberated to say what she wanted, but a lot of her chat emphasized the oppression and state of censorship in Mexico, her homeland. In a tone that quite rightfully sounded triumphant, she talked about how insidious and continuous efforts had been put in place to silence her in her country of birth. Clearly, the social oppression of dissenting and provoking voices in Mexico didn't work. She was here, and she was loud.

As an alternative to a midterm exam, students attended and reflected on the day long events. While some students connected the repression and marginalization as a Mexican migrant woman to previous Chicanx histories, others were inspired to write and perform poems or raps about their lives as immigrants, Latinas and people of color. Not only did this "alternative midterm" encourage students to gain knowledge from new sources and listen to new voices, but it provided a powerful model of self-expression.

Of course, one cannot decolonize a classroom, much less an institution, within a day. Thus, this concert also formed part of larger project of decolonizing Harvard as well as creating spaces for Latinx through a semester long Latinx Poetry and workshop series, the first of its kind on the campus. Through three performances, six poetry workshops; 12 Latinx poets representing diverse backgrounds graced Harvard's hallowed walls for the first time and drew increasingly large audiences. Although I was just a postdoctoral fellow at Harvard for a year, I felt it was important to disrupt Harvard's tradition of overlooking young, creatives's voices of color. And disrupt we did—the likes of Noel Quiñones, Ariana Brown, Elizabeth Acevedo, Peggy Robles Alvarado, Carmen Bardeguez Brown, Elisabet Velasquez, alongside three local Boston poets elicited laughter, tears, cheers and I'm sure shock in their irreverent English, Spanish and Spanglish performances. The events also collaborated with community organizations to bring a diversity of voices into Harvard as well as bring Harvard out into the community. We defied borders, broke open the gates of the Ivy League and then discussed it all in classrooms and workshops, in papers and dinners.

Thus, when thinking of colonization and decolonization, of coloniality and decoloniality, we think in conversation, with an attention that is much larger than the confines of the United States or of national borders. Like Harvard, borders stand for colonial markers. Hip-Hop transcends borders. In Audry Funk's words:

> El feminismo, porque ya ser migrante ya es bastante difícil, ser migrante y ser mujer en este mundo donde las oportunidades para las mujeres de clase trabajadora se nos acortan, es necesario alzar la voz por mí y por las demás, no en una posición de salvación, es entre otras cosas tomar ventaja de los pocos privilegios de los que he podido gozar, ser una mujer estudiada, tener voluntad, haber tenido una familia que me apoya y sobre todo estar legal en este país. [8]

The message of decolonial feminist hip-hop in the classroom and beyond is that it is important for women to speak for ourselves, to stop leaving our lives and our forms of evolving in this world in the hands of the great patriarchs of our communities. It is our time to shine, the time for history to reflect a new perspective, the perspective of all of us women who for centuries have been confined to oblivion, to marginalization, to the roles of tenderness and care, putting us in extremely vulnerable situations that steal the ground from beneath our feet that we need to survive in a capitalist world. Likewise, the decisions about our actions and our bodies have silenced us not only in a literal way, but also symbolically—and that is the most efficient way of closing us off, even though we are more than half of the human population. For this reason, we believe that rap combined with feminism is the most powerful way of reaching women who can't reach far, but who can listen to music, who have access to the internet. Rap produces a message so that every woman can understand and reflect upon. It has been our way of emancipating many compañeras and students who didn't even realize all the harm the patriarchy has caused in our lives and in the roles we develop. Lastly, to do feminism and hip-hop has caused us to reflect on the barrio, where, to be sincere, hip-hop is more important than universities or academies where fancy terms and magnificent theories stay only on paper and never in solidarity with the real people affected.

Notes

1 We acknowledge the reality that commercialized hip-hop today includes work by many artists who have been affected by colonialist structures of thought. We continue to deal with entertainment tyrannies where spaces are given to those creators who are perfectly aligned with the conventional western canons of both beauty and discourse. Nonetheless, we have begun to see more diverse representatives both in looks and in music, though they are often less commercially celebrated

2 As Cervantes (2015) argues, hip hop pedagogues continue to use the genre as a vehicle to: (a) critique social policies aimed at youth of color (Chang, 2005; Rose, 1994); (b) analyze linguistic hip-hop elements (Alim, 2007; Pennycook, 2007; Smitherman, 1997); (c) examine development of identity formation (Dimitriadis, 2001; Gin Wright, 2004; Hill, 2009; Petchauer, 2007); (d) promote critical literacy (Akom, 2009; Alim, 2007; Duncan-Andrade & Morrell, 2005); and (e) increase student engagement and critical consciousness (Dimitriadis, 2001; Mahiri, 1998; Pardue, 2004; Stovall, 2006)

3 As in the U.S., Latin (American) rap worked as an amplifier of concrete social realities, so it is not surprising that it was permeable to historical wounds (military regimes, feminicide, deep economic gaps) that the Latin American map experienced for a long time. In this way, along with the most playful expressions of the genre, a focus on resistance was developed from which rap was restored as a combat tool. It is on these margins that we find what we today identify as a boom of feminist rhymes, in which hundreds of females discover their power and decide to take action, claiming their role as active subjects within a culture that had displaced them for years

4 For more about reggaeton's development and popularity see Raquel Rivera et al. (2009) *Reggaeton* and Petra Rivera-Rideau's (2013) *Remixing Reggaeton*

5 For more on the complex histories of feminism in Latin America see Gargallo (2014), Lugones, Matos and Paradis, and Restrepo

6 Tricia Rose's *Black Noise: Rap Music and Black Culture in Contemporary America* continues to be studied and held up as the landmark it is in hip-hop studies. Nevertheless, following this basis, the study of hip-hop which now spans over two decades generally limits itself to Black popular culture as a backdrop. For example, more recently P. Khalil Saucier and Tyrone P. Woods, in their unfortunately titled

article, "Hip Hop Studies in Black," make an argument to "reintroduce hip hop studies to black studies" which they define as "the political project emanating from the context of black revolution in the 1960s. . . . It melds the rich archive of black letters back to the slave narratives with the Black Power generation's unwavering response to the structural impossibility of blackness" (271). Although this does not necessarily exclude Afro-Latinxs who participated in these movements, the article's emphasis on blackness does exclude the diversity of Latinx who participated in and identify with hip-hop as an identity. This continues to be the trend even in a global hip-hop context, as titles like *The Vinyl Ain't Final: Hip-Hop and the Globalization of Black Popular Culture* demonstrate. Following Rose, scholars in Black/African American studies including Michael Eric Dyson, Cornel West, Anthony B. Pinn, Nelson George, Bakari Kitwana, and Murray Forman were among some of the first scholars to give hip-hop legitimacy in academia. See Chang (2005), Dyson (1997), Forman (2002), George (2005), Kitwana (2005), Rose (1994). More recent areas of study are gender/feminism (see Morgan, 1999, 2006; Morgan J., 2009; Perry, 2004; Pough, 2004, 2007; Rabaka, 2011, 2012) regional trends (see Faniel, 2012; Miller, 2012; Schelling et al., 2010), and commercialization/mainstreaming (Asante, 2008; McWhorter & Watkins, 2005; Rose, 2008). A few scholars have focused on West Indian influences (Hebdige, 1987; Seyfu Hinds, 2004)

7 For more on this project visit her website: http://www.audryfunk.com/funky-beast.html
8 Why feminism? Because being an immigrant is already very difficult; being an immigrant and a woman in a world where opportunities for working class women are cut short, means it is necessary to raise one's voice for myself and for others. Not to save anyone; but rather to take advantage of the few privileges that I have been able to enjoy, to be an educated woman, to have free will, to have a family that supports me, and above all, to have a legal status in this country.

References

Akom, A. A. (2009). Critical hip-hop pedagogy as a form of liberatory praxis. *Equity & Excellence in Education*, 42(1), 52–66.

Alim, H. S. (2007). Critical hip-hop language pedagogies: Combat, consciousness, and the cultural politics of communication. *Journal of Language, Identity, and Education*, 6(2), 161–176.

Álvarez, S. (2013, Dec. 1). Krudas Cubensi: rap desde las trompas de Falopio. *Revista Píkara Magazine*. Retrieved from: http:www.pikaramagazine.com/2013/05/krudas-cubensi-rap-desde-lastrompas-de-falopio

Banks, T. L. (2006). Unreconstructed Mestizaje and the Mexican Mestizo self: No Hay Sangre Negra, So there is no Blackness. *Southern California Interdisciplinary Law Journal*, 15(2), 199–234.

Bouza, C. (2015, Oct. 30). Recuperar la voz: diez propuestas de rap feminista latinoamericano. *Revista Píkara Magazine*. Retrieved from: https://www.pikaramagazine.com/2015/10/recuperar-la-voz-diez-propuestas-de-rap-feminista-latinoamericano/

Cervantes, M. (2015). Teaching decolonial sounds on the margins: Reflections on a K-12 teacher workshop covering Black & Brown musical transculturation in Texas. *Multicultural Education, 22*(3–4), 8–14.

Chang, J. (2005). *Can't stop won't stop: A history of the hip-hop generation.* St. Martin's Press.

Davis, A. Y. (1998). *Blues Legacies and Black Feminism: Gertrude "Ma" Rainey, Bessie Smith, and Billie Holiday.* Pantheon.

Dimitriadis, G. (2001). *Performing identity/performing text: Hip hop as text, pedagogy, and lived practice.* Peter Lang.

Duncan-Andrade, J. M. R., & Morrell, E. (2005). Turn up that Radio, Teacher: Popular Cultural Pedagogy in New Century Urban Schools. *Journal of School Leadership, 15*(3), 284–304.

Durham, A. (2007). Using [Living Hip Hop] feminism: Redefining an answer (to) rap. In G. D. Pough, E. Richardson, A. Durham, & R. Raimist (Eds.), *Home girls, make some noise!: Hip hop feminism anthology* (pp. 304–312). Parker Publishing.

Durham, A., Cooper, B., & Morris, S. (2013). The stage hip-hop feminism built: A new directions essay. *Signs: Journal of Women in Culture and Society, 38*(3), 721–737.

Dyson, M.E. (1997). *Between God and Gangsta Rap: Bearing Witness to Black Culture.* Oxford University Press.

Freire, P. (1972). *Pedagogy of the oppressed.* Penguin.

Gargallo, F. (2014). *Feminismos desde Abya Yala. Ideas y proposiciones de las mujeres de 607 pueblos en nuestra América.* Mexico City: Editorial Corte y Confección.

Hernández-Cuevas, M. P. (2004). *African Mexicans and the discourse on modern nations.* University Press of America.

Hill, M. L. (2009). *Beats, rhymes, and classroom life: Hip-hop pedagogy and the politics of identity.* Teachers College Press.

Johnson, G. T. (2013). *Spaces of conflict, sounds of solidarity: Music, race, and spatial entitlement in Los Angeles.* University of California Press.

Krantz, L. (2016, March 3). "Harvard to honor slaves who worked, lived at Wadsworth House." *The Boston Globe.* Retrieved from https://www.bostonglobe.com/metro/2016/03/30/harvard-president-drew-faust-says-university-must-come-grips-with-ties-slavery/gzJe3dLomzuuXvayRQJZAN/story.html

Leong, N. (2014). Racial capitalism. *Harvard Law Review, 126*(8), 1251–2226.

Lugones, M. (2010). Toward a decolonial feminism. *Hypatia, 4,* 742–759.

Mahiri, J. (1998). *Shooting for excellence: African American and youth culture in new century schools.* Teachers College Press.

Maldonado-Torres, N. (2011). Thinking through the decolonial turn: Post-continental interventions in theory, philosophy, and critique—An introduction. *Transmodernity: Journal of Peripheral Cultural Production of the Luso-Hispanic World, 1*(2), 1–15.

Mariscal, G. (2005). *Brown-Eyed children of the sun: Lessons from the Chicano movement, 1965–1975.* University of New Mexico Press.

McFarland, P. (2013). *The Chican@ Hip Hop Nation: Politics of a New Millennial Mestizaje*. Michigan State University Press.

McFarland, P. (2017). *Toward a Chican@ Hip Hop Anti-colonialism* (Routledge Focus on Latina/o Popular Culture). Taylor and Francis. Kindle Edition.

Menchaca, M. (2002). *Recovering history, constructing race: The Indian, Black, and White roots of Mexican Americans*. University of Texas Press.

Morgan, J. (1999). *When chickenheads come home to roost: My life as a hip- hop feminist*. Simon & Schuster.

Morgan, J. (2006). Hip-hop feminism. In L. Heywood (Ed.), *The women's movement today: An encyclopedia of third-wave feminism* (pp. 172–75). Greenwood.

Navarro, J. (2015). WORD: Hip-hop, language, and indigeneity in the Americas. *Critical Psychology, 42*(2), 1–15.

Pardue, D. (2004). "Writing on the margins": Brazilian hip-hop as an educational project. *Anthropology & Education Quarterly, 35*(4), 411–432.

Peláez Rodríguez, D. C. (2016). Chicana hip hop: Expanding knowledge in the L. A. Barrio. In M. Castillo-Garsow & J. Nichols (Eds.), *La Verdad: An international dialogue on hip hop latinidades* (pp. 183–202). Ohio State University Press.

Pennycook, A. (2007). *Global Englishes and transcultural flows*. Routledge.

Pérez, E. (1999). *Decolonial imaginary: Writing Chicanas into history*. Indiana University Press.

Rivera, R. (2003). *New York Ricans from the hip hop zone*. Palgrave Macmillan.

Rivera- Rideau, P. (2015). *Remixing reggaetón: The cultural politics of race in Puerto Rico*. Durham.

Rose, T. (1994). *Black noise: Rap music and Black culture in contemporary America*. Wesleyan University Press.

Sandoval, C. (2000). *Methodology of the oppressed*. University of Minnesota Press.

Sheffield, C. L. (2011). Native American hip-hop and historical trauma: Surviving and healing trauma on the "Rez." *Studies in American Indian Literatures, 23*(3), 94–110.

Smitherman, G. (1997). "The chain remains the same": Communicative practices in the hip-hop nation. *Journal of Black Studies, 28*(1), 3–25.

Stovall, D. (2006). We can relate: Hip-hop culture, critical pedagogy, and the secondary classroom. *Urban Education, 41*(6), 585–602.

Tuhiwai, S. L. (2012). *Decolonizing methodologies: Research and indigenous peoples* (2nd ed.). Zed Books.

Vinson, B., & Vaughn, B. (2004). *Afroméxico: El pulso de la población negra en México: Una historia recordada, olvidada y vuelta a recordar* (C. García Ayluardo. Trans.) Fondo de Cultura Económica.

Toward Decolonial Teaching in Ethnomusicology: Learning Elements of Afro-Caribbean and Mexican Traditional Music as Participatory Pedagogy

ALEXANDRO D. HERNÁNDEZ

The field of ethnomusicology began as a discipline rooted in colonialism. Formerly known as comparative musicology, ethnomusicology was founded by scholars from the Global North that conducted research in the Global South, in areas such as Africa, East Asia, South Asia, the First Nations of the United States and Latin America through comparative analysis of indigenous sounds to Western art music (Merriam, 1977). Comparative musicology reinforced hierarchical structures in academia by favoring research and publications versus utilizing the world's musical traditions and its instruments for pedagogical instruction. As both a practicing musician and ethnomusicologist, I propose a pedagogy based on the principles of applied ethnomusicology (Sheehy, 1992) informed by critical race, ethnic and gender analysis (Delgado, 2002; Delgado & Stefancic, 2001) to create a transformative and decolonial educational space (Ochoa & Enrique, 2004).

In this essay, I expand on Freire's (2005) approach to decolonizing the teacher-student relationship through participatory teaching with music. In doing so, I establish a decolonial method to teaching ethnomusicology that is also inclusive, anti-racist and gender critical. I specifically focus on Afro-Cuban rumba guaguancó, Afro-Puerto Rican bomba, son jarocho zapateado, and the composition/performance of corridos in lecture. My goal is to engage students with internalizing the sounds and feeling of experiencing music while developing a decolonial critical race, ethnic and gender analysis to music as culture.

Throughout my journey in ethnomusicology, I've analyzed the contradictions of colonial-European methods of learning versus Indigenous applied modes of teaching/learning. I critique the work of music anthropologist Alan P. Merriam (1997), a foundational scholar of the Euro-American centric canon of ethnomusicology (Loza, 2006). Merriam (1977) declares that an ethnomusicologist is a scholar first who therefore relinquishes professional musical aspirations, such as becoming active in music performance with a band or solo project, becoming a recording artist, or achieving a good level of talent on a musical instrument. Following the demands of Merriam, an anthropologist of music is dedicated to European-colonial methods of scholarly work such as research, writing and publications. However, Merriam reveals one of the major trappings of hierarchy in the academy; his perspective resembles that of a scholar in a tier-one research institution where classroom pedagogy and students are not a priority. This framework is inherently capitalist in that it favors the production of scholarship rather than the creation of communal aspects of mentorship, collective teaching/learning and ignores that a classroom can provide a transformative experience for all.

Some students may unknowingly approach ethnomusicology courses with a colonial gaze. Since colonialism is deeply entrenched in our society, we are socialized to view Global North and Global South marginalized people with a colonial gaze, and fields of anthropology including ethnomusicology are no exception. For example, a UCLA student once asked why I do not cover "Western Art Music" (i.e., "Classical" music) in Latin America even though my course description for *Music of Latin America* emphasizes indigenous, traditional, and popular music. Although classical music has a place in the trajectory of music in Latin America, I choose to focus on indigenous, traditional, and popular music as non-nationalistic and decolonial modes that contest socio-political stratification by music creators from aggrieved communities. Furthermore, traditional modes of ethnomusicology reaffirm the expert-student divide in which the professor teaches "uninformed" students about music as culture. But I prefer to believe that undergraduate students take ethnomusicology courses to experience new sounds and musical genres or learn/contribute more about genres they are familiar with, plus the opportunity to critically engage music as culture. If the professor, teaching assistants, or students provide live performance or live musical samples – the latter being the most common for ethnomusicologists in the classroom to employ – then this provides the most engaging class experience. To better understand my perspectives toward decolonial pedagogy, it is best to explain how I navigate settler-colonialism in South Texas – where I was raised – and in higher education while uncovering the social power of music.

Positionality of the Author

I am a first-generation scholar-musician in higher education. My intention to remain in the academy is decolonial. My mother is from a rural pueblo in the Tierra Caliente (hotlands) region of Michoacán, México and worked in a shoe factory sweatshop in Los Angeles, as a nanny for a Jewish American family in Whittier and raised my brother and me. My father is Texas Mexican and a war veteran, former ranch worker for a White Texan family and retired Los Angeles School District teacher. My life is best described as migratory living between California, Texas and Washington, DC with extended stays in Michoacán and Mexico City with my family. To my knowledge, I am the first in my family to become a musician as well as attain a doctoral degree. However, music marks the tempo that guides my purpose ever since I became enthralled by the sounds of metal beginning with Black Sabbath. As I progressed into punk, hardcore, hip-hop, rock en español and Latin Alternative while learning to play boleros, son jarocho and Texas Mexican conjunto music, I learned the value of code-switching between various music styles. Furthermore, I learned to appreciate the cultural significance of these genres through ethnographic participant-observer study as a major in Mexican American Studies at the University of Texas at San Antonio (UTSA). My experience as a professional musician and nascent researcher at UTSA prepared me to become a critical ethnomusicologist.

My journey into higher education was difficult with many challenges beginning with the institutional, social, and politically conservative region in which I was raised. Along the U.S.-México border of South Texas, I learned to maneuver a racist white minority, local police, sheriffs, military recruitment centers, Texas Highway Patrol and the Border Patrol who uphold white supremacist practices regardless of the officer's ethnicity. I was met with institutionalized and peer racism my entire higher education journey from community college in Texas to graduate study at the University of California, Los Angeles (UCLA). During a yearly progress review in UCLA's Department of Ethnomusicology, an anonymous comment from a professor directed the following to me: "He has a difficult time conceptualizing in the English language. Spanish interferes with his learning abilities." This was emotionally devastating to read and showed me that the Department of Ethnomusicology had no protocol – or intention – to stop racist faculty from harming students through their microaggressions. The irony of the statement is that the department required graduate students to learn two additional languages aside from the English language. However, this did not reduce the colonial and white supremacist trappings of the academy toward students of color – especially Black, Chicanx-Latinx, women and LGBTQIA+ students – and its its classist discrimination. This hurtful statement ignited my survival instinct of maneuvering oppressive power structures. I did not allow this statement to hold enough power to keep me from achieving a doctoral degree. Rather than claim resiliency, my decision to continue to pursue a doctoral degree in a hostile environment resulted in post-traumatic growth: enduring psychological struggle and working through trauma to find personal growth (Collier, 2016: 48). Comparable to my own experiences, many students I've taught in the University of California and California State University systems come from similar experiences in socio-economic status, ethnicity and are first-generation students from immigrant families. Most students are bilingual in two colonial languages – English and Spanish, with the latter considered as students' first language in their homes.

I share a commitment to intersectional education and underrepresented communities with my colleagues at teaching-focused universities where students represent diverse genders, ethnicities, and physical abilities. As such, their experiences should be reflected in course content. My curriculum includes a critical race and gender analysis of Chicana/o/x, Latina/o/x, African, Arab, Euro-descendant, Jewish and Asian contributions to U.S., global, Chicana/o/x and Latin American cultural and creative expression. I build my courses on a foundation of anti-racist teaching and progressive socio-political thought to explore the issues affecting the Global South with critical analysis of gender, race and ethnic representation (see Herrera-Sobek, 1993; Ozuna, 2018; Prashad, 2012) . To challenge heteropatriarchal male contributions-stories to academia and narratives of struggle, I also center feminist analysis in my teaching practice. Finally, I incorporate critical race theory, which is a movement comprised of activists and scholars who study and seek to transform the relationship among race, racism, and power (Delgado & Stefancic, 2001: 2; Hernández Castillo, 2010; Isasi-Díaz & Mendieta, 2012; Marco, 2018; Pérez, 1999; Ramos, 2018; Scott, 1990). I guide students to apply critical race theory to understand class privilege, patriarchy, racial micro-aggressions, and institutionalized racism in professional, academic, and personal life.

As an ethnomusicologist, I utilize music-cultural research to enhance classroom pedagogy and discuss ethno-cultural intersectionality. The pedagogical method of applied ethnomusicology is the study and practice of music as culture, and as such, allows for students to merge creative learning with academic learning through audio-visual and kinesthetic learning that centers singing and playing instruments. In essence, the classroom should be transformative where students of diverse experiences, genders and ideologies will feel safe, creative, and intellectually enhanced.

The forthcoming examples about decolonizing the classroom with music are not methods that I claim perfection. Still in process, the examples of son jarocho and corridos tend to work at allowing the students to have a physical and sonic connection to instruments, dance, and songwriting in the classroom. In doing so, the student to professor divide is diminished in presenting opportunities to be musical. No matter the extent of musicality, bringing students to leave their seats and learn rhythms introduces an engaged approach to learning. These experiences enrich the classroom through lecture-demonstration-performance beyond the inherently colonial setting of a Western classroom.

However, classroom pedagogy and the following examples of music making are not presentations of mastering decoloniality in the classroom, but of methods that often work well in creating engaged teaching. Within the practice of engaged teaching/applied ethnomusicology (Dirksen, 2012, Sheehy, 1992), I incorporate decolonial thought for my students to consider, such as explaining accepted gendered elements in son jarocho dancing or in male dominated practices such as Afro-Cuban drumming but challenging these patriarchal practices by having all students participate despite gendered hetero-normativity accepted as "tradition". Consider the work of Julietta Singh and her critique of mastery over decoloniality: "For colonial thinkers, engaging the logic of mastery that had long since governed over the colonies was critical to restoring a full sense of humanity to the colonized subject, to building a thoroughly decolonized postcolonial nation-state, and to envisioning less coercive futures among human collectivities" (2018: 3). Yet also, "The mastery at work in this project was one whose political resonance resided in national sovereignty and the legal principle of self-determination, one that approached the dismantling of mastery through an inverted binary that aimed to defeat colonial mastery through other masterful forms" (Singh, 2018: 3).

The idea of a "master musician" or of "mastering" a method is polemic. In the still colonial Americas, the word "master" is deeply entrenched in asymmetrical relations of power enacted by white supremacy. Even the idea of a "master bedroom" became a much too casual reference of a white supremacist race, class, and gender divide. Let us eliminate the idea of "mastery" for all its racist trappings of power particularly as it relates to the idea of decoloniality.

In essence, I argue that an ethnomusicologist can be both a musician and scholar. One element does not need to be diminished in turn for the other. An ethnomusicologist – or any type of professor – can pursue both academic and musically professional trajectories that are enhanced by intellectual and creative reciprocity. To separate these elements is to follow an elitist belief of "mastery" that is extremely problematic due to European colonial legacy. However, there remains great opportunity for people of color and supportive non-POC faculty in the academe and our role in shaping the next generation of critical race, gender, and decolonial thinkers, scholars, and activists. The combination of music, culture and teaching provides a powerful opportunity to create a transformative education for students. The following examples are my own attempts to decolonize ethnomusicological teaching with applied pedagogy via rumba guaguancó and bomba.

Collective and Applied Learning with Rumba Guaguancó

Rumba is a foundational Afro-Cuban participatory music that emerged in urban centers such as La Habana and Matanzas, Cuba (Blank, 2005). The three forms of rumba honors stages of life beginning with the oldest form Yambú, a slower-paced rumba with a dance that honors elders. On the opposite side of the spectrum is rumba columbia with fast-paced rhythms and the energic movements of the youthful spirit (Acosta, 2006). Rumba guaguancó is perhaps the most disseminated form beginning with its heteronormative courtship dance and its rhythmic repurposing in salsa and Latin jazz music. I introduce rumba guaguancó to decolonize the classroom with its group participatory elements to show students what's achievable when synchronizing as a collective. It is important to learn how different rhythms are applied to function together, like a metaphor of how varying thoughts fit to achieve a greater goal. In addition, dancing rumba takes years of learning to allow the body to flow like the ocean and its waves, which I believe to be the essence of guaguancó dance through a non-gendered interpretation. I have not learned to dance rumba, but the heteronormative elements of its courtship dances remain perpetual.

Prior to its repurposing as one percussionist on tumbadoras (congas) in mambo, salsa or Latin jazz, rumba is traditionally a collective music played by a group of percussionists in musical conversation with each other. Key instruments such as set of tumbadoras from smallest to largest: quinto, conga and tumbadora are played by a group of three drummers. The rumba's foundation is a 3/2 clave pattern that is considered the "heartbeat" of the music. Other rhythms such as the cascara compliments the rumba clave. However, according to legendary Afro-Cuban percussionists Francisco Aguabella and Armando Peraza, a rumba can be played anywhere and on anything (2005). A rumba can begin with tapping the wall, a table, bottle or with the use of spoons or forks.

I was fortunate to assist percussionist/santero Francisco Aguabella at UCLA before his untimely passing due to cancer.[1] Considering that the Afro-Cuban percussion class consisted of students inexperienced in music, maestro Aguabella simplified many rhythms so students could learn basics of such complex percussive patterns. One of the simplified approaches to rhythms Aguabella taught us was rumba guaguancó, which I would go on to use as an exercise of applied learning for ethnomusicology courses. Since UCLA is equipped with sets of tumbadoras, I would borrow them for a lecture-demonstration on Afro-Cuban percussion for my *Chicana/o/x-Latina/o/x Music in the U.S.* course. I begin by teaching the class how to clap the 3/2 rumba clave rhythm and reinforce that perfection is not the goal of the music, but to "feel" and experience collective music making. Once a decent rumba clave clapping is established, I invite five students to learn a very simplified to the rumba guaguancó rhythm on three tumbadoras along with the cascara rhythm on the side of the tumba, the largest and lowest-pitch drum.

Then I invited students experienced on percussion. Student-musicians demonstrated how the full and complex rumba guaguancó rhythms sound. I got a sense of appreciation from the class by seeing/witnessing and hearing their classmates play rumba. Hence the professor-student breach was minimized by collective teaching/learning through rumba guaguancó. One of the methods of decolonizing rumba is through the intentional participation of women and LGBTQIA+ students as percussionists. Much like many elements of traditional and popular music, rumba practices remain spaces of male domination. It is important to explain these gendered dynamics and to emphasize the significance of women and LGBTQIA+ students as percussionists, if even for a few minutes of participation in class. Temporality does not define the significance of deconstructing and challenging heteropatriarchal practices in musical traditions.

Since I taught the cross-listed course *Cultural Impact of Development* in Pan-African Studies and Latin American Studies at California State University, Los Angeles (CSULA) – a predominantly first-generation and working class/working-poor student of color campus in comparison to UCLA – I modify this exercise since I didn't have access to tumbadoras through the aforementioned departments.[2] However, this gave room for creativity as I recalled famed congueros Francisco Aguabella and Armando Peraza's statement that an impromptu rumba can begin with any object or surface that makes sound

(Blank, 2005). With only drum sticks I teach simplified rumba patterns on classroom chairs. Granted that the sonic depth of congas is missing, however, the sound of the clave and cascara rhythm is easily duplicated on classroom chairs. Sometimes using a table to drum the rumba tumbadora pattern mimics two recurring guaguancó notes on the tumbadoras. When creativity results from necessity it is achievable by using equipment already in the classroom. Over the years, I've learned that my experiences and knowledge as a musician contribute to an engaging classroom experience. In essence, it is beneficial to be musician and professor at the same time, not only a scholar despite the over-exhausted prestige surrounding the title. As a form rooted in the African oral traditional of transmission, Afro-Cuban drumming is inherently a decolonial practice. When introducing rumba guaguancó to a group of students by demonstrating and encouraging how to play these rhythms, I believe it honors African ancestral knowledge, learning, and teaching through the language of drumming.

Collective and Applied Learning with Afro-Puerto Rican Bomba

Having connections to a grassroots musical community is also beneficial for student learning. Inviting musical guests to class helps dismantle the coloniality of knowledge by challenging the institutionalized elitism of scholars as experts of a field, which overvalues scholarly-intellectual analysis over embodied practice, which in this case involves talent with an instrument and nuanced cultural understanding of a musical tradition. Rather than spend an entire course interpreting the meaning of music as culture, it is important to allow students to encounter learning perspectives from music practitioners, performers, or student-musicians. For example, my classes often include guests such as Nuyorican percussionist Hector Luís Rivera, who enlightens my classes with foundational Afro-Puerto Rican rhythms such as sicá and yubá on barriles, the barrel drums of bomba music. As a community organizer and longtime bomba musician, Rivera contributes his experience in collective organizing to motivate students to learn bomba dance and rhythms.

Rivera incorporates examples of intersectionality between Black Atlantic Diaspora (Gilroy, 1993) practices similar to bomba. The decolonial project seeks to find the interconnectivity of Diasporic knowledge and is opposed to the violent and forceful separation of intersectional cultural practice like bomba and its relative practices in the Caribbean and beyond. For example, tumba francesa from Cuba, punta from Garifuna society in Central America, and Kalenda from the Kongo into the Caribbean show student's interconnectivity of Afro-Diasporic music and dance practices and places bomba within a greater Black Atlantic context. Yet, learning to dance and play simplified bomba rhythms demonstrates the value of applied teaching/learning versus spectatorship of a community musician. I believe this process not only dignifies bomba but humanizes the guest presenter as a valued member of their music of practice. Having a guest artist provides an unfiltered perspective that often removes rigid formality in the classroom. It allows students to be engaged with ideas from a "source" that's not a standard academic. This approach transforms a hegemonic space where only the scholar imparts knowledge and information. The informed musician can explain verbally or speak through the instrument to impart knowledge.

Some applied ethnomusicology scholars may insist that participatory teaching is already part of class pedagogy in ethnomusicology. However, I argue that conscientious anti-racist applied ethnomusicology deems the method decolonial. Just because one invites musicians to present during lecture does not automatically count as decolonial academics. For example, during graduate study I attended a lecture featuring a group of musicians from India. The White American professor only referred to the musicians by first name and did not interpret their exchanges because the classroom was not set up for dialogue, only demonstration. A fellow graduate student shook their head and made a statement about institutions and colonialism. This left me to truly ponder the meaning of this type of neo-colonial presentation and understand that the intent was to keep the musicians silent, who were only chosen to provide musical support while the professor presented himself as the expert of their tradition. It felt like a gross display of a traditional museum-like setting designed for spectatorship and reaffirmation of expert-scholar – an institutionalized form of white supremacy.

But there are methods of challenging spectatorship and colonial modes of teaching through applied-decolonial ethnomusicology. Corridos and son jarocho provide the classroom with practices of applied ethnomusicology. The forthcoming example of utilizing the composition and performance of corridos enhances the classroom through engaged pedagogy. Introducing elements of the corrido and son jarocho provides the educator an opportunity to decolonize hetero-patriarchal practices of both traditions.

The Classic Corrido Form as Applied Decolonial Pedagogy

My goal as an instructor is for students to understand that creative learning is a viable intellectual process alongside social theory and research in classroom pedagogy. A major objective is to further develop methods of applied ethnomusicology in my Chicana/o Studies class dedicated to the trajectory of the corrido tradition. The composition of corridos in the classroom is an excellent activity for creatively engaged learning. According to folklorist Américo Paredes, an emergent corrido began to form in México during the War of Reform during 1858–1860 (Paredes, 1958: 136). Texas Mexican corridos document the resistance of Texas/U.S. colonial projects by narrating the stories of Juan Cortina and Gregorio Cortez. Although the stories of Cortina and Cortez differ in their motives of resistance, both become archetypes of Texas Mexican male heroes against the brutality of White American settler-colonizers in Texas.

Although Paredes is a foundational scholar to the academic study of corridos in the U.S., his work reinforces settler colonialism in Texas and contains racist perspectives toward First Nations. In addition, Paredes romanticizes Mexican resistance in the colonial region of Nuevo Santander – the Mexican state of Tamaulipas into present-day South Texas – toward racist White American policing. However, Paredes makes Spanish settler colonialism seem non-hostile toward First Nations in "Nuevo Santander" and refers to some indigenous people as remaining "in a wild state" (Paredes, 1958: 8). These racist perspectives were long perpetuated by the Spanish sistema de castas (caste system) in México which privileged white and light-skinned people, including Paredes generations later. Despite limitations to the work of Paredes, it serves as an initial point of reference to interpret decolonial possibilities for corridos and Texas Mexican resistance to white supremacy.

Although the regional Mexican and Central American styles that utilize the corrido have changed considerably since the late 1850s, the corrido as a format of storytelling in song remains remarkably relevant. The structure and singing style of corridos have evolved into popular styles such as corridos verdes, corridos tumbados or trap corridos in the present moment. Corridos developed from Spanish-European musical storytelling elements like the *romance* and introduced via colonialism in México. Although corridos are proliferated during times of conflict and struggle, many issues remain prevalent due to its colonial and hetero-patriarchal gaze since their emergence in México.

One of the biggest issues with corridos remains constant. Bands and corrido composers are overwhelmingly cis-gender male, which is reflected in the patriarchal male gaze to misogynistic visual and lyrical content in regional Mexican corrido groups such as Fuerza Regida, Legado 7 and Arsenal Efectivo. This leaves ample room to remove patriarchal elements and create compassionate, feminist-centered corridos beyond an abusive commercial music industry replete of toxic masculinity. Regional Mexican artists like

Victoria La Mala and the late Jenni Rivera perform corridos and rancheras against male patriarchy, however, I would argue that feminist corridos and feminist rancheras remain limited within heteronormative relationship themes. Often deemed as a "feminist" corrido, Jenni Rivera's "Cuando muere una dama" expresses that she is "la mujer de los huevotes." This line problematically defines female empowerment through the comparison of male genitalia. I summarize that feminist corridos in commercialized Mexican Regional Music still lacks the thematics of liberatory messaging from greater societal, institutionalized, and gendered oppressions. However, like many established musical traditions from Latin America and the Caribbean, the corrido is rooted in colonial elements, but its foundational structure can be challenged by intentional content. Therefore, an anti-colonial classroom with a foundation of feminist and progressive thought is the perfect environment to cultivate corridos based on these values.

In my corridos courses at the University of California, Los Angeles (UCLA) and at California State University, Domínguez Hills (CSUDH), I introduce the basic structure of a corrido-tragedia (tragedy) that I learned from attending corrido writing workshops by musician- ethnomusicologist Juan Dies. According to Dies, the classic structure of a corrido-tragedia is comprised of 8 sections:

1. *Permiso*: Ask for permission
2. *Presentación de personajes*: Introduction of characters
3. *Advertencia*: Warning
4. *Desafío*: Description of challenge
5. *Confrontación*: Conflict-confrontation
6. *Tragedía: detalles*: How the tragedy occurs
7. *Moraleja*: Moral of the story
8. *Despedida*: Ending-conclusion

Furthermore, classic corridos are written in verse form as *cuartetas*, four octosyllabic lines that follow an ABCB rhyme structure. I believe that a corrido composition assignment as a group effort is best for sharing creative ideas to construct a narrative among students. Perhaps one of the most participatory traditions to lend itself to collective musicking are corridos. One of my favorite teaching moments during my first semester at CSUDH was in utilizing applied ethnomusicology. For example, at the Fall 2019 Día de Los Muertos/Day of the Dead event, my Special Topics class was invited to share group project *corridos* (narrative ballads) composed in class. I divided the class of eleven into three groups and allotted about 30 minutes each class to write original corridos. Students researched topics such as immigration, feminism and socio-economic class struggle to compose their corridos. Once ready for rehearsal, I encouraged a very shy, but dedicated group of students to sing their own corridos.

With the accompaniment of my only student-musician on a twelve-string guitar and myself on a nylon-string guitar, the class performed our three corridos and sang about feminist motherhood, immigrant rights and immigrant struggle. We were warmly received at the event and the students learned that they could apply critical knowledge, personal experience and creative writing into their own original musical text and experience collective music making. Furthermore, witnessing the students transform themselves from reluctant singers into collective performers proved that talent is cultivated and not inherent.

In addition, the class extended their research practice to compose individual corridos and wrote academic analysis to explain the significance of the topics discussed in their narratives. Singing the corridos completed the tenants of applied ethnomusicology, which rounds the learning experience by performing the academic material composed in class. Furthermore, I view this as a service to create a unified, positive, and culturally informed campus climate.

Performing the corridos at Día de Los Muertos as a class demonstrated the participatory element of applied ethnomusicology. Bridging the classroom to the campus community through performance is an applied methodology that I recommend to all students and professors. The value of intentionally anti-patriarchal corridos is not decided by commercial recognition of the toxic music industry, rather by the impact of these corridos on the community present at the event. The misogynistic colonial elements of the corrido were challenged by telling stories of women border-crossers with agency, dignifying the personal-familial stories led by women and queer students. Commercialized corridos are not representative of the decolonial process. However, writing feminist corridos in the classroom is one way to create a new catalogue of anti-patriarchal narratives absent from most commercial corridos. In cultivating a space for feminist corridos in the classroom, I hope these corridos can be professionally recorded to challenge societal patriarchy and misogyny in corrido culture.

An Applied Approach to Son Jarocho Zapateado in a Lecture-Classroom Setting

Son jarocho is one of the primary traditional string musics from Central to Southern Veracruz, México into neighboring areas.[3] The music arose out of the Spanish colonial experience in present-day México and approximately began to take form in the late 1700s and especially into the 1800s. Since the music and practice is a result of the violence that is colonialism, the practice of son jarocho is heavily informed from elements of struggle, protest, and transgression to the colonial order: the Spanish Crown and the Catholic Church. Like most music traditions from the Americas and the Caribbean that were forged since European invasion, the intertwining of African, First Nations and European musical-cultural elements shape the son jarocho.

From approximately 1571 until the early 1800s, the Holy Inquisition in colonial México brutally punished anyone believed to be subversive to the Catholic Church (Katz, 1996: 3). Banning sones of early son jarocho practitioners was thoroughly enforced. According to the Instituto Veracruzano de la Cultura (IVEC), the official cultural institution for Veracruz – which also hosts a son jarocho research website – a large group of sones and dances were banned between 1571 and 1820: "El catatumba," "El currimpamplí," "El fandango," "El pan de jarave," "El pan de manteca," "El mambrú," "El saranguandingo," "El temor," "El toro," "El toro nuevo," "El torito," "El zacamandú," "La cosecha," "La maturranga," "Las boleras," "Las lloviznitas," "Las pateritas," "Las seguidillas," "Las teranas," "Los chimisclanes," "Los garbanzos," "Los merolicos," "Los panaderos," and "Los perejiles." During the Holy Inquisition, intolerance of religious and ethnic diversity was extensive, therefore targeting First Nations and African spiritual and creative practices. Accused practitioners of sorcery, heresy, and blasphemy were burned to death, and even lesser crimes against the Church were punishable by strangulation (Knoll, 1890: 483). In essence, activities not approved by the fundamentalist Catholic Church resulted in torture or death of its practitioners. In regard to music censorship, The Holy Inquisition attempted to silence the subversive dance, poetry, and some instrumentation of the emergent son jarocho during the colonial period (Hernández, 2014: 45).

Beyond the well-accepted boundary of placing son jarocho within Veracruz, the tradition is not limited to imagined state borders. It has longstanding connection to neighboring areas such as Oaxaca, Tabasco, Chiapas and is heavily practiced in Yucatán, Mexico City, Coahuila, Baja California and more. Son jarocho ensembles remain present in the United States, primarily in California since the mid-1940s (Hernández, 2014: 58). Given its trajectory of over 70 years in the state of California, there is some presence of the tradition in K-12 classrooms and in higher education. While there are consistent lecture-demonstrations of son jarocho, there are limited ensemble programs in public schools or universities aside from Frida Kahlo High School and the Claremont Colleges in Los Angeles County and at the University of California, Santa Barbara Department of Music.[4]

However, I would like to present an activity I learned from my mentor César Castro, a musician from Veracruz, México who is a respected son jarocho maestro in Los Angeles. Castro begins lectures about son jarocho with "El siquisirí," the son that initiates a fandango and allows for participants to introduce themselves in sung verse.[5] This technique allows for Castro to not only introduce himself in song, but also dismantles the colonial trappings of the classroom through the rigidity of lecture. The classroom is geared toward applied learning when Castro asks the class to learn basic steps of the zapateado, the percussive dance of the son jarocho.[6]

The exercise begins with walking in place with a "1-2-1-2" percussive step, albeit a simplified version of the zapateado for beginners or previously non-musical students. Once a steady rhythm is established, Castro then asks the class to double the step as a "1-1-2-2" pulse with the feet stomping "right-right, left-left, right-right, left-left." This creates the opportunity to introduce the duple-meter son "El colás" and connects with the established rhythm performed by the students.

If the class is ready to be challenged further, the zapateado in triple meter can expand their creative-corporal learning experience through dance. Although it is more challenging to learn in one teaching, the zapateado for sones in triple meter is phonetically introduced as a repetitive "café con pan, café con pan, café con pan." The phonetic description can be translated to the feet moving "right-right-left-right, left-left-right-left" in steady repetition of triple meter. Applying to the classroom what I learned through many years of performing alongside Castro at concerts, community gatherings, social actions and through cultural practice fandangos, has enriched my pedagogy in academic courses and in music ensemble courses. The basic or simplified steps of the zapateado add an activity to enhance the classroom with engaged pedagogy.

As the zapateado in Latin America danced its way through colonialism, it also functions as an anti-colonial resource for applied learning. Nonetheless, it is imperative to remain critical and move beyond the hetero-patriarchal limitations in the son jarocho. The established sones de a montón, sones danced by a group of women, and sones de pareja, sones danced by a woman (or group of women) and a man, resemble the hetero-patriarchal conditions from which the zapateado emerged. When introduced to a class of varying genders or students who are gender non-conforming, this allows for an intentional and applied decolonial approach to the practice of the zapateado.

Everyone learns to dance together as a collective of diverse gender representations (Díaz-Sánchez & Hernández, 2013; Flores, 2020; González, 2020; Miranda, 2009).

Furthermore, I am thinking of ways to make the zapateado activity accessible to students with ability challenges. As I continue develop decolonial and creative applied pedagogy, there is much for me to learn regarding accessibility and students. Diversity of abilities in students opens the opportunity to create accessible and equity-driven classrooms for students to be engaged with creative learning. In comparison to the son jarocho zapateado activity, the collective or individual aspects of a corrido writing assignment is perhaps more accessible and inclusive in consideration of students with physical ability challenges.

Conclusion

Collective songwriting will be incorporated in my future class projects that places student creativity as the center to the educational process. This will allow for students to work with their own interest in genres such as regional Mexican music, cumbia, hip-hop or punk rock to apply social analysis in lyrical content. When students learn to merge creativity with research practice grounded in critical race and gender analysis, this allows for the transformative, decolonial principles of Chicana/o/x-Central American-Latina/o/x Studies to be enhanced with applied ethnomusicology.

Furthermore, advising and mentorship serve to enrich teaching performance with consideration of student feedback. I am very proud to have mentored two students from my corridos course to apply to the 2020 National Association for Chicana and Chicano Studies annual meeting. Both students were accepted to present their analysis of the corridos composed in class. I will continue to mentor according to the aspirations of my students as they move forward in their professional and academic goals. My courses are intentional about dismantling the colonial teacher-student hierarchy (Freire, 2005) by cultivating a community of active learners where all are "holders and creators of knowledge" (Delgado Bernal, 2022). In addition, there's the layer of decolonizing the very genres I teach such as corridos where a lot of its commercial content is toxic and son jarocho which long reinforced its cisgender norms and heteronormativity and heteronormative. However, this is no longer the case with active decolonial son jarocho practitioners in our respective communities and in the classroom.

Notes

1 A santero/a/x is a practitioner of Yoruba spirituality commonly known as santería, candomblé or vodún in the Caribbean and Latin American African Diaspora, but originally referred to as Ifá in the Yoruban communities of Nigeria, Togo and Benin
2 There is an Afro-Latin Ensemble at CSULA directed by Dr. Paul De Castro that I did not get to connect with while I was a lecturer on campus
3 Son huasteco is distinguished by its huapango rhythm, falsetto singing and lead violin, and is also a string music tradition. It is primarily practiced from central to northern Veracruz into neighboring states such as Tamaulipas, San Luís Potosí, Querétaro and Hidalgo
4 Granted that my practice of son jarocho is primarily in the Los Angeles, Orange County, Central Coast area and in various parts of South Texas, I am certain there are examples of the tradition in San Diego, the Central Valley and Bay Area public schools and in other parts of California. However, I hope to learn more about son jarocho's presence beyond the Los Angeles metro area in further ethnographic research
5 A son jarocho fandango – sometimes referred to as "huapango" – is a communal practice of gathering practitioners to play sones and dance on a tarima (percussive wooden platform) most often beginning at night and into the next morning
6 The son jarocho zapateado is a regional iteration of percussive dance throughout African Latin America such as the zapateo in the joropo llanero of the Orinoco plains of Colombia and Venezuela, or the zapateo of Afro-Peruvian music

References

Acosta, I. (Director). (2006). *Cómo se forma una rumba*. MVD Entertainment Group.
Blank, L. (Director). (2005). *Sworn to the Drum: A Tribute to Francisco Aguabella*. Flower Films.
Collier, L. (2016). Growth after trauma: Why are some people more resilient than others and can it be taught? *American Psychological Association, 47*(10), 48.
Delgado, B. D. (2002). Critical race theory, Latino critical theory, and critical raced-gendered epistemologies: Recognizing students of color as holders and creators of knowledge. *Qualitative Inquiry, 8*(1), 105–126.
Delgado, R., & Stefancic, J. (2001). *Critical race theory: An introduction*. New York University Press.
Díaz-Sánchez, M., & Hernández, A. D. (2013). The Son Jarocho as Afro-Mexican resistance music. *The Journal of Pan African Studies, 6*(1), 187–209.
Dirksen, R. (2012). Reconsidering theory and practice in ethnomusicology: Applying, engaging, and advocating beyond academia. *Ethnomusicology Review, 17*, 1–35.
Flores, X. (2020). *Rewiring ourselves and our spaces of presupposed justice: Building sites of true liberation with the Son Jarocho/Fandango Community in Los Angeles* (Master's thesis). Pacific Oaks College.
Freire, P. (2005). *Pedagogy of the oppressed: 30th anniversary edition*. Continuum.

Gilroy, P. (1993). *The Black Atlantic: Modernity and double consciousness*. Harvard University Press.

González, M. (2020). *Chican@ Artivistas: Music, community, and transborder tactics in East Los Angeles*. University of Texas Press.

Hernández, A. D. (2014). *The Son Jarocho and Fandango amidst struggle and social movements: Migratory transformation and reinterpretation of the Son Jarocho in La Nueva España, México, and the United States* (Doctoral Dissertation) University of California, Los Angeles.

Hernández Castillo, R. A. (2010). The emergence of indigenous feminism in Latin America. *Signs: Journal of Women in Culture and Society, 35*(3), 539–545.

Herrera-Sobek, M. (1993). *The Mexican amidst: A feminist analysis*. Indiana University Press.

Isasi-Díaz, A. M., & Mendieta, E. (2012). *Decolonizing epistemologies: Latina/o theology and philosophy* (1st ed., Transdisciplinary Theological Colloquia). Fordham University Press.

Katz, L. (1996). Rare documents shed light on Grisly Mexican inquisition. *Jewish Bulletin of Northern California, 29*, 1–5.

Knoll, A. H. (1890). The inquisition in Mexico. *Overland Monthly and Out West Magazine, 16*(95), 483.

Loza, S. (2006). Challenges to the euroamericentric ethnomusicological canon: Alternatives for graduate readings, theory, and method. *Ethnomusicology, 50*(2), 360–371.

Marco, D. D. (2018). Vibing with blackness: Critical considerations of *Black Panther* and exceptional black positionings. *Arts (Basel), 7*(4), 85.

Merriam, A. P. (1977). Definitions of 'Comparative Musicology' and 'Ethnomusicology': An historical-theoretical perspective. *Ethnomusicology, 21*(2), 189–204.

Miranda, M. K. (2009). Dancing to "Whittier Boulevard": Choreographing social identity. In N. Cantu, O. Najera-Ramirez, & B. Romero (Eds.), *Dancing across Borders: Danzas y Bailes mexicanos* (pp. 66–79). University of Illinois Press.

Ochoa, G. L., & Enrique, C. O. (2004). Chicana/o and Latin American Studies and community struggles. *Latin American Perspectives, 31*(1), 59–80.

Ozuna, A. (2018). Rebellion and anti-colonial struggle in Hispaniola: From Indigenous agitators to African rebels. *The Journal of Pan African Studies, 11*(7), 77–95.

Paredes, A. (1958). *"With His Pistol in His Hand": A border ballad and its hero*. University of Texas Press.

Pérez, E. (1999). *The decolonial imaginary: Writing Chicanas into history (Theories of representation and difference)*. Indiana University Press.

Prashad, V. (2012). *The poorer nations: A possible history of the global south*. Verso.

Ramos, J. G. (2018). *Sensing decolonial aesthetics in Latin American arts*. University of Florida Press.

Scott, J. C. (1990). *Domination and the arts of resistance: Hidden transcripts*. Yale University Press.

Sheehy, D. (1992). A few notions about philosophy and strategy in applied ethnomusicology. *Ethnomusicology, 36*(3), 323–336.

Singh, J. (2018). *Unthinking mastery: Dehumanism and decolonial entanglements.* Duke University Press.

Mapping el Movimiento: Decolonizing the Classroom through Chicano Musical Performance Pedagogy

Noe Ramirez

This chapter presents the utilization of musical performance as a pedagogical approach to promote and build student awareness of South Texas Chicanx/a/o activism in response to conditions stemming from colonization of Mexican-Americans in this area. To do this, I draw from music that I composed, referencing the Chicano Movement in South Texas—a four-county area situated in the southernmost part of the state, adjacent to Mexico, also referred as the Rio Grande Valley, or the "Valley" ("El Valle"). I augmented my musical compositions and performances in two of my university level courses and connected to the broader context of colonization associated with research findings, including rationale for the movement in El Valle, establishing ethnic identity, call for government response to socioeconomic condition in South Texas, historical perspectives of the Chicano movement in El Valle, and community organizing strategies utilized by Chicana/o/x activists. For instance, my compositions call for re-igniting the cause ("La Causa"), uprising in response to Texas Ranger atrocities, which are expressed in two corridos (ballads), and Chicano identity, a principle objective of the movement (Kanellos, 1979; Zepeda, 2018). I am gradually incorporating the music I composed as part of the curriculum in two courses: "Social work Practice with Latinos" and "Social Work Practice with Diverse Populations."

In this chapter, I use the term "Chicano" given its expansive-use in the Chicano Movement literature. Recognizing the vital roles that Chicana women made to the movement (Mirande & Enriquez, 1979; National Latino Communication Center, 1996[1]), as needed, I use the term "Chicana/o." I also recognize and use the gender expansive term Chicana/x/o and Latinx/

a/o where applicable. Finally, I use the term "Mexican-American" as a general identifier for this population group.

By extending a decolonial curriculum that centers musical performance in my courses, the engagement between instructor and students enables students to gain a deeper understanding of the effects of U.S. colonization on Chicana/x/os as an ethnic group in the U.S. I also draw from experiential learning, engagement in critical thinking and critical consciousness via group discussions, and adult and audio-based learning. This pedagogical approach serves as a foundation for life-long learning while facilitating a process for decolonization. Although the music's aim targets undergraduate and graduate students' learning at the University of Texas Rio Grande Valley, the music's message can be utilized to cultivate decolonial knowledge in the general population, for example, via presentations in conferences, human services organizations, cultural arts music centers and festivals, workshops on community organizing and activism, and classroom settings in public schools.

In view of the emphasis placed on teaching our students to develop cultural competence in their service to Latinos and diverse populations, the songs that I wrote (N = 12) are written in English and Spanish, although the wording for the two compositions presented in this writing are in Spanish. The performance of the music is integrated in these courses' units, consisting of scheduled weekly sessions, primarily, during the latter part of a semester while re-iterating the history of colonization of Latinos in general and, specifically, Chicana/x/os/ or Mexican-Americans. As an educator, I use music inspired by the Chicano Movement to engage students in understanding content that is rooted in decolonial Chicana/x/o poetics. Therefore, the use of music helps me to supplement the curriculum content that is designated by the social work program. I do this by providing students the content of the songs, relating the song themes to the Chicano Movement and its struggles for decolonization, and performing the songs with guitar arrangements in order to enhance the lecture by targeting the students' audio-based learning (Branford, Vye, Stevens, Kuhl, Schwartz, Bell, Meltzoff, Barron, Pea, & Reeves, 2005; Greany, 2018).

My approach to integrating music in classroom pedagogy is grounded on inductive and deductive reasoning/logic (Moore & Bruder, 2005). Inductively, a lecture on understanding Chicana/x/o identity and oppression is broadened with discussion of selected songs that correspond to the subject of discussion. My songs "La Estación del Soldado (Tribute to Brown Berets)" ("The Soldier's (train) Station") (Ramirez, 2018b) and "Recuerdo el Movimiento En El Valle (Identidad Chicano/a)" ("Reminiscing the Movement in the Valley" (Chicano/a Identity) (Ramirez, 2018c), allow for further examinations of oppression of Black, Indigenous, and People of Color (BIPOC) stemming from social policies derived from institutions in the U.S., its capitalist ideology and the overarching dynamics of imperialism which led to the colonization of people in nations throughout the world. I utilize this inductive approach to discuss systems of oppression involving the formation of assumptions about Chicanxs/as/os/ or Mexican- Americans, labeling, stereotyping, prejudice, discrimination and racism leading to oppression (Lum, 2011). In reverse order, using a deductive approach, I present the music themes as content within the curriculum from a general-to-specific approach. For instance, a lecture on understanding social work practice with Latinos and diverse populations is, broadly, presented in the context of U.S. ideology, its connection to colonization, conquest, violence, assimilation and the Chicana/x/o identity experience in a colonized social environment.

My pedagogical approach is derived from the Movement's realization in El Valle and its significance to social work education since it is scantly reported in scholarship (Ramirez, 2015). To address this knowledge gap in the profession, I began by investigating the organizing strategies and tactics that were utilized by Chicano Movement activists of the late 1960s/early 1970s and cross-referenced them with organizing models reported in the social work profession in order to enhance community practice curriculum in social work. As the research progressed, beginning in 2005, I planned the writing of music compositions for inclusion in curriculum to promote and build student awareness of Chicanx/a/o activism and its resistance to colonization. After considerable time directed at composing 12 songs and their musical arrangements, I gradually began utilizing their themes to enhance the content presented in the courses. From 2015 to more recent times, I have presented research findings at conferences on the utilization of music in my courses, which at the present time, is a work in progress.

I am professor of social work in South Texas' Rio Grande Valley (RGV) where students of Mexican-American origin comprise 89% (University of Texas Rio Grande Valley, 2017). They report being unfamiliar with the Chicano Movement in general and, particularly, its occurrence in this area, although there is a rich and important history of Chicano Movement activism in the valley (Ramirez, 2012, 2015). The student's unfamiliarity with Chicana/x/o activism may be associated with multiple factors, including diminished exposure to community organizing by Chicana/x/os particularly after the late 1970s when the Movements' momentum slowed and the professionalization of Mexican Americans took hold (Gutierrez, 1998) as college education opportunities for Mexican American youth expanded (Montejano, 1987). Other factors associated with the student's unfamiliarity with Chicana/x/o activism include the current generation gap and its acculturation status which is typically bi-lingual, bi-cultural or highly acculturated (Cuellar, Arnold, & Maldonado, 1995), and the marginality of content associated with the Movement's activism delivered in non-Chicana/x/o Studies in higher education (Ramirez, 2015). As Albert Memmi (1965) writes, the colonized are often condemned to lose their memory of the past, their folk heroes, popular leaders, and sages as "the most serious blow suffered by the colonized is being removed from history and from the community" (p. 91).

I base this chapter on the need to promote awareness among undergraduate and graduate students on ways in which colonial structures (Acuña, 2004; Blea, 1988; Montejano, 1987; Quijano, 2000; Subedi & Daza, 2008) and the power of institutions (Curiel, 1995; De Hoyos & Ramirez, 2006; Gonzalez, 1990) have succeeded in erasing Mexican-American or Chicana/x/o history from the thought processes and conceptual reality of students in the Valley and beyond (Acuña, 2004). The teaching and learning of Chicana/x/o history, culture,, and identity remains consistently influenced by mainstream US exceptionalist values instilled in education (Gonzalez, 1990). Frantz Fanon (1963) writes, "[v]alues are, in fact, irreversibly poisoned and infected as soon as they [the colonist] come into contact with the colonized" (p. 7). To counter this condition, I have developed a curriculum that integrates the study of the Chicano movement through music (Duran & Bernard, 1982). Through course content, supplemented with Chicano music performance and analysis, I aim the curriculum towards dismantling and decentering colonial epistemologies through a mapping of the Chicano Movement to its present day with music, highlighting decolonial resistance.

The Research Setting: El Valle

With a population of 1,370, 424 comprising 89% (1,219,677) of Mexican-American or Chicanx/a/o origin (US Census, 2018), El Valle is a four-county area located in the southernmost region of the state, adjacent to the Mexico border—a borderlands region (Anzaldúa, 2012). The oppression of populations in El Valle are historically connected to its status as an internal colony of the U.S. (Blea, 1988). Within the colonial institutions of South Texas, Mexican-Americans experience conditions that remain marginally alleviated, including high school drop-out in higher education, chronic health problems such as diabetes and heart disease, illiteracy, poor access to health and other services, substandard housing, poor infrastructure, especially in rural unincorporated communities referred as "colonias" (Cohen, 2013; Mhpsalud.org, 2018). This region also contends with shifting socioeconomic trends, variables that form a core area of study in the social work profession (Karger & Stoesz, 1994; Popple & Leighninger, 2011). They comprise changing demographics, including a decreasing household size, cultural values stemming from the power of institutions, such as the education system and the family affecting the socialization of the people, acculturative stress (De Hoyos & Ramirez, 2006), fragmentation of the family, and increased mobility stemming from the mechanization of agriculture in the area (Mhpsalud.org, 2018; Ramirez, 2015; Ramirez, 2018a).

The economic conditions in South Texas have resulted in a family structure experiencing poverty that often relies on institutional-based resources to meet basic needs. This problem is compounded by the fact that families are essentially becoming increasingly fragmented due to migration from the area in search of economic opportunity (Ramirez, 2018a). Other trends affecting this area include an increasing life-span and growth in elderly population living in isolated conditions with marginal extended family support (Ramirez, 2018a), and the expansion of human service organizations which has incrementally led the greater reliance on its resources to meet the population's needs (Ambrosino, Hefferman, Shuttleswork, & Ambrosino, 2001; Cohen & Cohen, 2000; Garcia, 1999; Lower Rio Grande Valley Development Council for South Texas, [Council of Governments], 2018; Ramirez, 2015, 2018a).

Essentially, in the last 50 years, these trends have affected the local Mexican-American population in South Texas, and they have implications for enhancing curriculum content in social work education with decolonial pedagogies. In my utilization of Chicano music, as a component of curriculum, I work to enhance the students' learning as they connect the content from social work practice with Latinxs/as/os and social work practice with diverse population courses. This pedagogical approach aims to serve as a catalyst for decolonizing the students' current perception of oppressive conditions in the area as they build insight on the oppressive consequences of the Mexican-American War (1846–1848). In effect, this war fostered the creation of an internal colonial system that oppressed Mexicans (Baca Zinn, 1975; Barrera, Muñoz, & Ornelas, 1972; Garcia, 1999). As the U.S. accelerated its expansion of capitalist interests in South Texas during the mid-1800s (Montejano, 1987), its population experienced atrocities committed by the Texas Rangers, forceful acquisition of their lands, lynching, repression of their civil rights including voting due to the poll tax, economic hardship, their utilization as cheap labor, discrimination in the legal system, institutional racism, and oppression. As Chicano historian David Montejano (1987) notes, "the Rio Grande settlements experienced trauma of war and annexation" (p. 25) and continue to contend with the legacies of U.S. settler colonialism.

Decolonizing through Education

Chicana/x/o and Indigenous scholars have laid important groundwork that pronounces the importance of decolonial curriculum content (Barrera et al., 1972; Blea, 1992, 1988; Perez, 1999; Waziyatawin & Yellow Bird, 2012). As noted by Blea (1998), the politics of social sciences quells its responsibility for addressing the effects of social-historical imperialistic practices (i.e., colonization with use of violence, force, conquest, subjugation, slavery, institutionalized oppression); "[t]his is why Chicano studies have been so important in the battle of ideas" (p. 146). With a focus on Chicana third space feminism, Chicana historian Emma Perez (1999), posits her groundbreaking term "decolonial imaginary" as a theoretical tool for uncovering the hidden voices of Chicanas that have been relegated to silences, to passivity, to the third space where agency is enacted through third space feminisms" (p. xvi). While Perez's writing remains grounded in Chicana feminist activism, this work has been vital to understanding ways colonization has inflicted all Chicanx/a/o communities.

Notably, in social work practice with Latinas/xs/os and diverse population engaging students in understanding the cultural characteristics of the Latino or Mexican-American family by relating the intersectionality of multiple systems of oppression, stemming from the historical experience with colonialism, U.S. ideology and post-colonial conditions, is of major importance because it builds on areas of knowledge which are necessary for development of culturaly competent practice in performance of direct and indirect service roles; for example, strategic use of Spanish in the helping process and administrative decision-making based on addressing the unmet needs of the family and its members (Lum, 2011). This content is particularly important because it also provides students with an understanding of institutional forces whose impact on the family is traceable to colonization. From development of the students' knowledge, one of four principles in the social work profession (Council on Social Work Education, 2015; Krogsrug, O'Melia, & DuBois, 2011), on the Chicano/a family, coupled with addition of Chicano music in the classroom, critical consciousness is facilitated in ways that students feel confident and optimistic, as key agents of change, in addressing the breakdown of the family, particularly, via community organizing (Netting, Kettner, & McMurtry, 2004).

Arguably, the internal colonization model offers a more accurate perspective in teaching students an understanding the historical effects of colonization on Chicanas/xs/os. As cited in Barrera et al., (1972) it is more realistic "in the kinds of solutions it suggests. It also serves better to organize information about Chicano politics, and thus 'make sense' of it" (p. 286). Yet, the internal colonization model has its drawbacks. As Blea (1992) writes, its precepts are questioned on several premises; (1) the extent it clearly articulates what to replace the model with; (2) its distinct objective on social change (reformist vs revolutionary) needed to be realized; and (3) which specific intervention strategies are feasible to achieve desired change. In view of these questions, my work as an educator and performance-based scholar presents avenues to dismantle colonial epistemologies for my students in the RGV by promoting the integration of social work principles in practice—namely, *knowledge* on the connection of colonial structures to oppressive conditions experienced by the people provided services by social work practitioners, *skills* that are drawn from the knowledge base, and *ethical standards* and *values* from which to integrate the knowledge and apply skills (Council on Social Work Education, 2015).

Decolonizing Education through Movement-Inspired Music

A major aim in decolonial praxis is to instill in students a healthy and vibrant awareness of who they are as cultural-racial-ethnic beings equipped with critical consciousness and critical thinking skills. As an example of initiatives undertaken to build knowledge on ethnic awareness, with a colleague, I studied the benefits of having a healthy cultural-based identity by examining the association between shame and acculturation (De Hoyos & Ramirez, 2006). Knowing and understanding one's identity and maintaining a historical consciousness adds confidence and optimism in looking towards the future (Jimenez, 1994). In effect, my work, involving my performance of music in the classroom setting, is expected to serve as a medium that facilitates building the students' awareness of their ethnic origins and their capacity to think critically about Chicana/x/o$_i$s' livelihood in a colonized world. Towards this aim, since 2018, I have gradually integrated musical performance in my courses, which students have received positively, i.e., "[b]est Zoom lecture, loved the fact that you incorporated the Latino family, corridos (ballads), and the history. . . . yes! [t]he corridos were great . . . [y]es, Dr. Ramirez they really caught my attention!"

As a self-taught musician I started creating Chicano Movement compositions in summer 2005. As mentioned earlier, the themes for these songs emerged from a qualitative research project (Ramirez, 2015). The compositions were created, simultaneously, with melodies and chord arrangements determined suitable for each song. I selected the chord arrangements based on musical scales for each song suitable for my vocal range. During the process of writing this manuscript, I also applied rhythms, ranging from slow and rock rhythms-to-free-style/rap and corrido ("Ballad"), to establish genres for each composition. I rehearsed the songs consistently on weekends, or as time permitted, to perform in class as a part of my curriculum. Although until Fall 2020, I have solely performed the music in the classrooms, during the 2020–2021 academic year, I plan to include students in the music's performance by issuing them the words to the compositions for analysis. During this time, I plan to develop an assignment that requires students to write and choose to perform songs related to the colonial experience of Latinas/xa/os and Chicanas/xs/os. Ultimately, I plan to record these 12 songs and distribute CDs to students and the general public to promote awareness of Chicana/x/o culture, and tracing histories of colonization.

In social work education, scholars have introduced music for instruction on multiculturalism, social problems in contemporary urban life, poverty and disparity in distribution of resources, co-optation in "selling out" to conventional society, chronic illness, the hopes and dreams of working people, resistance and empowerment strategies, loneliness and isolation of persons with disabilities and veterans, depression era and Social Security, importance of the extended family, the Black spiritual experience, and feminist practice (Brown, Graham, Lawson, Martin-Robbins, Santos, & Seidl, 1995). Although these narratives are covered via musical performance, they are limited to promoting awareness of conditions that many persons accessing services form social workers are experiencing. In contrast, I work to transcend this limit by applying music as a classroom intervention that, supplemented with regular curriculum content, creates insight on the colonial position of Chicanas/xs/os, which carries with it systems of oppression, institutionalized racism and other injustices (Lum, 2011).

Towards this end, as a social work professor, I wrote two corridos ("Ballads"), one of which is presented in the writing, from the investigation on the Chicano movement in South Texas; this genre expands methods being utilized for decolonization-based instruction in that it embodies a revolutionary versus reformist agenda (Baca Zinn, 1975). As a genre, the corrido originated during the Mexican-American War era (1846–1848) as the deeds of individuals who resisted the American incursion and Texas Ranger atrocities were reflected and sung in this format (Paredes, 1958; Rodriguez-Puertolas, 1975). The reformist portrayal in the corrido presents an opportunity for me to talk about South Texas as a colonial project needing reform. I align this awareness with the social work profession which in the past, had a dominant reformist agenda (Reisch & Andrews, 2002) which gave way (1920s) to a focus on the individual, or micro social work practice (Krogsrug et al., 2011).

There are numerous compositions of the corrido which correspond to characteristics in South Texas during the post-Mexican-American War era (Montejano, 1987). Accordingly, as Anglos intermarried with wealthy Mexican land/ranch owners, the first generation dominated the area until the 1870s; the second generation of Anglos and elite Mexican-Tejanos governed through the 1910s and 1920s; "[t]he tenure of this pioneer elite would not be broken until the early twentieth century with the immigration of Anglo farmers from the Midwest and the South" (p. 98–99). Within this time span, corridos were written about Juan Nepomuceno Cortinas around 1859, a soldier-general-activist who fought in the Mexican-American War in El Valle and led uprisings against American incursions during the war and the Texas Rangers in the aftermath (Paredes, 1958). The corrido was expanded to pay tribute, among others, to Los Sediciosos ("Seditionists") who promoted the 1915 "Plan De San Diego" in El Valle, led by Aniceto Pizaña, Luis de la Rosa, and Basilio Ramos (Johnson, 2003; Paredes, 1958). Within this anti-colonial tradition, I wrote a remake of "El Corrido de Jacinto Treviño" ("The Ballad of Jacinto Trevino"), who avenged his family with the killing of one, possibly two, Texas Ranger(s) in 1919 (Garcia Ordaz, 2018). My two corridos, which I perform in the classroom, offer a spring board to decolonial conversations in that they are reflective of the history of South Texas and the local population's response to oppression which stems from the internal colonization of the Mexican-Americans in this area. The other compositions presented in this writing consist of themes associated with Chicano identity, the current status of the Movement and its re-instatement in the present era.

Utilization of Music Compositions

In lectures utilizing Chicana/x/o music, I strategically select themes from the music compositions, communicate them to students and recite their verses to express their relatedness to the subject of the lecture. The recital of the music is conducted, primarily, during the latter part of a semester. At this time the primary content of social practice with Latina/x/s and social work practice with diverse populations will have been delivered. As the content is delivered, I illustrate verses from the songs and discuss their relatedness to the subject of the lectures. This approach frames an understanding of the subject from a general-to-specific and specific-to-general levels of understanding (deductive and inductive reasoning). As the song verses are shown to students I discuss their connection to the colonization of Latin America, including Chicanas/xs/os in South Texas, and the importance of critical thinking and consciousness of locality. As such, this instructional approach is expected to serve as a catalyst for decolonial thought.

"La Estación Del Soldado" (Tribute to Brown Berets) ("The Soldier's Station"), is a ranchera (fast cut-time) type "corrido" (ballad) derived from observations of reported scenes and battles of the Mexican Revolution and the train stations, where soldiers convened to be transported to their garrisons and areas where the battles occurred. I wrote the song to portray the Mexican soldier's experience in the 1910 revolution, embodied and symbolized with the Brown Beret persona as a "soldado" (soldier) in the Chicano Movement. Initially formed by David Sanchez and other activists, including Vietnam veterans, in California and spreading to other region in the U.S. (Parra, Rios, & Gutierrez, 1979), as a revolutionary organization in the late 1960s, during the onset of the Chicano Movement, among other purposes, the Brown Berets served as security for Chicano youth involved in the Chicano movement, especially, the school "walk-outs" (National Latino Communication Center, 1996[2]). Of major significance, the Brown Beret organization collaborated with other organizations to realign their standing to a more militant and "compatible position in terms of *la causa* ("the cause")" (p. 301). The organization was, and remains, active to the present day with various branches taking distinct names throughout the U.S. For example, in California the Brown Berets organization is commonly referred as "La Causa" ("The Cause"), wherein Texas a major chapter is referred as "Carnalismo" ("Brotherhood"), Texas Brown Beret Cemanuach in Dallas, and Chuco in El Paso (Ramirez, personal communication with Brown Beret members). Aside from its paramilitary posture, the Brown Berets' activism revolved around farm worker's struggles, educational reform, anti-war activism, and its members also organized against police brutality.

Self-identified as "Soldados" ("Soldiers"), the Brown Berets' mission is connected to decolonial content in delivery of curriculum because one of its aims, during its origins, countered the colonization of the Mexican-Americans in the Southwest. In more recent times, the Brown Berets, particularly in Texas chapters, have expanded their mission to include service to local communities and the people, including promotion of civic-engagement and services involving fund-raising to provide assistance to poor families, school supply drives for youth, anti-gang campaigns, community/barrio clean-ups, immigration advocacy, collaboration with Black Lives Matters and other Black activist groups protesting policy brutality, demonstration organizing, lobbying, and other causes (Ramirez, personal communication with Brown Beret members). Throughout, the evolution the organization's major objectives has remained, namely, a commitment to preserving the Mexican-American or

Mapping el Movimiento: Decolonizing the Classroom 155

Chicana/x/o culture and assisting communities in creating a future throughout Aztlan. Of note, my composition was distributed to Brown Beret activists in Texas, and read at their conference (September, 2016).

In my classroom, I use the song "La Estación del Soldado" (Tribute to Brown Berets), by sharing its lyrics to students and creating discussion on their meaning by connecting the themes to ongoing struggles, and performing it with guitar accompaniment and/or vocals. The theme of the song is highlighted in the context of conditions which sparked the Chicano Movement (i.e., student walk-outs, police brutality, farmworker struggles, discrimination in the barrios, etc.), conditions that Chicanas/xs/os experienced as persons living in an internal colonial system. I wrote the song and selected its use in my curriculum for reasons associated with the social work profession, including its structural components comprising social work functions, which, in this case, would involve assessing the clients' experience in the historical context of colonization, acculturative stress, experience with oppression and racism. Lyrics:

> Al recordar de los años
> Cuando estaba en la estación
> Esperando con las tropas
> Del General Obregón
> Para llegar a Ciudad Juárez
> Y intervenir en los hechos
> Del General Pancho Villa
> Que esta contra del gobierno
> Chorus
> En México se ha grabado
> Estos hechos del soldado
> Es por eso que a la orden
> Se realiza la batalla
> Esto son los resultados
> Del famoso Plan de Ayala
> Dentro de varios encuentros
> Muchas vidas se perdieron
> Se oyen los trenes silbando
> Y los soldados gritando
> Chorus
> En México se ha grabado
> Estos hechos del soldado
> Estado de Guanajuato
> En la región de Celaya
> Pelearon los Federales
> Con las modernas metrallas
> Se fue acabando muy pronto
> Las fuerza de Pancho Villa

No le sirvió la estrategia
De usar la caballería
Chorus
Yo regreso a la estación
Casi sin alma y sin vida
En California La Causa
Y en Tejas El Carnalismo
Está de acuerdo la gente
Sobre el plan del activismo
Al confrontar la injusticia
Sobre las comunidades
Se implementa la estrategia
De protestar en las calles
Chorus
El Brown Beret es soldado
En la historia se ha grabado
Desde El Valle hasta San Diego
Esta aclarada la causa
El Brown Beret activismo
En mi mente está conmigo
La Causa y El Carnalismo
Se está poniendo de acuerdo
En mejorar estrategias
Para defender nuestro pueblo
Chorus
El Brown Beret es soldado
En la historia se ha grabado

Integrating this song in the curriculum, I discuss with students the Brown Berets' organizing which involved confrontation and paramilitary strategies that were also employed by earlier Texas Mexicans in response to oppressive conditions experienced leading up to, and after, the Mexican American War; for example, armed resistance used in the Cortina Wars (Moore, 1970) and Jacinto Trevino's confrontation of Texas Rangers (Montejano, 1987). Of note, I provide content on other organizing strategies and tactics, which are derived from social work practice models, including collaboration, social planning, canvassing, and negotiation (Homan, 2004), for comparative analysis. The verses in "La Estación Del Soldado" generate conversations that offer opportunities to decolonize established views on the Chicana/x/o experiences in South Texas. Overall, students have acknowledged the relevance of its verses to the profession's mission which addresses dismantling oppressive conditions in communities.

"Recuerdo el Movimiento En El Valle" ("Recalling the Movement in The Valley"), a slow "bolero"-type rhythm, accentuates Chicana/x/o identity, cultural conscience, and recall of the activist's involvement in the Chicano movement in El Valle. The verses confirm Chicano identity stemming from participation in the movement and la causa ("the cause").

The theme of this song that I wrote portrays an activist's efforts to retain the memory of the movement as its recollection is gradually fading from the conscious of many people in South Texas as the use of Chicana/x/o self-identifier in the present era is diminishing (Gutierrez, 1998), especially among social work students (Ramirez, 2012). My song frames the Chicana/x/o term as a positive identifier to counter colonial identification. As cited in Guzman (1974), through formal channels numerous attempts were made to characterize Chicanas/xs/os as Mexican immigrants, "illiterate, unclean, peonized masses who stemmed from a mixture of Mediterranean blood Spanish peasants with low grade Indians who did not fight to extinction but submitted and multiplied as serfs" (p. 23). Furthermore, the expanding birth rate of Chicanas/xs/os was perceived by the colonizer as a threat to their homogenous coloration and race; "Chicano children were considered a hybrid race of inferior quality" (Guzman, 1974, p. 25).

I wrote the song to direct attention to identity issues stemming from the colonial experience of Chicanas/xs/os and how the Movement in El Valle, in the current generation, is scantly mentioned and, in some cases, non-existent in the students' curriculum or collective memory although a major tenet the movement addressed was the forging of a unique ethnic identity in the U.S., one which had been demoralized through colonization (Escobar, 1993; Muñoz, 1989). In sum, the overarching theme in the song that I wrote consists of a person, an activist, reminiscing his role in the Chicano movement and drawing from the inspiration that the movement generated in activists forging a positive self-image of his cultural heritage and unique identity in a colonial-imposed society (Paz, 1961).

As noted in Muñoz (1989) Chicana/x/os were typically perceived as being non-Mexican nor American. In response, ethnic identity issues were stipulated in Chicanismo, the major ideology of the movement (Cuellar, 1974), which depicts the Chicanas/xs/os as a conquered people who were forced out of their lands and "transformed into a rootless economic commodity, forced to depend on migrant farmwork or to sell his labor in the urban centers, where his fate dependent upon the vicissitudes of the economy" (p. 151). As reflected in the song I wrote, the Chicano self-identity symbolized self-determination and ethnic pride (Escobar, 1993; Muñoz, 1989), which was called for by the movement, despite the atrocities inflicted upon Chicanas/xs/os from the colonial apparatus.

I've introduced this song in my curriculum and classroom teaching to enhance students' knowledge of Chicanas/xs/os' colonial status and utilize it to engage students as change agents, either at the macro level through community organizing and/or as advocates at micro level/direct practice. Towards this aim, I discuss with students the framing of the activist's identity in the context of organizing strategies and tactics (i.e., confrontation, use of strikes, marches and protest demonstrations) that characterized the Chicano Movement in South Texas responding to oppressive conditions instilled by the colonial history of the area. Similar to a Chicana/x/o activist framing their identity within the cause ("la cause"), students are taught to develop a professional identity within the social work profession, for example, by utilizing the integrative method in social work practice which, as an educational standard (Council on Social Work Education, 2015), calls for applying social work principles (knowledge, skills, ethics and values) in practice with Latinos, diverse populations and other groups. Lyrics:

> Estado yo en el movimiento Chicano
> Y yo recuerdo el poder de tus manos
> Estado yo contemplando y te extraño
> Solo al pensar del movimiento Chicano
> Recuerdo que tú me enseñaste quien era
> Dentro la historia de mi raza en la tierra
> Yo sé quién soy dentro la causa en el Valle
> Mi identidad es Chicano lo sabes
> La juventud no sabe de tus hechos
> Cuando el Chicano peleo por sus derechos
> La gente no sabe de tu historia Chicana
> La causa en Valle que recuerdo y extraño
> Chorus
> Nunca me olvidaré de ti
> Del movimiento Chicano fui
> Tú me ensenaste mi identidad
> Dentro la causa y la sociedad
> Chicano estoy consiente
> Dentro de este sol ardiente
> Que en El Valle ya ni se miente
> La causa de nuestra gente
> Nunca me olvidaré de ti
> Del movimiento Chicano fui
> Nunca me olvidaré de ti
> Del movimiento Chicano fui
> Nunca me olvidaré de ti
> Del movimiento Chicano fui
> Tú me enseñaste mi identidad
> Dentro la causa y la sociedad

During analysis and discussion, students made connections to the social work profession as the song theme reinforces the importance of Chicana/x/o identity within curriculum content. The utilization of the integrative method addresses oppressive conditions in communities; for example, through community organizing and other macro-level roles, including administration and supervision, and as advocates in direct practice with individuals. In turn, at the micro level social work interventions, among others, include providing psychosocial education on cultural identity to address negative self-image and shame associated with Mexican cultural origins (De Hoyos & Ramirez, 2006), and emotional disorders in clinical settings (Ramirez, 2001).

Implications Music Compositions: Conclusions

In my classes, I perform compositions that I wrote via various methods; for example, through music and poetry readings. I utilized these expressions in student group exercises to build critical thinking and critical consciousness about the Chicano Movement, aimed at decolonizing my courses. As I work towards this paradigm shift, in sequence, I use the students' insight to promote civic engagement and community organizing in a continuous effort to dismantle the systems of oppression stemming from the colonization of Chicanas/xs/os in South Texas (Ramirez, 2015). Similarly, in an activism course, which I developed and is cross-sectioned with undergraduate and graduate enrollment, I use the songs to develop the students' understanding of the effects of local conditions on our communities by discussing their historical connection to colonization.

Although I have not utilized the songs in other courses, the compositions and others like them, have the potential to be used across social work curriculum in order to supplement the understanding of our communities and persons accessing assistance from social workers. For example, students enrolled in another course would be taught to challenge the unresponsiveness of human service organizations in meeting the public need (Cohen & Cohen, 2000) by engaging in planned change (Netting et al., 2004) via community organizing in order to address disparities in resource distribution, barriers in service access, discrimination, racism, and oppression—essentially, conditions connected to colonization of people in this area.

The utilization of music in my courses has implications for practice. Upon students participating in decolonization-based instruction, it is conceivable that the compositions may enhance their initiative to engage in community practice and organizing, a major strategy Chicana/x/o activists used to direct attention to conditions affecting the community in order to formalize them as problems and mobilize target systems to address them (Ramirez, 2015). It is possible using Chicano Movement themed music in the class will generate collaboration with others to plan development of community organizing proposals (Ramirez, 2015). This work would include identifying organizing models, strategies, and tactics that translate into actual practice in their communities, for example, service learning, volunteer service, field practicums, and employment in human service organizations. Also, within this macro practice level, the students' exposure to the music may lead them to integrate their understanding of concepts in leadership roles in organizations experiencing unmet needs. At the micro-direct practice level with clients experiencing unmet needs, the music compositions in decolonial-based instruction may enhance students' understanding of coloniality and promote culturally-competent practice skills (Lum, 2011) to empower clients accessing services from organizations (Ramirez, 2010, 2015).

The utilization of decolonial approaches using Chicano music has exciting possibilities in how we approach education. Employing music in the classroom, challenging histories of colonization, may lead educators to test and document its effectiveness in meeting student learning objectives. This work would include assessing the extent that colonial knowledge is internalized for integration in practice and life-long learning. Student exposure to music in decolonization-based instruction could be further developed by educators exploring curriculum delivery methods that enhance its effectiveness in pedagogy. Towards this aim, educators could collect data on its utilization and disseminate findings in conferences and other forums to build collaborative networking in refining its use. In effect, this decolonial-based instruction engages students, as well as educators, in questioning conventional epistemologies rooted in higher education. Once provided with content aimed at decolonizing education, students have the potential to critically think about their relation to colonial histories and expand their knowledge base and clarity in perception of their environment and that of the persons they serve in the social work professions (Karls & Wandrei, 1995).

References

Acuña, R. (2004). *Occupied America: A history of Chicanos* (5th ed.). Pearson Longman.

Ambrosino, R., Hefferman, J., Shuttleswork, G., & Ambrosino, R. (2001). *Social work and social welfare: An introduction* (4th ed.). Wadsworth/Thomson Learning.

Anzaldúa, G. E. (2012). *Borderlands/La Frontera: The new Mestiza* (4th ed.). Aunt Lute Books.

Baca Zinn, M. (1975). Political familism: Towards sex role equality in Chicano families. *Aztlán: International Journal of Chicano Studies Research*, Spring 197, 5 6(1), 13–26.

Barrera, M., Muñoz, C., & Ornelas, C. (1972). The barrio as an internal colony. In F. C. Garcia (Ed.), *La Causa Política: A Chicano Politics Reader* (pp. 281–301). University of Notre Dame Press.

Blea, I. I. (1988). *Toward a Chicano social science*. Praeger Publishers.

Blea, I. I. (1992). *La Chicana and the intersection of race, class, and gender*. Praeger Publishers.

Branford, J., Vye, N., Stevens, R., Kuhl, P., Schwartz, D., Bell, P., Meltzoff, A., Barron, B., Pea, R. D., & Reeves, B. (2005). Learning theories and education: Toward a decade of synergy. In P. Alexander & P. Winne (Eds.), *Handbook of educational psychology* (2nd ed., p. 95). Erlbaum.

Brown, P., Graham, M. A., Lawson, T., Martin Robbins, S., Santos, D., & Seidl, F. (1995). *Concerned in concert*. HRI Records.

Cohen, R., & Cohen, J. (2000). *Chiseled in sand: Perspective on change in human service organizations*. Wadsworth/Brooks Cole.

Cohen, J. (2013). Rio Grande Valley Tops List of "America's Poorest Cities." Retrieved April 13, 2022, from https://www.texasmonthly.com/articles/rio-grande-valley-tops-list-of-americas-poorest-cities/.

Council on Social Work Education. (2015). *Education policy and accreditation standards for Baccalaureate and Master's Social Work Programs*. Retrieved October 30, 2020, from https://www.cswe.org/accreditation/standards/2015-epas/.

Cuellar, A. (1974). Perspective on politics: Part I. In F. C. Garcia (Ed.), *La causa política: A Chicano politics reader* (pp. 36–52). University of Norte Dame Press.

Cuellar, I., Arnold, B., & Maldonado, R. (1995). Acculturation scale for Mexican-Americans-II: A revision of the original ARSMA scale. *Hispanic Journal of Behavioral Sciences*, *17*(3), 275–304.

Curiel, H. (1995). Hispanics: Mexican Americans. In R. L. Edwards (Ed.), Encyclopedia of social work (19th ed., pp. 1233–1244). NASW Press.

De Hoyos, L. R., & Ramirez, N. (2006). The relationship between shame and acculturation among Latino/Chicano students: Implications for social work education. *The Journal of Ethnic & Cultural Diversity in Social Work*, *17*(1/2), 147–166.

Duran, L. I., & Bernard, H. R. (1982). *Introduction to Chicano studies* (2nd ed.). Macmillan Publishing Co., Inc.

Escobar, E. J. (1993). The dialectics of repression: The Los Angeles Police Department and the Chicano Movement, 1968–1971 (PDF). *The Journal of American History*, *79*, 1483–1514.

Fanon, F. (1963). *The wretched of the earth* (R. Philcox, Trans). New York.

Garcia, A. (1999). The Latino family in transition. In M. Sotomayor & A. Garcia (Eds.), *La familia: Traditions and realities*. National Hispanic Council on Aging.

Garcia Ordaz, D. (2018). *Will the real Jacinto Treviño please stand up?* Retrieved December 29, 2018, from http://www.angelfire.com/poetry/ mariachi /writing/jacinto.html

Gonzalez, G. G. (1990). *Chicano education in the era of segregation*. Associated University Press.

Greany, K. (2018). *6 sound strategies for using audio in your elearning*. https://www.elucidat.com/blog/6-audio-elearning-strategies/

Gutierrez, J. A. (1998). *The making of a Chicano militant*. The University of Wisconsin Press.

Guzman, R. (1974). The function of Anglo-American racism in the political development of Chicanos. In F. C. Garcia (Ed.), *La causa política: A Chicano politics reader* (pp. 19–35). Notre Dame.

Homan, M. S. (2004). *Promoting community change: Making it happen in the real world*. Thomson/Brooks/Cole.

Jimenez, C. M. (1994). *The Mexican-American heritage* (2nd ed.). TQS Publications.

Johnson, B. H. (2003). *Revolution in Texas: How a forgotten rebellion and its bloody suppression turned Mexicans into Americans*. Yale University Press.

Kanellos, N. (1979). Folklore in Chicano theatre and Chicano theatre as folklore. In A. West, & J. Macklin (Eds.), *The Chicano experience* (pp. 165–206). Westview Press, Inc.

Karger, J. H., & Stesz, D. (1994). *American social welfare policy: A pluralist approach* (2nd ed.). Longman.

Karls, J. M., & Wandrei, K. E. (1995). Person-in-Environment. In R. L. Edwards (Ed.), *Encyclopedia of social work* (19th ed., pp. 1818–1827). NASW Press.

Krogsrug, K., O'Melia, M., & DuBois, B. (2011). *Generalist social work practice: An empowering approach*. Pearson Education, Inc.

Lum, D. (2011). *Culturally competent practice: A framework for understanding diverse groups and justice issues* (4th ed.). Brooks/Cole.

Memmi, A. (1965). *The colonizer and the colonized*. Beacon Press.

Mhpsalud.org (2018). Inside Texas communities: What are Colonias? Mhpsalud.org. Retrieved April 13, 2022 from https://mhpsalud.org/inside-texas-border-communities-colonias/.

Mirande, A., & Enriquez, E. (1979). *La Chicana: The Mexican-American woman*. The University of Chicago Press.

Montejano, D. (1987). *Anglos and Mexicans in the making of Texas, 1836–1986*. University of Texas Press.

Moore, B. N., & Bruder, K. (2005). *Philosophy: The power of ideas* (6th ed.). McGraw Higher Education, Inc.

Moore, J. W. (1970). Mexican Americans. In M. M. Gordon (Ed.), *Ethnic groups in American life series*. Prentice-Hall, Inc.

Muñoz, C. (1989). *Youth, identity, power: The Chicano movement*. Verso.

National Latino Communication Center & Galan Productions, Inc. (Producers). (1996[1]). *Chicano: History of the Mexican-American Civil Rights Movement: Quest for a homeland (Video tape)*. (Available from NLCC Educational Media, P.O. Box 39A60, Los Angeles, CA 90039).

National Latino Communication Center & Galán Productions, Inc. (Producers). (1996²).
Chicano: History of the Mexican-American Civil Rights Movement: Taking back the schools (Video tape). (Available from NLCC Educational Media, P.O. Box 39A60, Los Angeles, CA 90039).

Netting, F. E., Kettner, P. M., & McMurtry, S. L. (2004). *Social work macro practice* (3rd ed.). Longman.

Paredes, A. (1958). *"With a pistol in his hand": A border ballad and its hero*. University of Texas Press.

Parra, R., Rios V., & Gutierrez, A. (1979). Chicano organzations in the Midwest: Past, present, and possibilities. In A. West & J. Macklin (Eds.), *The Chicano experience* (pp. 291–312). Westview Press, Inc.

Paz, O. (1961). *The labyrinth of solitude*. Grove Press.

Perez, E. (1999). *The decolonial imaginary: Writing Chicanas into history*. Indiana University Press.

Popple, P. R., & Leighninger, L. (2011). *Social work, social welfare, and American society* (8th ed.). Pearson.

Quijano, A. (2000). *Coloniality of power and eurocentrism in Latin America*. Sage Publications. Retrieved September 08, 2018, from tp://journals.sagepub.com/. https://doi.org/10.1177/0268580900015002005

Ramirez, N. (2001). Supervisors' personal-professional attributes and approaches to supervision in organizations providing clinical services to Mexican-American persons. *The Clinical Supervisor*, *20*(2), 117–131.

Ramirez, N. (2010). The immigration movement and demonstrations: Implications for social work practice. *Perspectivas Sociales/Social Perspectives, Bilingual, Bi-national Journal*, *12*(2), 85–109.

Ramirez, N. (2012). *Student awareness of Mexican-American-Chicano cultural history and activism in the Rio Grande Valley of South Texas*. Unpublished raw data. University of Texas Pan American Social Work Department.

Ramirez, N. (2015). Integration of community organizing curriculum and content on Chicano activism: An instructional approach in South Texas. *Perspectivas Sociales/ Social Perpectives, Bilingual, Bi-national Journal*, *17*(1), 151–168.

Ramirez, N. (2018a). *The breakdown of the Mexican-American family as a supportive resource*. Unpublished raw data. University of Texas Rio Grande Valley School of Social Work.

Ramirez, N. (2018b). La Estación Del Soldado (Tribute to Brown Berets). *The Chachalaca Review*. Spring, 2018 Issue; http://www.chachalacareview.com/la-estacion-del-soldado-tribute-to-brown-berets

Ramirez, N. (2018c). Recuerdo el Movimiento En El Valle. *The Chachalaca Review*. Spring, 2018 Issue; http://www.chachalacareview.com/Recuerdo-el-Movimiento

Reisch, M., & Andrews, J. (2002). *The road not taken: A history of radical social work in the United States*. Brunner-Routledge.

Rodriguez-Puértolas, J. (1975). La problemática socio-política chicana en corridos y canciones. *Aztlan: International Journal of Chicano Studies Research*, *6*(1), 97–116.

Subedi, B., & Daza, S. (2008). The possibilities of postcolonial praxis in education. *Race Ethnicity and Education*, *11*(1), 1–10.

University of Texas Rio Grande Valley. (2017). *Brownsville, Edinburg, Harlingen, TX. Institutional Summary 2017–2018*. Retrieved March 08, 2018, from: https://www.utrgv.edu/sair/_files/documents/instsummary2017.pdf

US Census. (2018). *Population estimates of Texas Counties, 2010–2017: Arranged in alphabetical order*. Retrieved December 29, 2018 from https://www.tsl.texas.gov/ref/ about tx/popcnty2010-11.html

Waziyatawin & Michael Yellow Bird. (Eds.). (2012). *For indigenous minds only: A decolonization handbook*. School for Advanced Research Press.

Zepeda, C. (2018). *Folklore of the Rio Grande Valley: Jacinto Treviño*. Retrieved December 29, 2018, from https://melabordeypereztrevino.wordpress.com/author/melaborde ypereztre vino/page/3/.

Reflections on the Path to Decolonial Pedagogies

Reconstructing Music Education: One Chicana's Journey

Rachel Yvonne Cruz

I read about the history of Western music and the lives of great composers––Bach, Mozart, and Beethoven––upon embarking on my course of music study at the University of Notre Dame. There I was taught Western European music, "classical music" or music that has stood the test of time per European scholars and set the universal standard for formal music study. As a result, I thought it the only type of music worthy of academe and scholarly research. There was no mention of Mexican born composers and musicians, nor the music or notational systems of pre-Colombian civilizations in the Americas, any type of world music––traditional and folk music not derived in the Western European style. It wasn't until I began working on my doctorate at The University of Texas at Austin (UT), that I supplemented my study of Western European music with classes covering the music of Mexico and the Caribbean and Chicanas/xs/os in the school process. I wanted to enhance my education with knowledge and understanding of what was relevant to me, my culture and heritage, and pertinent to my new job as choir director in a school where the student body was predominantly of Mexican descent.

In those elective courses at UT, I learned the Aztecs and Mayans had a ritualistic, rigorous musical regime including music for a 260-day religious calendar of which missed drum beats were punishable by death (Stevenson, 1952, pp. 17–19). It's logical, understanding the vital role of music in indigenous society, that they had composers, a tuning system, and a form of musical notation. According to Frances Karttunen (n.d.), specialist in Mesoamerican languages, there remain two manuscripts of song lyrics published shortly after the Spanish Conquest. However, aside from a few syllables representing drum beats, there is no type of musical notation in those books that can be used to musically interpret how the songs were sung or performed. The history of the music of the indigenous people, and world music in general it seems, went predominantly undocumented by European settler-colonialists; its historical significance and importance disregarded, erased, and subjugated as a means of settler-colonization.

In this chapter, I reflect on my experiences as both music student and music educator. I look back at the lack of options I had when pursuing music as a formal field of study. As an aspiring singer studying at the university level, only Western European *bel canto* singing was taught; hence, my doctorate in classical vocal performance. I never questioned what I was taught, until I became a teacher. I then understood that even though I'd done well in academe and obtained a terminal degree in music, I had been the victim of a perfectly orchestrated take-over. Juliet Hess (2015) in her article on decolonizing music education explains " ... Western music in music education acts as a colonizer" (p. 1), a manner of manipulating Indigenous into thinking the ways of the colonizer are the best ways. Music curriculum in the United States not only favors Western European musical study, for the most part, it's the only form of musical study. Because there were no alternative forms of music in which I could major, I assimilated into the Western European musical tradition––I was colonized. Western European colonialists successfully erased and robbed me from the history and *conocimiento* of my ancestors and until the very recent past, I never questioned it. As a Chicana music scholar and educator, my work is to shift the paradigm for others like me by deconstructing this imperialistic model and reconstructing music education so that it is authentic and concise, incorporates Indigenous and mestizo culture and thought (passed in the oral tradition), and centers Chicana/x/o students.

Music Student

My family, my mother especially, has always been influential in my love for and taste in music. The rancheras and corridos of José Alfredo Jimenez, Lola Beltrán, Vicente Fernández, and Ramón Ayala were staples in my home. As a child, my first lessons in music were given by my great-grandfather, who taught me to sing Spanish language songs; *Cielito Lindo* was the first one I learned. My great-grandfather and his brothers were musicians who played in the *salones* and *cantinas* in the late 19th century in South Texas. He taught me in the oral tradition (as most world music is taught), the same way he and his brothers learned. They passed on their art and culture, their songs and musicianship, from one generation to another, with words and by example; they had no formal music training or ability to read musical notation

(Western European music notation). In my family, I was the first to be musically literate in the Western tradition.

I was born and raised in Seguin, Texas. I attended Briesemeister Middle School and Seguin High School where the mascots were the "Toro" and the "Mighty Matador," respectively. Within the Anglo context, naming the mascots with Spanish language words was probably an attempt at cultural inclusivity; however, the mascots at both schools were Eurocentric as were their music programs. While I would have preferred to take a mariachi or conjunto class, music with which I was familiar, Briesemeister didn't offer those courses. Instead, I played the clarinet in the band. I didn't really want to play the "stupid" clarinet, if I had to be in the band, I wanted to play the soprano saxophone like Kenny G! However, at the time, I didn't know the name of the instrument. I thought it looked a lot like a gold clarinet, so I told the band director I wanted to play the gold clarinet. He said I should start with a wooden one. It made sense to me at the time. I know now I was probably being patronized. He likely assumed my family couldn't afford a clarinet made of gold. My parents and grandparents combined their resources and purchased a Normandy clarinet—an expensive clarinet. Unlike many of my friends and cousins (other Chicana/x/o kids), my family supported my musical endeavors. Many of the other Chicana/x/o students had to use loaner instruments if they wanted to participate in band class and finding transportation to and from extra-curricular activities also presented a problem for many. I was fortunate my parents and grandparents always got me where I needed or wanted to be. Throughout middle school and high school, I continued to learn Mexican and Tejano music (Mexican music that evolved in the state of Texas) outside of school. And while I didn't know the difference between a clarinet and a soprano sax, I could identify the guitarrón, vihuela, guitarra de golpe, acordeón and the bajo sexto.

In middle school, I also participated in sports. I thought myself to be an amazing athlete! If it had not been for the coach from hell, a white woman, I never would have ended up a Doctor of Musical Arts. According to the coach, I was not as good as I thought I was in athletics. Apparently, I was expendable on the volleyball court. I was not, however, expendable in Texas Future Problem Solvers (TFPS), the extra-curricular activity for people in the Gifted and Talented Program. TFPS did well at University Interscholastic League (UIL) competition, so I, along with another volleyball player, missed volleyball practice to attend the state competition. The white coach told me I would be excluded from the next away game for missing practice. She said I was strictly B-team as an athlete and wouldn't be missed. However, she did allow my white best friend, in the same circumstance, to attend. My friend told the teacher who sponsored TFPS (the TFPS teacher went to school with my mom) of the unjust differentiation in treatment, and the teacher called my mother. First thing in the morning, my mom went in to see the school principal regarding the injustice I had experienced the day before. The coach was called into the office, and my mother told her "a teacher's job is to build up students, not to tear them down! No one has ever been able to break Rachel's spirit, her confidence, and you're not going to be the first!" The coach, in tears because my mom pointed out her obvious bias towards the white student and let her have it in front of the principal, asked me to get on the bus for the tournament. I didn't. Instead, I turned in my uniform and joined the choir. My mom was actively involved in my education. She knew how to navigate the public school system, she spoke English, and she advocated on my behalf. The public school experience wasn't the same for many of my friends and family; they didn't have parents with either the courage or the grasp of the English language to face off with a teacher, especially a white teacher. This was the first time I experienced racism in public school; however, I didn't really understand it or see it for what it was back then. My mother did a good job of sheltering me, steering me away from the negative and keeping me on the college track.

As a 16-year old sophomore, I was the youngest person at Seguin High School to make the Texas All-State Choir and the only one to do it multiple times! Who knew? My mom was right, I could sing! However, even though I was an exceptional singer, I began in the Girls' Choir, the junior varsity ensemble where the not so good singers started rather than the varsity or Honor Choir. My first year in high school, I did well at the Texas Music Educators Association (TMEA) competition and it was then my choir director took notice of me, my potential. Only then was I given extra help learning solfege (a system for learning to sight-read using only the voice), a skill reinforced in honor choir that kept me from being an All-State winner my freshman year. I do not remember auditioning for the high school choir. Perhaps my counselor assumed because of my Spanish surname, the Girls' Choir was where I belonged. I can't help but think had I begun in Honor Choir, where music reading was reinforced daily, I would have been more successful as a freshman in competition.

In their book, *The Learner-Centered Classroom*, McCombs and Whisler (1997) describe an optimal learning environment as one that considers factors such as the learner's heritage, experiences, perspectives, background, and needs. They note that all content is learned better when understood relationally, including music. While I was in high school, my mother began creating an optimal learning environment for me by supplementing my public school education with music classes that celebrated my *Mexicanismo*. She began deconstructing my colonialized education by integrating cultural experiences and classes that fostered in me an appreciation for my ethnicity and heritage; they were tailored to my needs, comfortable and familiar, and afforded me the resources that I as a Mexican American girl needed to be successful in academe.

According to my mother, "I was singing before I was speaking." This is why she encouraged me to audition for an all-star ensemble slated to tour the world, "*Mariachi 7-Up USA.*" I won a spot in the ensemble, and even though *Mariachi 7-Up* never fully formed, I was able to continue studying mariachi in San Antonio, Texas, throughout high school. My mom drove eighty-miles twice-a-week to get me to mariachi classes in San Antonio, because Seguin High School didn't provide the culturally relevant education she saw I needed. She supplemented my education with experiences that helped me become a well-rounded individual with a sense of pride in my heritage and an overall sense of self-worth. My mother, realizing the importance of this musical experience, asked Teatro de Artes de Juan Seguin, a Mexican American cultural center in Seguin, to umbrella a mariachi education project in Seguin, where it was so desperately needed for others like me.

Studying music, in a familiar context that celebrated my culture and heritage, impacted my academic success. My mom supplemented my education with cultural learning experiences ranging from the predominantly Mexican American church we faithfully attended to taking me to see Mexican movies and supporting mariachi lessons. At my high school graduation, I was acknowledged with a couple of different awards: Outstanding Student Award (voted on, unanimously, by the school faculty) and Best Female Vocalist (voted on by the student body). I also received the largest amount of scholarship money in my graduating class, a one-hundred and thirty-six thousand dollar scholarship to The University of Notre Dame, where I earned a Bachelor of Arts degree in Music/Vocal Performance and then the Master of Music and Doctor of Musical Arts degrees at The University of Texas at Austin. I was also accepted to the University of Rochester's Eastman School of Music, Princeton University, Westminster Choir College, and Rice University. One would think these accomplishments and overall academic success would have been an incredible boost to my confidence as a student and as a musician. However, I remember hearing someone (a white parent) at my graduation ceremony questioning whether I received the awards because of my scholarship and talent or because of affirmative action (a government policy put in place to support, favor ethnic groups that have been marginalized and excluded from education). Years after I graduated from Notre Dame,

I read an article in the University's magazine defining the designation "Notre Dame Scholar," of which I was one—a Notre Dame Scholar is someone who earns a scholarship based on their academic credentials, not someone who fills an ethnic or racial quota. McCombs and Whistler's notion that enriching student learning models with lessons that consider the learner's heritage and background is indeed essential in cultivating academic growth and empowerment; it did mine.

University Music Student

My mother's upbringing was typical of Mexican Americans in her community. She was schooled by white teachers who thought it okay to anglicize her name (born Maria Luisa, her first teacher called her "Mary," and it stuck) and lived in a home where the man was king and could do as he pleased—women were considered less than, a burden, property. Even her marriage to my father was based on a racist caste system; he was a good catch because he was *güero* (light-skinned) and my great-grandparents thought he had money because of how he dressed and the car he drove. This is why it was acceptable for her to drop-out of school and marry at 16 years of age. Considering the values, the culture in which she was raised, how did she know educating me would shift the patterns of race, class, and gender inequities in which she and my father were raised? She took notice of how the white people were "getting-out." They were going to college. My mom never had the opportunities she and my father gave me. On the contrary, her grandmother, the woman who raised her, thought differently about education, especially for Mexican women. When I left to the University of Notre Dame in August of 1988, my great-grandmother thought my mother was the " . . . most horrible mother in the world. If she has to go to college, she can go in Seguin," she said. Mexicans didn't go to college, especially not Mexican girls. I graduated from high school and that was enough. She really believed it would have been better for me to be at home, in Seguin, where I would get married and have children as previous generations had done before me. My great-grandmother didn't speak to my mother for weeks (they typically spoke several times a day), maybe months; however, even without my great-grandmother's approval, she and my dad drove me to Notre Dame.

On our way to Notre Dame in South Bend, Indiana, was probably the first time I realized how atypical it was for a Chicana to be going to college, especially a university like Notre Dame. We made a stop for gas, and I met a girl about my age named Mari who greeted me in Spanish. While I understood her, speaking back to her in Spanish was a challenge for me. My mom helped us communicate. Mari asked me if I was on my way to *"los pepinos."* I thought it was a place, maybe a community college somewhere. She was on her way to pick cucumbers. I was almost ashamed to tell her I was going to college; however, she appeared to be genuinely happy for me when I did and told me when she wasn't picking with her family, she took classes at the community college in the Texas Mexican Border region (The Valley). After this experience, I asked my mother why she didn't teach us to speak Spanish. She told me she was punished in school for speaking Spanish. It wasn't allowed because non-Spanish speaking teachers convinced themselves Mexican kids were speaking derogatorily about them. I think it was just another form of colonialist behavior meant to keep Mexicans marginalized, in their place. Luckily for me, my great-grandmother only spoke to me in Spanish and insisted I respond in Spanish, however poor my grasp of the language.

I'm not sure I truly understood or appreciated the anomaly that was my upbringing, that it wasn't the norm for Chicanas/xs/os. I had two loving parents and was groomed (as best as possible) for higher education, even though they had to acquire those values on their own. I was also unaware we were not rich—far from it. I can only imagine what it was like for my parents to gather enough money to drive me to South Bend from Seguin, Texas (thirteen-hundred miles one-way), leave me each semester with a check for twenty-five hundred dollars (this was the parent contribution required of them towards my tuition), and then send two children to college once my brother enrolled at Notre Dame when I was a senior. They struggled so we never had limits placed on our potential. On the contrary, what was drilled into us was "do your best." We didn't worry about money, food, or having a home in which to live while school was out-of-session. We were to concentrate solely on our schooling.

I wonder how many students, Chicanas/xs/os like me, had parents unable to afford the parent contribution towards college tuition. Was this a form of institutional racism? You have been accepted to the university based on your academic credentials and awarded a scholarship. However, your parents will still have to contribute twenty-five hundred dollars a semester (may as well have been twenty-five thousand dollars), two-to-three times the cost of your local community college for you to attend. This could be construed as a form of institutional racism. I never thought for one moment I wasn't going to go to college. I knew I would go to college. The choice I was given, wasn't whether-or-not I was going; it was where I was going. While neither of my parents was raised in a home where education was a priority, they understood that education was synonymous with success, independence, and self-sustainability; a college degree was the tool I needed to end the cycle of poverty and the legacy of systemic racism my ancestors experienced as Mexican Americans in South Texas.

At Notre Dame, I was the only vocalist out of five music majors in the freshman class; the others were pianists. Our first day in Music Theory class, we were given a placement test. If one didn't score a minimum of seventy-percent, we were advised to drop the music major. I got sixty-nine percent of the answers correct. The test was easy for my peers who had all begun piano lessons between the ages of three and five. I would love to have taken piano lessons; however, we didn't have a piano. It didn't seem reasonable for me to ask my parents to pay for lessons, and besides, I had only seen pianos in the homes of my rich white friends and at church. Western European music theory is built into piano method books, to which I was never exposed. I played the guitar and sang, began my learning in the oral tradition. There was no written music involved. While I had learned to read simple rhythms and notes in middle school band and solfege in the high school choir (probably how I earned the sixty-nine points), I didn't know how to build chords using musical notation. I drew guitar chord symbols above the staff, used those symbols as a guide, and drew the notes where I thought they belonged. My chords were built correctly, however, I had no idea how to notate key signatures. I was called into the professor's office. He showed me the score and asked if I'd ever considered majoring in anything else. I told him I was born singing and that I was at Notre Dame to study music, only music. With what I perceived as many reservations, he allowed me to stay in the class. My peers tutored me and I remediated my deficit within the semester. I passed the course and progressed through the degree. I also registered for piano lessons, as passing a proficiency test in piano was required for completion of my degree; the pianists, however, didn't have to pass a vocal proficiency examination. I always thought this to be a form of discrimination; however, that is a first world problem not pertinent to this chapter. I promised myself if I was ever in a teaching position, I would do just that, teach; no student of mine would show up to college unprepared.

Interestingly enough, chord progressions I learned studying mariachi music helped me pass the Graduate Record Exam (GRE) in Music and progress to The University of Texas at Austin. I used the same knowledge (common mariachi chord progressions) to pass the harmonic analysis and listening components of the Texas Music Teacher Certification Exam and my doctoral comprehensive exams. Because my mother began enriching my education with cultural music from my early childhood, it isn't much of a leap to understand why, after studying music in the western European tradition through a doctorate in vocal performance, my life changed course.

Music Educator

I began my work in music education in 1996 at Fulmore Middle School, an inner-city school in Austin, Texas where a significant percentage of the students were migrant students of Mexican descent. While the school was unique in that it seemingly went to great lengths to prioritize student needs by requiring all of its teachers be English as a Second Language (ESL) certified, that effort did not extend to the fine and performing arts. Only band, choir, and orchestra (western European ensemble types) were offered as options for learning music, similar to what I experienced in middle-school. I was hired to direct the choir, where those migrant students of predominantly Mexican descent were being dumped when the art classes reached their capacity. I realized quickly, the choir didn't provide a suitable learning environment for those students, and with the encouragement of the Fulmore principal, I began Austin's first middle school mariachi ensemble, *Mariachi Halcon* (for the Fulmore Falcons).

It wasn't long before the mariachi program rivaled the band, choir, and orchestra. Mariachi transcended language, cultural and socioeconomic barriers faced by the students. To be part of an ensemble celebrating their culture and offering them a secure learning environment inspired them academically. The question for me remained, how was it that in 1996, a school district in one of the most progressive, liberal cities in the United States, making attempts at preparing teachers to work with Spanish language speakers by offering ESL courses, wasn't providing culturally relevant courses in the performing arts? By this point-in-time, mariachi classes were making their way into public schools, sometimes as extra-curricular or afterschool programs and sometimes as actual classes in the core curriculum.

While working for the Austin Independent School District, I was a contributor for a choral textbook called "Texas Choral Connections." I was on a committee of certified music (choir) teachers who were using the Texas Essential Knowledge and Skills for Music to create standards of music education for choirs Pre-Kindergarten-12th Grade. It was curious to me the amount of energy being spent on developing choral curriculum when I never had a problem finding good examples of such when lesson planning for my choir classes. I couldn't say the same about finding mariachi curriculum. Until the very recent past, mariachi was considered the music of the working class, devoid of art or significant value. With the exception of ensembles like Mariachi Vargas de Tecalitlán, who insist their musicians be musically literate, Mexican folk music has been primarily passed in the oral tradition. Because I couldn't find mariachi standards of education or Texas Essential Knowledge and Skills (TEKS) written for mariachi specifically, I applied the standards of music education I worked on for choir, with some adjustments that took into consideration instrumentation and style, to mariachi. I was familiar with the research compiled by the National Association for Music Education (2020) that acknowledged the positive relationship between studying the fine and performing arts and academic achievement. I knew learning music worked to promote academic success; however, the paradigm has been that the pedagogical tools that facilitate success (repertoire, curriculum, and credentialed teachers), have not always been afforded to mariachi ensembles. So, I began drafting curriculum, incorporating state and national standards of music education in mariachi class. This was how I began to deconstruct and reshape a Eurocentric, imperialist music education system: by applying those principles of Western music, that were proven to foster higher-order thinking skills and improve academic scores, to Mexican music.

Music Professor

After graduating from UT Austin, I was offered a position at Texas A&M International University (TAMIU) in Laredo, Texas—derogatively called "Tamale Tech" or "Mariachi Tech" because the student demographic was predominantly Mexican American. This racist nomenclature aimed at making Mexican Americans inferior dates back to circa 1848 when Texas, which had been a part of Mexico following its independence from Spain, became a part of the United States. Property and U.S. citizenship agreements that were guaranteed to Mexicans as part of the Treaty of Hidalgo were overlooked as white settler-colonialists continued to do what they do—erase and bury heritage and culture to either force Mexican Americans to assimilate or disappear. The racism and marginalization of Mexican Americans in Laredo still poignant and palpable in the year 2000, and "mariachi" (my area of specialty) remained synonymous with negative stereotypes and racial epithets that dated back to the aforementioned period. I thought, however, the job was totally within my skill-set, and I was going to change the derogatory perception of mariachi. My thought was that by creating a music program focused on integrating mariachi as a university discipline worthy of scholarly attention, I would accomplish this.

The challenge and the reward of working at TAMIU, a brand new university, was one and the same—the challenge to build a program from the ground-up and the reward to build a program of my own design. While there existed a mariachi program, it was not directed by a tenure-track faculty member familiar with mariachi music, not like the string ensemble or the choir, for example. I drafted a syllabus for the class, began to develop curriculum, and initiated the recruitment process. I went on Spanish language, local television to sell my program. I did my best in broken Spanish to be enthusiastic and excite prospective students about enrolling at TAMIU. When asked what courses I would be teaching, I responded with " ... voy a ofrecer 'cursios' en musica y mariachi!" What I meant to say was that I would be offering courses in music and mariachi. What I actually said was that I would be offering "diarrhea" in music and mariachi. I guess it worked. I had a line of students ready to sign-up, if not to learn, to make fun of me. Not kidding! They wanted to meet the new professor who said "diarrhea" on television.

I recruited not only college students, but high school students from Zapata, Texas as well. I became interim director of the *Mariachi Halcon* at Zapata High School when their director had a heart attack. Traveling back and forth from Laredo to Zapata, about two hours each day, became a bit of a challenge for me. So instead of making myself crazy juggling a part-time high school schedule with my full-time university appointment, I began working together with the director of enrollment management to bring the Zapata students to TAMIU. I recently spoke to her, and we are confident we were one of the first universities to create an early admissions program—a roadmap for success as it was coined by TAMIU, specifically for high school mariachi students. Using mariachi as a recruitment and retention effort worked. Creating an environment comfortable, safe, and familiar was conducive to learning. Bringing the Zapata students on campus and tailoring the university experience to them by validating Mexican music as equal to Western European music made students part of a learning and social circle that helped them be successful.

Upon enrolling those Zapata high school students at TAMIU, something serendipitous and incredible happened—we began to win international university-level mariachi competitions! Moreover, we did it with an enrollment that was over fifty-percent high schoolers! "Mariachi Tech?" The term no longer seemed quite so derogatory. The first time *Mariachi Internacional* of Texas A&M International University competed in a national arena and won, I was compelled to forget about my own budding operatic career and give those students the opportunity I never had in college—to formally study the music of their culture and heritage as part of their university education.

While at Texas A&M International University (2000–2004), I was selected for the Texas A&M System Regent's Initiative for Excellence in Education program where I presented on several occasions about concurrent enrollment and the transition into higher education and on the importance of culturally specific ensembles, like the mariachi. I also presented at The Texas

State Historical Society's annual convention about the development of the traditional mariachi, concurrent enrollment, and its impact upon higher education success. Through my work at TAMIU, I continued preparing future mariachi educators and developing curriculum that met state and national standards for music education. In the summer of 2001, I received a fellowship to begin developing mariachi curriculum; I began writing, *The Art of Mariachi* (2017). The fellowship legitimized mariachi as an art form deserving of academic study—its history, development, evolution—from a historical, cultural and musical perspective. Dr. Jeff Nevin (Chula Vista College in California) and Marcia Neel (music education consultant), amongst others, also began writing, developing, and presenting on the importance of mariachi curriculum in the early 2000s. TAMIU, the fellowship, and other academics finding value in mariachi pedagogy gave me the support I needed to be able to attest that mariachi deserved its proper place in academe.

In 2004, I began an appointment at Our Lady of the Lake University (OLLU) as assistant professor of music education. I was charged with creating the first degree of its kind in the U.S., a Bachelor of Arts degree in Music with All-Level Teacher Certification and a Specialization in Mariachi Performance and Pedagogy. Using my experience as a certified Secondary Music teacher and the curriculum I began developing at TAMIU, I offered courses in music pedagogy and mariachi methods and directed another award-winning ensemble, *Mariachi OLLU*. This degree was innovative and important. It began an effort quickly followed by other universities like Texas State University in San Marcos, Texas, to prepare future teachers with the requisite tools to teach Mexican American music in public schools.

In 2008, I left OLLU to open my own business, the International Academy of Music and the Arts (IAMA). I never, however, truly left academe. I continued my work to standardize mariachi education by notating mariachi repertoire (in the Western tradition) and presenting on the importance of mariachi education. I also offered professional development workshops for mariachi directors and schools working to develop mariachi programs. Under my direction, IAMA sponsored *Mariachi Internacional de IAMA*, a mariachi of university students from San Antonio area colleges that quickly became award-winning, competing against programs with full university support. I set the same academic bar for *Mariachi Internacional de IAMA* as I had when working for a university. My focus on challenging systemic, institutional injustice remained steady and my strongest tool, creating a reconstructed model for teaching music that centered Mexican American learners.

In 2012, I formed a partnership with Main Plaza Conservancy, a non-profit organization charged with preserving San Antonio culture and heritage. They contracted me to produce a mariachi festival. I proposed *Mariachi Corazón de San Antonio* (MCSA), a visual and audial showcase of the city's very heartbeat: its youth. Through the *Mariachi Corazón de San Antonio* program, whose membership was derived from a yearly festival and competition, San Antonio high school students were given an opportunity to audition for an all-star ensemble led by a Mexican American doctor of musical arts. Participation in MCSA exposed these students to a quality, cultural music education, where emphasis was placed on facilitating student success and higher-education preparedness. Through my work with MCSA, I was invited to present on standardizing mariachi curriculum at the Texas Music Educators Association Convention in 2016 and 2017, the largest music educators' convention in the world, and both times, MCSA was invited to showcase in the company of the best of the best in school level ensembles (Western European ensembles). The MCSA program, with a 100 percent matriculation rate of its graduates into higher education, created a significant impact in the high school graduation and participation rate of San Antonio's mariachi students in higher education supporting Rocco Landesman's, (chairman of the National Endowment for the Arts) statement that "Students who have arts-rich experiences in school do better across-the-board academically and they also become more active and engaged citizens,..." (National Endowment for the Arts. The arts and achievement in at-risk youth: Findings from ... (2012), p.5). Through participation in MCSA, San Antonio's historically underserved students had an opportunity to be involved in an urban cultural arts environment that otherwise may have been unavailable to them, especially if they were from low-income school districts with underfunded music programs. Through the *Mariachi Corazón de San Antonio* program, I worked to bridge the gap for those students of Mexican descent by providing a musical opportunity equitable in terms of quality (led by a state-certified educator), cost-free (no charge to the student in addition to earning scholarship money for participating), and that highlighted San Antonio's predominantly Mexican American culture and heritage. MCSA graduates have attended schools ranging from The University of Texas at San Antonio, University of Houston, and Texas A&M University to Stanford University in California.

Reconstructing Music Education

In 2017, I finished writing my book, *The Art of Mariachi: A Curriculum Guide* (2017). The book was written as resource for mariachi specialists who may or may not be certified teachers needing pedagogical tools and for those certified teachers of band, orchestra, and choir being challenged to teach mariachi. Although I mention standardizing and making equitable mariachi education to its Eurocentric counterparts in the book, I make no mention of what it means to "decolonize" music education. While my book offers curriculum ideas for making mariachi music education consistent with state and national standards for band, orchestra, and choir, it doesn't incorporate decolonial pedagogies for restructuring music education. I understood that music education in U.S. schools has been and remains dominated by antiquated, Eurocentric, middle class, learning modalities that are not learner-centered. And throughout my years of teaching, I thought that "decolonizing" was exactly what I was doing, even though I was unfamiliar with the term. I believed that by living the mantra "to create an inclusive and culturally sensitive learning environment" and using buzzwords like "diversity" and "equity" that I was decolonizing education.

As a Chicana music scholar and teacher, I ask "what does it really mean to decolonize music education and how do we begin the process of decolonizing music education?" Isn't this what I have been doing all along? According to Tuck and Yang (2012), "Settler colonialism is different from other forms of colonialism in that settlers come with the intention of making a new home on the land, a homemaking that insists on settler sovereignty over all things in their new domain" (p. 5). Settlers do this to ascertain their ways are the best ways while erasing indigenous epistemologies and cultural practices of which music is a part. As musicologist and music pedagogue, Margaret Walker (2020) notes, when we only teach Western European music, which is now recognized as the universal standard for music literacy, we are quite possibly delivering a message of white superiority (p. 13). I believe that we are, and by doing so, we are rationalizing and justifying the erasure of everything Indigenous by labeling it inferior. Decolonizing music education is not the same as making it equitable, inclusive or diverse. Tuck and Yang (2012) remind us that decolonizing education isn't synonymous with other forms of social justice movements used to diversify and integrate education, but it is " . . . about the repatriation of Indigenous land and life; it is not a metaphor for other things we want to do to improve our societies and schools" (p. 1).

If to decolonize music education does not mean to diversify, integrate, or make equitable, what does it mean? And, how does one decolonize when the majority of what is written and taught is done so in the colonialists' language (the "universal" language) of Western European music? In her book, *Decolonizing Methodologies*, Linda Smith (2021) reminds us that "Decolonization . . . does not mean and has not meant a total rejection of all theory or research or Western knowledge. Rather, it is about centering our concerns and world views . . . " (p. 39). Decolonizing music education does not necessarily mean eradicating Western music theory, history, and notation from music curriculum. This wouldn't be conducive to preparing musicians for careers in the world as it is today. Decolonizing music means deconstructing Eurocentric perspectives of what constitutes "good" music or music worthy of study. Defining what is "good" music is subjective and shouldn't apply to any one genre as it has been to Western music. It means deconstructing music curriculum that marginalizes students by aggrandizing Western music and omitting all other non-Western music and experiences. Decolonizing music also means developing pedagogical approaches and methods for teaching music from a position that meets students where they are and tailoring music education models that validate and introduce genres of music relevant to who they are, their heritage, history, and *conocimiento*.

I was recently appointed in a tenure-track position in the Mexican American Studies program at The University of Texas at San Antonio, not in the music department as my credentials might suggest. I've been tasked with developing a Mexican American Music Concentration as an option for students pursuing a bachelor of arts degree in Mexican American Studies and to pave an Early-Admissions/Dual enrollment pathway into the University for MCSA and other San Antonio area high school students. Our purpose is to facilitate the academic success of Mexican American students by providing an academic atmosphere that celebrates Mexican American cultural assets, heritage, and musical traditions. We are poised to educate current and future teachers and professional musicians to express Mexican American music in public spaces, schools, and universities with an appreciation of Indigenous Mexican American epistemologies, understanding of the Mexican American diaspora, and the importance of music in Mexican American society and culture.

There are many challenges for students of Mexican descent when it comes to learning in American public schools, particularly the lack of culturally relevant curriculum and pedagogical models that are Chicana/x/o student-centered. I recently attended an event for Latina leaders where one of the speakers remarked about Latinx children, "If they can't see it, they can't be it." And sadly, " ... only one-tenth of 1 percent of Latino students attend a school system where the portion of Latino teachers equals or exceeds the percentage of Latino students" (Meckler & Rabinowitz, 2019). For those of Mexican descent, achieving academic success is exponentially more difficult as their faces and histories are not reflected in those of their educators or school curriculum. I was one of the students of which she spoke. I wasn't like my white peers at Notre Dame who had taken piano lessons. Had my mother not created opportunities for me to study under the tutelage of exceptional *Mexicanos*, I would have never reached my potential as a musician and scholar, nor begun my work shifting the paradigm for other Mexican American students.

The work of decolonizing and reconstructing music education is not easy. White, Euro-classicist co-workers (I find it hard to call them "colleagues") have challenged me at every turn and continue to do so. Several years ago, a white, male, doctor of musical arts (the same degree I have), not only questioned my ability to notate using appropriate time signatures, but had the audacity to challenge my knowledge of rhythmic patterns I have proficiently played since I was 12 years old. How could I possibly notate music, Mexican music at that, more accurately than he? How dare I say mariachi music is as worthy of study as a Beethoven symphony, of which with an appropriately notated arrangement, a mariachi can play, and play well. When I spoke to another *doctora*, Latina colleague, about him, she pointed-out something I had never realized. She said, "You have been working twice as hard your entire life, to be perceived of as half as much." This was a crazy, thought-provoking, and sad revelation for me. Was I running myself ragged because I thought I was only worth half of him? Because I'm of Mexican descent? Is that what I have always done? While this was a poignant idea to consider, I realized that for whatever the reason, all of the extra effort was paying-off. Albeit unknowingly, I was making headway in the process of deconstructing, decolonizing, and then reconstructing music education. I knew my effort was working because I was making the Western European music scholars uncomfortable. They were getting mad!

I merged Western European music methods with Mexican music practices. I earned the discipline of Western music's highest credential, a doctorate in musical arts, and blended that knowledge with the *conocimiento* passed to me by my great-grandfather and others like him to Mexican music curriculum. As a result, my ensembles have been academically sound, popular, and award-winning! How dare I out-perform them, the Eurocentric classicists, by deconstructing their narrow-sighted approach to music teaching. I reconstructed mariachi education from its foundation and tailored what worked, made it comprehensive, especially for those who choose mariachi instead of band, orchestra, or choir. My students learn everything that those students in Eurocentric ensembles learn; however, they also learn the history of the music of Mexico, the accomplishments of the indigenous Mexicans and those of Mexican Americans and Chicanas/xs/os that through social activism, resistance, and perseverance paved the way for them.

Epilogue

Despite my parents' effort to protect me from the racism they experienced being Mexican Americans in Texas, I have struggled with believing my own self-worth and in the value of what I have accomplished as a musician and as an educator. Western European music was all I could see; it encompassed the totality of my formal music education. Hence, I always questioned that if the type of music I was good at was indeed equal, why wasn't it offered in school? Why is it that Eurocentric music scholars continue to fight me at every turn when the only music validated is theirs? Why is music an either/or and not a combination of both Western European and Mexican music in academia? Today, and for centuries now, Western European music is the standard for music theory, notation, quality, and artistry; it has become a universal language. That is what colonization does, it erases other forms of knowledge, in this circumstance, music; it executes a "universal" truth through an absolute annihilation—epistemic colonization[1]. Gary Ingle (2017), a national leader of music teachers writes "The common thread of colonization, whether it's the old kind of colonization or the new, is an 'either/or' mentality. One music reigns supreme, while the other is neglected at best or dies away at worst. The 'either/or' 'colonial' approach is not healthy or even desirable for a flourishing culture. Thus, the necessity to decolonize our music" (p. 17).

Mexican American music contains a hybridity of Indigenous Mexican elements and those brought by European colonizers. Mariachi, for example, derived from the Spanish theatrical orchestra of harps, violins, and guitars that was introduced to the now extinct Coca people in what is Cocula, Jalisco, Mexico. Post-Spanish conquest, the Spanish theatrical orchestra became transient and was used as instrumental accompaniment to dance. The name "mariachi," however, is indigenous to Mexico and in the language of the Coca.[2] Also indigenous to Mexico, are the guitarrón or "heart-beat" of the mariachi, the vihuela, and the guitarra de golpe that have percussive sounds that complement the foot-work of folkloric dancers. Another example is the conjunto that incorporates the accordion that was introduced in Texas by German and Polish immigrants who fled Mexico as a result of the revolution. Mexican American music is a cacophony of styles that incorporates the music and instrumentation of many different cultures. However, Eurocentrics continue to devalue indigenous elements of Mexcian music because it threatens Western Europe's epistemic dominion over music; the term that best describes this reaction is "white backlash[3]."

My mother, having grown up in a public school system that stripped her of her culture, her identity when they changed her name from Maria

Luisa to "Mary," knew innately that education was my path to success. When confronted with the inequities, the gaps in my public schooling, she supplemented it with cultural learning opportunities, experiences that helped me build a sense of self, community, and pride in my heritage. Starting on the lap of my great-grandfather, where I learned my first song, to sitting in the *cocina* listening to Lola Beltrán as she made us a breakfast of *frijolitos, huevos rancheros*, and homemade *tortillas*, she provided me with the cultural armor[4] I needed as a young Mexican American to be successful in Anglo academia.

I will proudly receive Maria Luisa's baton and continue the work she began of tearing down walls of institutional racism. And, as a reaction against colonial and capitalist material inequities, oppressive ideologies in education, and "white backlash," I will continue deconstructing the racist, Eurocentric archetype that is American music education. Furthermore, I will continue constructing music programs that allow educators to introduce the culture, music history, theory, and artistic ideas of colonized people in the Americas. I will educate and lead a "brown-wave" of musicians, teachers, and activists empowered by the *conocimiento* of our ancestors to be seen by young Chicanas/xs/os so they know their potential has no limits, that if they can see it, they can be it.

Notes

1. Epistemic colonization is synonymous with establishing control over knowledge: factual, conceptual, procedural, and metacognitive (Tapia, 2018)
2. There are many misconceptions regarding the etymology of the word "mariachi." The most common misconception is that the word is derived from the French word for "marriage." The earliest known reference to the word "mariachi" is found in a document written by a priest, Cosme Santa Anna, in 1852; the document antedates the French occupation of Mexico (Jáuregui, J., 2007)
3. In his article, *How White Backlash Controls American Progress*, Lawrence Glickman (2020) defines white backlash as a white counterreaction to all social movements and any type of cultural transformation. The term was coined in the 1960s; however, according to Glickman, the act of white backlash dates back to at least the Reconstruction
4. Patsy Torres, Tejano superstar, uses this term when she describes her traje de charro

References

Cruz, R. Y. (2017). *The art of Mariachi: A curriculum guide*. Conocimientos Press.

Glickman, L. (2020, May 22). *How white backlash controls American progress*. The Atlantic. http://www.kolumnmagazine.com/2020/05/22/how-white-backlash-controls-american-progress-the-atlantic/

Hess, J. (2015). Decolonizing music education: Moving beyond tokenism. *International Journal of Music Education, 33*(3), 336–347. https://doi.org/10.1177/0255761415581283

Ingle, G. L. (2017). Decolonizing music: The music forum of the Americas. *The American Music Teacher, 67*(2), 16–18. https://search.proquest.com/openview/7a28cba5800ebc7d3516db075b3c1159/1?pq-origsite=gscholar&cbl=40811

Jáuregui, J. (2007). *El Mariachi: Símbolo musical De México.* Instituto Nacional De Antropología e Historia.

Karttunen, F. E. (n.d.). *Aztec Song.* Mexicolore. https://www.mexicolore.co.uk/aztecs/music/aztec-song

McCombs, B., & Whisler, J. (1997). *The learner-centered classroom and school: Strategies for increasing student motivation and achievement* (1st ed.). Jossey-Bass.

Meckler, L., & Rabinowitz, K. (2019, December 27). *America's schools are more diverse than ever, yet teachers are still mostly white.* The Washington Post. https://www.washingtonpost.com/graphics/2019/local/education/teacher-diversity/

National Association for Music Education. (2020). *Music education and academic achievement.* https://nafme.org/advocacy/what-to-know/all-research/

Smith, L. T. (2021). *Decolonizing methodologies: Research and indigenous peoples.* Zed Books Ltd.

Stevenson, R. M. (1952). *In music in Mexico: A historical survey.* Thomas Y. Crowell Company. https://archive.org/details/musicinmexicoahi007091mbp/page/n41/mode/2up

Tapia, D. (2018, April 27). 4 types of knowledge. https://learningstrategist.org/2018/03/01/4-types-of-knowledge/

Tuck, Y. and Yang, K.W. (2012). *Decolonization is not a metaphor. Decolonization: Indigeneity, education & society, 1*(1), 1–40.

Walker, M. E. (2020). Towards a decolonized music history curriculum. *Journal of Music History Pedagogy, 10*(1), 1–19. http://www.ams-net.org/ojs/index.php/jmhp

"Haz Algo": Reading and Writing in a Chicanx Punk Pedagogy

Olivia Jean Hernández

Punk has always been there for me. It was there before I knew it. It will probably always be there.

My favorite uncle decided it was his personal job that I received a musical education. He is my mother's youngest brother and her family had worked for years through generational poverty in the Midwest, the kind where no one had time to do much of anything, let alone waste time listening to music and collecting records. There was music on my dad's side, sure. But it wasn't quite rock and roll, let alone punk rock. My abuelito, who had moved to the U.S. from the estado of Coahuila when he was young, kept up a steady musical diet of rancheras that often reverberated through the home, and well throughout my childhood. My abuelita, who was born in Eagle Pass, Texas, had children to raise and has never even told me if she has a favorite song.

So my uncle decided it was his job. We started with the Ramones, and then the Clash, and then the Sex Pistols. I sat listening to these bands on the floor by my uncle's record player, or by the computer while songs slowly downloaded onto our mostly broken desktop. I was immediately energized and entranced by classic punk songs that were at once full of rebellion and angst, as well as the underpinnings of joy. I loved that they were songs that invited you to yell back. And so I did. And then I went off the rails of the "classic" songs recommended by my uncle. I found The Slits. Bikini Kill. Sleater-Kinney. I latched onto these feminine voices that held joy and community, but also righteous anger that my emerging feminist self understood very well. By the time I finished high school, I was a walking encyclopedia of 1970s and 1980s punk and riot grrrl. I was a young girl possessed. These songs were so resonant because they helped me cope with the ways that I was also isolated. I was a confused girl from Eastern Washington who was angry and did not yet know that there were songs just for me.

I first heard Chicana punk around the same time I gained the language to talk about my own identity. Learning what it meant to be Chicana liberated me from an insecurity that I had dealt with my whole life. I had struggled to find meaning in my experience as the granddaughter of both Mexicano migrant workers and a poor white family by way of Kansas. A Chicana identity gave me a language to describe myself.

But Chicana punk. Chicana punk is where I found a purpose and a place for action.

Punk as Decolonial Text

Punk has always had an inherently anti-colonial potential. In a 2019 interview with Rick Castro from *Another Man*, Alice Bag of the legendary 1970s Los Angeles punk group The Bags summarized the experience of women of color in punk from its inception to now:

> Punk rock has evolved over time and there have been periods when it seemed to be dominated by aggressive, straight white male energy, but those periods didn't last. I think women, people of colour, queers, and anyone who identified as 'other' were always involved. Even when bros in leather jackets were trying to push us off the dance floor, we've persisted. Punk has found its way back to its roots, which means inclusivity, diversity, a rejection of conservative patriarchal values and challenging the things we want changed in our world. (Castro, 2019).

Punk has always been rooted in the possibilities of liberation for marginalized peoples. While mainstream histories of the genre have so often focused on the cis, straight, white, male anger that has often characterized a popular understanding of punk's sound and image, the parallel narratives of punk's history show different aspects of the genre.

Gaye Theresa Johnson's *Spaces and Conflict, Sounds of Solidarity: Music, Race and Spatial Entitlement in Los Angeles* (2013), outlines the key possibilities of Black and Chicano punks that emerged from the social and political unrest in Los Angeles in the 1970s and 1980s. Through examining the relationships between young people of color in these communities, Johnson shows how the creation of musical coalitions enabled new social relations. By claiming both physical and discursive spaces for their own, young punks were able to rewrite the meanings and possibilities of their communities from within the space that they created. Johnson writes, "These harsh new realities produced new forms of political resistance, mobilization, and struggle that had a cultural corollary in the emergence of the politicized punk music produced by disaffected youth of color. Their frustration with and anger at urban decay and persistent racism, led them to struggle to create new collective identities" (Johnson, 2013, p. 196). As reactants to the inequalities of race, class, gender, and location that played out in L.A. at this time, young people were and are still able to use punk music and punk-centered music spaces to spark and share coalitional efforts toward change. In these opportunities for "interracial and antiracist congregation" (Johnson, 2013, p. ix), punks created new visions of their future outside of the oppressive structures that had marginalized them from the outset.

Johnson's analysis of the work of young punks of color in earlier decades still rings true in the present. At a contemporary moment that sees major movements and activism on behalf of immigration protections, antiracism, livable wages, and queer and trans recognition and safety, it is not surprising that some of the most crucial work for advocacy is being done through cultural forms such as music and social media. In particular, the immediate availability of music from underrepresented bands has enabled a rush of artists, many of them Chicanx[1] and Latinx artists, who are politically and socially transparent in both their sound and their lyricism.

While punk has clearly been a space to engage in anti-colonial expression, the genre and community are also rife with opportunities to practice anti-colonial and decolonial action. Punk communities offer coalitional spaces for listeners to engage with each other and take action toward the liberatory messages and anti-colonial arguments of artist-activists. Do-It-Yourself practices, such as the sharing of zines or social media activism, enable punk fans to share and enact anti-colonial thinking and activism in their own local communities. The contemporary artist activism of Chicanx punk from bands like Providence's Downtown Boys and San Antonio's Fea provides a clear example of the anti-colonial praxis and dialogues by and for punk communities.

Chicana Punks y La Onda

In the realm of music, Chicana and Latina identities have often been omitted from the dominant narratives of artistic creation and invention. The role of the punk biographer has often been occupied by white, male journalists who replicate colonial understandings of power in the punk scene and focus on white, male artists as the key players in the development of the punk image and identity. A major project of Chicana scholarship has been to recover and revive various artistic narratives in order to reveal the stunning contributions of Chicanas to various musical genres, including punk rock. In *Loca Motion: The Travels of Chicana and Latina Popular Culture* (2005), Michelle

Habell-Pallán questions the omission of Chicana contributions to punk music. She concludes that "Perhaps these women do not register in non-academic accounts because of the way they disrupt fixed, one-dimensional notions of identity ... [Fixed] notions of Chicana identity framed by the dominant culture do not allow for recognition of these women in discussions of subcultural musical practices or in discussions focused on countering the shrinking of the public sphere" (Habell-Pallán, 2005, p. 153). At a critical moment for the development of social space and political order, Chicana punks have and continue to contribute to a reworking of understandings of identity and activism. Much like Johnson and Habell-Pallán, the editors of a recent issue of the journal *Social Text* see potential in the critical birthplace of punk music, particularly for punks of color: "Like queer, the adoption of punk as an individual and collective descriptor was a hand-to-hand struggle within and against violently demeaning language, against social and economic orders that marginalized and policed difference. This history that the word encodes continues to matter, insofar as it resonates within social spaces still striated with violent relations" (Brown et al., 2013). Even as these narratives are waiting to be widely uncovered, the contributions of Latinx and Chicanx punks to the genre have been invaluable.

Chicana feminist scholarship has established a space to read the contributions of Chicana punks over the last several decades. Depending on the shifting categories of what punk means, this is a legacy that goes far back into the disruptions of dominant genres and narratives by transgressive femininity in the rancheras of Chavela Vargas up to the punk aggression of Alice Bag or the queer indie rock of Girl in a Coma. All of these artists, and many beyond them, are engaged in the feminist project of reconstructing Chicana identities in the borderlands. In *Dissonant Divas* (2012), Deborah Vargas engages the figure of the "dissonant diva," of the Chicana artist working against dominant narratives of both history and of social imagination in order to contribute to la onda—the wave of a sonic Chicana movement (Vargas, 2012). Vargas explains:

> Diva dissonance illuminates musical productions and representations that reveal the ways non-normative gender and sexuality have been foreclosed around la onda's sonic imaginary of the borderlands. Moreover, dissonant divas also represent a methodology for articulating musical sound as more than audible through vocals and tunes, but also audible and visible in the female body. Divascapes filled with class, race, and sexuality tensions and alliances are differently gendered musical configurations of sound that cannot be overdetermined by geographic nation-state borders or canonical musical genres. (Vargas, 2012, p. 225–226)

The divascape described by Vargas, whether it is through bolero, or ranchera, or pop, or punk, is a space from which Chicana artists are able to reform the expectations of their gender and the social allowances of their cultural identity. It is a divascape that many Chicana punks have entered through their own configurations of performance. By enacting what Emma Pérez calls the "decolonial imaginary," Chicana artists are able to use their work of performance and lyricism to redefine what it means to act, and sound Chicana in the shifting borderlands that typically problematize expressions of Chicana selfhood (Pérez, 1999).

Chicana punk artists are also building off a long genealogy of sonorous rasquache in Chicana punk.[2] In *Loca Motion*, Michelle Habell-Pallán explains, "The appeal of punk to rebellious Chicana and Chicano youth makes sense for several reasons. First, the D.I.Y. (Do-It-Yourself) sensibility at the core of punk musical subcultures found resonance with the practice of rasquache, a Chicana/o cultural practice of "making do" with limited resources; in fact, Chicana/o youth had historically been at the forefront of formulating stylized social statements via the fashion and youth subculture" (Habell-Pallán, 2005, p. 150). Chicana punk artists redefine the project of Chicana feminism and rewrite it on their own terms, and in their own necessary spatial and sonic spaces.

It must be acknowledged that Chicana punk, much like the Chicano movement and Chicanx studies, is flawed in its pursuit of decolonial objectives. In Aimee Carrillo-Rowe's "Settler Xicana: Postcolonial and Decolonial Reflections on Incommensurability" (2017), she writes "Mexicans, Mexicanxs, and Chicanxs often have a complex relationship to Indigenous identity: on one hand, families often share 'stories that speak of abuelas indígenas with pride,' while on the other hand, they engage in 'fierce denials of Indianness that elevate European ancestral ties.' Beneath such vacillations between desire for and rejection of our Nativeness is a settler consciousness that compels us to undertake a critical examination of Chicanx relationships to land and Native dispossession" (Carrillo-Rowe, 2017, p. 530). In "Studying in Relation: Critical Latinx Indigeneities and Education," Dolores Calderón and Luis Urrieta Jr. (2019) explore the equity work to be done in education through Critical Latinx Indigeneities to recenter Indigenous students. In particular, they address how Latinx studies and Chicanx studies replicate colonial discourse and frameworks that silence Indigenous communities in regards to expressions and exploration of mestizx identity. They conclude that "[Recognition] of multiple genealogies of indigeneity, especially for Chicanx Studies, encourages the disruption of the Mexica (Aztec)-centric approach to indigeneity of the 1960s and 1970s that often, even today, appropriates and essentializes what it means to be Indigenous in ways that resemble indigenismo" (Calderón & Urrieta, 2019, p. 233). Ultimately, scholars engaging in this critique of Chicanx studies remind us that anti-colonial work in many overlapping disciplines must work to uplift Indigenous voices. While a foundational scholar like Gloria Anzaldúa's articulation of Chicana voice in *Borderlands/La Frontera* (1987) is highly influential, critical scholars today remind us to acknowledge that Chicanx identity is far more racially complicated than the colonial framework of mestizx identity. Crucially, contemporary conversations should center the experiences and histories of Indigenous and Black people in Latin America and the identities of Afrolatinx people, in addition to mestizx experiences. In the context of an anti-colonial pedagogy, it is necessary to expand upon the appropriative and anti-Black conceptions of mestizx race in the work of many Chicanx scholars. A truly anti-colonial pedagogy must center the experiences, voices, and languages of peoples indigenous to the Americas, as well as people of African descent who are so often erased and marginalized in conceptions of racial, cultural, and linguistic identity in the Americas.

In this very reading of how Chicana punk bands have anti-colonial postures in their performance, I recognize that there are clear impediments toward decolonial action that are imbedded in the figuring of Chicanx identity. While continued labor and reflection is necessary for non-Indigenous Chicanxs and Latinxs to participate in decolonial action, punk music remains a uniquely liberatory anti-colonial medium toward this work because it is so inclined toward requiring action and intersectional coalition for artists and listeners. While Chicanx and Latinx artists must continue to reflect on their relationship as settlers to Indigenous land, they can and should continue to bring audiences and communities together toward anti-colonial action in their music.

The coalitional punk activism of madrinas of the genre such as Alice Bag, as well as the contemporary works by artists such as Providence, Rhode Island's Downtown Boys and San Antonio's Fea, reflects how Chicana identity and feminist politics have a bearing on contemporary performance of gender and race for an increasingly widespread audience seeking the transformative physical and discursive spaces that punk music allows for. In particular, the work of Chicana punks today demonstrates the crucial ties of language, rasquache practices of sound, racial and gender performance, and the anti-colonial possibilities of Chicana feminist projects. For women in the spatial and psychic borderlands, punk music, as an inherently mixed form that engages elements from multiple strands of musical and cultural influence, continues to be used as a necessary tool for rearticulating shifting identifies, being heard, and sharing and listening to productively dissonant voices and stories and histories.

Chicanx Composition

While punk has an inherently anti-colonial potential, composition studies should strive toward a decolonial intention. Composition studies has historically been dominated by the values of a white, male scholars. However, scholars and educators in the field have made strides toward establishing composition pedagogy that is inclusive, responsive, and that decentralizes Standard Academic English from reading and writing curriculum. Yet this does mean that composition studies is enacting a decolonial praxis. In the context of the composition classroom, punk music is a critical resource that can make anti-colonial thinking, anti-colonial action, and anti-colonial expression a reality. Punk music can be used both text for analysis and expressive model in a composition classroom in which anti-colonial practice and possibilities are introduced to students.

The use of punk in the composition classroom is not at all new. In "Pedagogy of the Pissed: Punk Pedagogy in the First Year Writing Classroom" (1998), Seth Kahn-Egan advocates for the establishment of a punk pedagogy that supports students in DIY composition and in critical thinking about institutions and power. Kahn-Egan concludes, "I'm advocating a classroom where students learn the passion, commitment, and energy that are available from and in writing; where they learn to be critical of themselves, their cultures, and their government—that is, of institutions in general and, most importantly, where they learn to go beyond finding out what's wrong with the world and begin making it better. The punk classroom helps them move from being passive consumers of ideology to active participants in their cult" (Kahn-Egan, 1998, p. 100). Kahn-Egan's work is helpful in establishing the value of punk music broadly as a text in the writing classroom, but it does not fully engage with the anti-colonial models provided by punk music by punk artists that were historically marginalized.

While the place of punk in the classroom has been explored by others, the use of Chicanx punk as an alternative history and linguistic site for critical anti-colonial thinking is underexamined. One bridge between Chicana feminism, Chicana composition pedagogy, and Chicana punk is found in the work of the Chicana scholar Gloria Anzaldúa, a Tejana feminist scholar, who wrote of Chicana identity as an accounting with multiple cultures that intersect in borderlands spaces. In her work *Borderlands/La Frontera* (1987), she shows ways of accounting for multiple identities, cultures, and voices, and Anzaldúa focuses immensely on the work of language to enable Chicanas to speak their identities into existence. Andrea Lunsford (2009) describes Anzaldúa's work as a theorist and writer as being in constant dialogue with the multiple selves, audiences, readers, and texts that emerge from her anti-colonial conceptions of the border space and the borderlands constructed around her. Lunsford describes Anzaldúa's work across language and genres as a feat of textual weaving that Anzaldúa later clarifies as an act of critical composition, or "compostura" (Lunsford, 2009, p. 1402). This work helps to conceive of the Chicana voice as part of a movement that rewrites, through composition projects, corrupted histories and thoroughly asserts resilience and survival. Within the distinct context of working with Chicanx and Latinx students, a critical, inclusive orientation toward pedagogy makes certain types of writing and reading available for them. Further, the work of Chicanx composition scholars shows that Chicanxs have been instrumental in the development of a multilingual, critical, and anti-colonial orientations toward composition studies. This articulation of Chicana identity helps to provide pathways for students and artist-activists to take up anti-colonial expression into their own work. Punk artist-activists provide rhetorical models for readers and students to enact anti-colonial action in their own expression and to create community connections that unite students in activism and thinking that can resist and perhaps even dismantle colonial structures in the classroom and beyond it.

Chicanx Punk Pedagogy

Chicana punk has become a central part of my own pedagogy for students in first-year composition. Chicanas in punk have created something material for Chicanx and Latinx students that want to encounter history, theory, activism, and identity expression in motion through vocal and live performance. Building off the work of Eve Tuck and K. Wayne Yang (2012), I recognize that it is vital that truly decolonial pedagogy be centralized around structural change within the classroom, and extending towards the structures of the college and the surrounding community. Decolonial pedagogy in the classroom should create space for students to hone their tools for dismantling systems, recognizing sovereignty of indigenous peoples, and establishing communities of recognition and resistance that extend beyond the classroom space. Punk helps bridge these contradictions of a decolonial pedagogy by showing students how to move from complacency in the face of anti-colonial criticism toward using the rhetorical and material tools to stay angry and motivated and engaged in community resistance on behalf of decolonial objectives.

As an instructor of composition, I've found that, through an anticolonial composition pedagogy that introduces theory and then asks students to watch theory in motion through punk performance, students are able to grasp, visualize and clearly articulate how the work of Chicanx artists cements the fractured lines of colonized experience through punk expression.

In the composition courses that I've taught, I have worked to center the voices and expressive possibilities of Chicanx creatives and my pedagogy has centered Chicana punks as a resource and a site for analysis and understanding of Chicanx identity and anti-colonial action. I used these texts in my own curriculum, specifically as a central part of a dissertation case study in a first-year composition course at the University of Washington.

In my case study class, which was an intermediate composition course offered to first-generation college students, I asked students to look to Chicanx authors as models for multilingual, multicultural self-composition of fractured, colonized identities. They looked for the ways that these authors use creative expression as a way of asserting and remaking their identity for a public audience. Chicana composition, and particularly Chicana composition practices informed by punk music, encouraged students to take up the genres and model possibilities available to them and to infuse their own voices and experiences within these expressive forms. In the class, students looked at foundational Chicanx theories and concepts by Gloria Anzaldúa and Cherríe Moraga to examine at how Chicanx identity has been expressed across many genres—poetry, short fiction, memoir, ethnography, comedy, children's literature, comics, painting, and music. I asked students to think about the power and function of "Yo Soy, I Am" texts in the field of Chicanx literature and other creative expressions. Tey Diana Rebolledo, a Chicana literary theorist, reveals the importance of self-making in Chicana literature in her book *Women Singing in the Snow* (1995). She writes, "Chicanas had to be able to name: name themselves, their ancestors, their environment ... [a] surprising number of "yo soy" or "I am" texts exists in Chicana literature, texts that name in an attempt to articulate who Chicanas are, what they stand for, what they are made of" (Rebolledo, 1995, p. 152).

To start their engagement with these "Yo Soy, I Am" texts, students in the course first engaged with and critiqued the work of Gloria Anzaldúa (1987). Though her work is far more accessible, and personable, than a lot of cultural theory, students still often struggled with her moves across genres and within academic jargon, a language they were not always equipped to understand or critique—especially in an early composition course. They often expressed frustrations with academic expressions of Chicanx identity and activism, especially in their own precarious role as first-year composition studies students.

But music is a language that they know. And it is a language they speak with confidence. They know this language with passion and intimacy and the joy of remembering their favorite songs and their meanings and their histories. So, we then considered how Chicanx identity is expressed in the Tejana pop of Selena. We looked at the Chicanx practice of repurposing and remaking older texts in Las Cafeteras' cover (2012) of the Richie Valens's breakthrough "La Bamba," (1958), itself a son jarocho folk song with Afro-Indigenous roots in the state of Veracruz (Meraji, 2018). Students beamed over the Latinx electropop declaration of confianza in "Soy Yo" by Bomba Estéreo (2016). And they all got a good swoon in over Miguel asking "What's Normal Anyway?" in the experience of being Black and Mexican (2015).

And then we got to talk about punk.

First, punk was contextualized. We discussed the history of punk. They knew about England and New York and all the white guys. I would ask them what they knew about punk and we would outline our collective understanding of what "punk"—as they broadly considered it—looked like, sounded like, acted like. They were uniformly surprised to learn that's not all of the history of punk. In lecture, we discussed how marginalized folks, and particularly Black and Latinx people, have been involved in punk since near the beginning. They were introduced to the L.A. punk scene of the 1970s that gave audiences The Brat and The Zeros and Alice Bag and The Bags. We watched clips of performances by Alice Bag in the 1970s (Spheeris, 1981) and I outlined some scholarly discussion from Habell-Pallán of Bag's role in the history of Latinx artists in punk. By the end of our discussions, they came to see how punk has always been a genre uniquely equipped to accommodate the community needs and communicative desires of Latinx and Chicanx youth. Through our critical analysis of lyrics and performance, we saw the "Yo Soy, I Am" punk performances in motion.

Reading Downtown Boys

The first primary Chicanx punk text that the class focused on was a performance by Providence, Rhode Island based Downtown Boys. Because Downtown Boys, and vocalist Victoria Ruiz in particular, are so transparently motivated by their political ideals in their work and in their interviews, it was easy for me as an instructor to fully contextualize their work in this activism for students.

As part of a composition pedagogy that focused on rhetorical awareness and analysis, the students first looked into some biographical information about the band and the main lyricist. Victoria Ruiz engaged in the Providence, Rhode Island punk scene along with future band mate Joey La Neve DeFrancesco when they were both employees of the Renaissance Hotel in Providence—and where they later fought to unionize the hotel workforce in the city. Along with their labor activism, Ruiz and DeFrancesco started Downtown Boys. Since the beginning, the band has engaged with explicit politics that are sustained by their loud and eclectic sound.

In terms of genre, the band sounds like a fairly conventional punk band. They have a pounding rhythm section and straight-forward guitar sound. Ruiz's vocals are shouts, sometimes offbeat and out of tune, and frequently buried under the din of her bandmates. A listener must sometimes strain to hear her underneath the raucous sound that surrounds her words. They are a band that hits hard and revels in being rough around the edges, and Ruiz knows and acknowledges how this sound works in their favor. In an interview with *The Le Sigh* online magazine, Ruiz remarked, "We're a really pretty nasty band and I don't think that we're finessed at all. Even our political message is very active and constantly influenced by what is going on in the status quo . . . I think my involvement in political issues very much came from my experiences as a person of color, a woman, an educated person of color coming from a poor family, and realizing that those experiences are part of a greater context" (Macon 2014). And what she isn't able to express through her work with the more traditional punk sounds of Downtown Boys, she is able to work through in her other collaboration with DeFrancesco—the electronic group Malportado Kids (2015). In their musical collaboration, Ruiz and DeFrancesco's sounds and lyrics redefine expectations of both punk music and the various genres that they embody and inhabit through their work. Ruiz creates, through her music, a kind of aural space that accounts for the music of her cultural roots, but also adjusts and rewrites in order to integrate the sounds of her adolescence and future.

For Ruiz, a revolutionary reality is one that is necessarily multilingual. This kind of multilingual approach to audience engagement is a necessary one that wraps up a much larger audience in a discourse of intimacy and mutual intelligibility over their shared ideological beliefs and activism. While Spanish is a language of colonial influence for Latinx people, it is also a language that is heavily discriminated against in the United States, and has also been historically marginalized in education and writing studies in particular. Bilingualism is not necessary to an anti-colonial pedagogy, but the possibilities of bilingualism in the context of a composition classroom models for students how their multilingualism can be used as a tool of rhetorical resistance toward anti-colonial and even decolonial purposes.

In class, I asked students to first read the lyrics to the Downtown Boys songs "(Brown and Smart)" and "Monstro" and then we listened to the studio recording from their 2015 album *Full Communism*. At the top of this song, Ruiz shouts out to her audience:

> Why is it that fear always wants us to go looking for more?
> So when people are brown, when people are smart, white hegemony wants us to go looking for this third thing.
> Why is it that we never have enough with just what's inside of us?
> Today, we must scream at the top our lungs.
> That we are brown, we are smart.
> That third thing is only fear.
> Push it away. (Downtown Boys, 2015)

As a class, we started with a close reading of the song, and then listened to the song together. First, we discussed how the sound of the song and Ruiz's voice contributed to their understanding of the song's lyrics. Finally, as a pair-share activity, I asked students to consider these questions: What other authors (from this class or beyond it) do you see this song connecting with? What does Ruiz mean by "push[ing] [fear] away" in this song? What does pushing fear away look like? What kind of action does this song make you want to take? Students discussed how these lyrics fit into the emerging patterns we had seen of Chicana authors and artists asserting their own identities against the pressures to assimilate and the barriers constructed against Latinx and Chicanx people, particularly in higher education.

We then watched Ruiz sing the song in performance in a Youtube video from 2017 for *PressureDrop TV*. In performance, this song takes on greater importance in the ways that Ruiz rewrites the lines in a moment of instruction for her audience. The introduction to this song, as well as many others, is different in almost every performance. Here, I asked students to consider how Ruiz's spoken word framing of the song prior to the performance enhances its meaning and resonance in the ways that she is expressing her identity. I also asked them to examine how Ruiz uses her body through performance to further support the messages about autonomy, identity, and expression. Nina Mashurova, in a review for *Impose Magazine* (2015), describes the important critical construction of Ruiz's performance style: "Victoria Ruiz prefaces every song with a micro teach-in, taking the opportunity to speak honestly about police brutality, the prison-industrial complex, racism, sexism, gentrification, etc. In punk tradition, these teach-ins are meant to educate and empower, to unify the crowd, make people think before they rage" (Mashurova, 2015).

These teach-ins, these performative moments of critical intervention and educational practice, form the crux of Ruiz's highly-constructed and self-aware stage presence. Through her performance, students were able to see the clearest illustration of how Ruiz is enacting what Cherríe Moraga calls "theory in the flesh." Moraga writes, "A theory in the flesh means one where the physical realities of our lives—our skin color, the land or concrete we grew up on, our sexual longings—all fuse to create a politic born out of necessity" (Moraga, 1981, p. 23). Through her flagrant displays of self-assured Chicana identity as it becomes part of her political and musical performance, Ruiz enacts this kind of theory of the body and of personal and communal history. She performs, and shares, and educates within performance space the kind of theory that she physically embodies through necessity.

Students discussed how Ruiz's work as a lyricist and bandleader speaks to the crucial ties of language, rasquache practices of sound, racial and gender performance, and the anti-colonial motivations of Chicana feminist projects. Further, they discussed the rhetorical impact of the song being bilingual. Though the opening call to action is in English, the rest of the song that follows, articulates, in Spanish, that white supremacy and the pressure to assimilate is the "monstro"—the monster—of the title. Through performance, and voice, Ruiz clearly shaped her own identity for the audience of students in my class and this helped them to consider their own identities freed from the pressure of the "third thing" that attempts to control their own agency in identity in spaces of colonial and white supremacist influence.

The articulation that "I'm brown, I'm smart" helped us as class to reconsider what it would look like to be unafraid of the racist, sexist, and classist assumptions that white supremacy tries to place upon marginalized people, particularly in educational spaces. The song emerged as a clear articulation of a liberatory politic for my students. Students recognized the "Yo Soy, I Am" project in Ruiz's lyrics and the fearless, reclaiming gestures of her performance.

For many of the students in my classes, this marked their first introduction to the possibilities of punk. But in a genre like punk, there are always more variations of the punk rock performance.

Reading Fea

After our discussion of Downtown Boys, we then moved into close reading and visual analysis of another Chicana punk band. In this course, students had already been asked to look at various visual or multimedia texts toward analysis of rhetorical choices. Their analysis of lyrics and a music video from the band Fea asked them to connect the rhetorical choices of one band to various "Yo Soy, I Am" texts they had analyzed throughout the course. Based in San Antonio, Fea is comprised of former members of the Chicana rock group Girl in a Coma. Deborah Vargas describes the musical genealogy of Girl in a Coma's discography, saying "Girl in a Coma's musical sound represents a sonic circuit that moves through the place of San Antonio, the bodies of *mexicanas* in rock, and across borders of nation and gender" (Vargas, 2012, p. 217). While Girl in a Coma was recognized for their queer and bilingual approach to remaking rock (Contreras, 2011), Fea solidly positioned the necessity of a queer Chicanx, and Tejanx, punk voice.

Fea formed in 2016 after the apparently permanent hiatus of Girl in a Coma. In this group, Girl in a Coma's Phanie Diaz and Jenn Alva were joined by lead vocalist Letty Martinez. In this group, Fea builds from the Tejana rock of Girl in a Coma toward a more punk and aggressively political voice. On their self-titled debut, *Fea* (2016a), the band directly question and rail against structures of gendered violence against Latinxs and Chicanxs ("Feminazi" and "You Can't Change Me"). They raise the specter of one of Chicana folklore's most maligned figures and question the legitimacy of feminine monstrosity in "La Llorona." Through their bilingual punk voice in "No Hablo Español," Fea examines the loss of language through assimilation for generations of Latinx and Chicanx people. However, the main crux of their work on their album is to direct audiences to understand and to value the legitimacy and safety of Chicanxs.

In class, after the lyrical and performance reading of "Monstro," I screened the music video for Fea's "Mujer Moderna," the first single released off their 2016 self-titled album. "Mujer Moderna" is both a vehicle for lyrical analysis and visual analysis of the symbolically rich music video.

The video is set in a nightclub full of a diverse representation of Latinx and Chicanx identities. In the video, the audience is able to visually recognize that there are queer women, fat women, trans women, women who love to drink, women who love to flirt, women who love to dance and sing, all kinds of women. And as an audience, all of these women are united in looking up into the performance and listening to the voice of Letty Martinez as she sings from her space on the stage. The men of Piñata Protest, a ranchera punk band from Texas, (gamely) play the role of "Los Necios," the fools, hitting on women in the club and getting repeatedly rejected.

In the video, these men set up Martinez's direct retort to rape culture and patriarchal machismo that attempts to control the looks and behavior of mujeres, even in a space that should be as safe as a punk club. She sings:

> So what if her shirt is low cut
> And her jeans are tight
> Tell me why, tell me why do you think that it's alright
> When she puts up a fight?
> Abre las piernas
> No soy culpa, ni ramera
> Ni soy puta, mujerzuela
> No soy sola, no soy perra, solo soy mujer moderna (2016)

In these lyrics, she directly calls out to men and women that make gendered assumptions about women "asking for" assault and also placing labels and expectations upon women and their identities. In Spanish, she echoes the voices of men that ask her to open her legs, as if this is her only value. And then, she takes up the powerful voice of "Yo soy" to assert that no, she is not a bitch (and students note how many different words here all mean "bitch"). Here, she is not these things, she is not what other people make her out to be or expect her, she says "soy mujer moderna"—I am a modern woman—and the implication is that a mujer moderna is whatever that woman wants herself to be.

Often, in the video, the perspective of the audience switches to a shot of Martinez as she sings underneath a neon bar sign in the shape of La Virgen de Guadalupe. She sings, literally basked in the protective light of La Virgen, a resonant religious and cultural figure for Mexican Americans and Chicanxs, a symbol of purity and womanhood and motherhood. Using this symbolism, Fea directly asks the audience to see la mujer moderna as one who is still linked up to la Virgen as both a woman, and a woman always deserving of respect.

Fea calls for audiences to recognize a different kind of "Yo Soy, I Am" text, affirming that modern women can't be told what to do or what they are or how to be. For my students, who had been thinking about the contours and nuances of Chicanx identity throughout the course, and considering the simultaneously uplifting and colonially damning influence of La Virgen on Chicanas, this song was a direct breakthrough. It's a clear articulation of selfhood and Chicana womanhood that directly critiques and describes the assumptions of others. In the reading list for the course, students have seen other artists do this work—the visual art of Alma López (1999), the poetry of Sandra Cisneros (1994), the young adult fiction of Isabel Quintero (2014)—but this song establishes for them the clearest articulation of what a modern Chicana can be through the act of self-expression and self-advocacy in the face of gendered and racialized oppression that is a function of white supremacy and colonialism. Students were asked to outline the intertextual connections between the lyrics and visuals of the video to other texts they had read in the course. I asked students to focus on particular lyrics and images in the video and connect them to previous readings. Next, I asked students to describe whether the medium of information of a punk song and performance impacts the strength of these messages about feminism, bodily autonomy, or language. Through this conversation, students were left considering the impact of punk expression as a rhetorical option for activism.

Supplementing Noise of Fiction, Zines, and Social Media

These possibilities of punk in articulating Chicana identity have been recorded in the memoir work of Alice Bag in *Violence Girl* (2011) and Michelle Cruz Gonzales in *The Spitboy Rule* (2016). These emerging narratives have been published and perhaps made palatable for the audience of readers and scholars in the academy. But young adult literature, which like punk is another similarly underappreciated and underestimated genre, is also doing work to affirm the possibilities of punk art, activism, and voice in the imaginary of Chicana readers and skeptical academics in the field of composition.

In *The First Rule of Punk*, a 2017 young adult novel by Celia C. Pérez, the young protagonist, Maria Luisa, or Malú, tries to use punk music, and punk identity, as a way of taking control over her own identity as a bicultural, biracial, and bilingual young Chicana. She takes up punk as her primary identity at first before recognizing that punk, punk music, and the punk ethos, gives her a tool for connecting with and reclaiming her identity as a young Mexican-American, and as a Chicana.

In the novel, Malú feels caught between the values and identity expectations of her white father and her mother, an effortlessly bilingual Chicana studies professor. When she moves with her mother to a new town, she begins to spend time with the tattooed Chicana owner of a local café. Sitting in the café, Malú scans the walls, seeing pictures of Teresa Covarrubias of The Brat. Mrs. Hidalgo, the café owner tells Malú, "I'll make you a mix sometimes ... You should know all punk has to offer, not just the standards. And you should know your people's influence on the genre. It's a part of your history" (Pérez, 2017, p. 163). This moment of generational intervention gives Malú the language to talk about her own identity, which had been so fraught up until this point in her experience. From this turning point in the novel, Malú approaches her Chicana identity, and her punk identity, with pride. Recognizing The Brat, and The Bags, and other Chicana punks, instills her with the confidence that she's been missing to define herself against the pressures and aggressions that she has encountered as a young student in school and in the community.

I assigned excerpts from this novel to my students in support of our discussions of Downtown Boys, Fea, and Chicana identity and punk performance. We read sections of *The First Rule of Punk* to see the fictionalized development of Chicana punk voice and also in order to consider Malú's other hobby: making zines. The book contains several photocopied zines "created" by the main character. These texts become yet another pathway for students in composition classes to consider the possibility of rasquache/DIY composition informed by Chicana punk. After looking at Malú's fictional zines, we also looked at work by Los Angeles photographer Devyn Galindo in the photo book and zine project *We Are Still Here/Todavía Estamos Aquí* (2016). On the final page of the bright red zine, alongside a self-portrait of the author, Galindo writes "Everyday! We fight to reclaim space, document our existence, & preserve our culture" (Galindo, 2016). In another zine titled "Women Who Rock!" (2014) students engaged with the collective publishing practices of Girls Rock Dallas and their celebratory centerfold featuring a biography of Alice Bag, alongside her punk contemporaries Poly Styrene, Siouxsie Sioux, and Patti Smith (2014). Girls Rock Dallas also introduced students to the dynamic possibilities of playlist-making, as a holdover of mixtapes, as a punk-centered genre with argumentative potential (Girls Rock Dallas, 2014). Finally, we examined the "Zine Album: Phase One" (Fea 2016b) zine created as a supplement to Fea's first album (2016a). This zine works as a lyrical booklet for songs on the album as well as autobiographical expression for members of the band in which they detail their experiences as Chicana punk musicians.

While not every student is enthralled by the punk rock sound, almost every student is immediately captured by the possibilities of zine-making. For the final project in the composition course, students were invited to craft a final project in any of the genres that we had read in class together. In this project, they were asked to make a statement about their own communities in any genre and with any rhetorical choices that they wanted to make. A short reflection paper concerning their rhetorical strategies also supplemented the creative final project. More than half of the students in the class chose to create their own zines that reflected experiences and issues within their own communities of belonging. Many also used the zine genre as a way to analyze and engage with the activism art of their own favorite musical artists.

Perhaps most valuably, students were introduced to zines by way of punk. By understanding the punk ethos of community-building and accessibility, they were further inspired by the possibilities of the zine as a feature of the punk community. In her thesis "Grrrls in the Underground: Punk Feminism in Composition Studies" (2015), Loren Skye Roberson argues:

> The benefit of zines is students can produce their own text, engaging in metacognition along the way about the choices they make in selecting images and designs. Because most zines are short, students must also decide how to tell their story in a way that meets the limitations of the medium. Once the zine is created, students can pass their zine out to friends and family in order to share their work, something which is difficult to encourage in first-year students. Zines can also be helpful in establishing agency, with students having pride in a physical product versus something they might perceive as limited by the page (Roberson, 2015, p. 39).

Zines are the composition project that establishes the most possibilities for students creating their own community change. As part of our discussion of zines, students outlined the possibility of zine making, and the affordability and accessibility of zines, as a tool for social and community change.

Beyond the zine, we also looked to social media as another emergent technology of access and punk possibility. Punk artists like Victoria Ruiz take up all of the technologies made available to them. She and her other bandmates are dedicated to raising consciousness and providing educational pathways outside of the spaces created through their music. Unlike their counterparts of the 1970s and 1980s described by Gaye Theresa Johnson, Deborah Vargas, and Michelle Habell-Pallán, punks like Victoria Ruiz have the instant access and reach provided by the internet and social media. On January 9th, 2019, the Downtown Boys twitter account posted with a link to the band's song "A Wall" off of their 2017 recording *Cost of Living*. The tweet assured followers, "A wall is a wall, and nothing more at all. That means borders are inherently violent. It also means that walls are built by humans and can and must be torn down by humans" (Downtown Boys, 2019). In moments of the ongoing colonial violence by white supremacists in the United States and beyond, Chicana punks continue to use their music, and their rasquache platforms, as a means of resistance. Punk artists provide pathways for anti-colonial action. While colonial tongues may now be the only language that punk artists like Fea and Downtown Boys can sing in, their expressive power provides models and pathways for students seeking possibilities to turn their own anger into activism that can uplift indigenous communities and all marginalized peoples. As Michael Dominguez writes, a decolonial pedagogy must "Displace colonial epistemologies and foreground epistemologies reflective of youth and community wisdom" (Dominguez, 2017, p. 233). Punk music and expression, as a rhetorical centerpiece to a composition curriculum, can offer up students the freedom to restructure the classroom, the institution, and beyond, with their own epistemological values and possibilities.

Poder Elegir

For Ruiz, punk as an action means to care deeply and work hard for what a person cares about. In her case, this means taking up the feminist Chicana project of those who came before her in order to create new spaces for safe and productive engagement with contemporary political and social forms. In an interview for *Vanyaland* (Dugay, 2015), Ruiz describes an early Downtown Boys song called "Haz Algo" as one of the primary tenets of the band's purpose. She explains, "Whatever language the song is in, the message is the same — it's to *do something*, it's to *say something*. Say what you think and how you feel and choose it and stand by it and don't be worried about people liking you or disliking you. It may hurt or it may not be easy and it may not be fun in the short term but in the long term it really does make an impact and it does shift power" (Dugay, 2015). These are the punk ideals that Ruiz supports, and it intersects with the world of Chicana feminism that she embodies and enacts through her work. These are the punk ideals that students are able to internalize and use as pathways for their own voices in composition projects across various genres.

In their own dynamic cover of Los Prisioneros 1987 protest track "Poder Elegir" (1987), Victoria Ruiz builds off and retunes the voices of the Chilean group in order to remind her listeners that, for those in power in colonial systems, "su poder es nuestra ignorancia," and that power should be reclaimed in the punk tradition of direct questioning and intellectual engagement with social and political problems, followed by personal and community action. Her crucial message, for both the broad reach of her audience, is haz algo. Do something, do anything. Recognize the knowledge and voice inherent to the marginalized people in this colonized system and to do something in coalition with others in the same fight.

At the end of *The First Rule of Punk*, after singing her own punk rock cover of "Cielito Lindo," Malú comes to a certain kind of conclusion about punk in her life as a young Chicana: "Even punk music felt more like a mismatched quilt than I had ever considered. Being punk meant a lot of different things, just like being Mexican meant many things. Sometimes those things didn't seem to match. And that was okay because I'd discovered that maybe the first rule of punk was to make your own rules" (Pérez, 2017, p. 310).

This is what punk music can provide for students, especially marginalized students, students of color, and Latinx and Chicanx students, as part of an anti-colonial pedagogy in praxis. Punk music and performance provide a model and a pathway for showing students that as members of academic institutions, we are able to take up what we have, the voices we have, the genres we have, the resources we've been given, and use them as sites for empowerment and rule breaking and remaking of the oppressive colonial structures around us.

In the future, I plan to further develop curriculum that uses punk music as the central text in a first year composition course. Instead of focusing only on Chicanx artist-activists, I would like to extend this study to punk music in the Americas by Indigenous artists, Black artists, and other artists of color. In particular, I intend to construct a course around the community activism of Xingonas in the Pit, the "San Antonio-based D.I.Y decolonial feminist punk collective," and their Black & Brown Punk Fest, which has been held in 2018 and 2019. The community fundraising and organizing tactics of this collective, along with their curated punk performances for the festival, would make a rich primary text for a composition course that prompts students to develop their own social media tactics or community organizing team as anti-colonial praxis. Through the creation of zines, and social media, punk artist-activists working today offer so many more sites of analysis and models for rhetorical expression and resistance for students.

As a Chicana punk, I am continually inspired in my own expression by the artists who gave me a voice, and a set of words, with which to assert myself. As a Chicana punk educator, and my attempts to establish an anti-colonial punk pedagogy, punk expression continues to provide pathways for resistance of my own frustrations with educational institutions. Punk reminds me that, as we find our voices and construct ourselves, we can also disassemble and reconstruct the constraints of the classroom, the academy, and the world around us.

Notes

1 The use of the "x" as a suffix for the word Latino has been circulated in academic and activist communities to be inclusive of transgender and non-binary people. For many, the o/a suffix reinforces the gender binary of male/female, and the "x" suffix or "e" suffix has been used to refer to the spectrum of gender identities that exist for people who identify as Latinx, Chicanx, Mestizx, and for other communities. In this paper, I will use the "a" suffix to refer to individuals who identify as female, the "o" suffix to refer to male-identified individuals, and will use the "x" suffix when talking about larger communities to be inclusive of non-binary individuals

2 Rasquache has long been used as a descriptor of the Chicano/a aesthetic practice of "making do" with social, economic, and material scarcity. In "Rasquachismo: A Chicano Sensibility" (1989), Tomas Ybarra-Frausto describes rasquache as "An attitude

rooted in the resourcefulness and adaptability yet mindful of stance and style" (Ybarra-Frausto, 1989, p. 3). Chicana theorists like Amalia Mesa-Bains (1999) have added that the practice takes on feminist dimensions in that "Chicana rasquache (domesticana), like it male counterpart, has grown not only out of both resistance to majority culture and affirmation of cultural values, but from women's restrictions within the culture" (Mesa-Bains, 1999, 161).

References

Anzaldúa, G.E. (1987). *Borderlands/La Frontera: The new mestiza*. San Francisco: Aunt Lute Books.

Bag, A. (2011). *Violence Girl: East L.A. Rage to the Hollywood Stage, a Chicana Punk Story*. Feral House.

Blackheart Records. (2017, May 17). Fea-Mujer Moderna. *Retrieved from* https://www.youtube.com/watch?v=fv4yHCASirU

Bomba Estéreo. (2016, September 7). Bomba Estéreo-Soy Yo (Official Video). Retrieved from https://www.youtube.com/watch?v=bxWxXncl53U

Brown, J., Deer, P., & Nyong'o, T. (2013). Punk at its afterlives: Introduction. *Social Text*, *31*(3), 1–11.

Calderón, D., & Urrieta, L. (2019). Studying in relation: Critical Latinx Indigeneities and education. *Equity & Excellence in Education*, *52*(2–3), 219–238. https://doi.org/10.1080/10665684.2019.1672591

Carrillo-Rowe, A. (2017). Settler Xicana: Postcolonial and decolonial reflections on incommensurability. *Feminist Studies*, *43*(3), 525–536.

Castro, R. (2019). L.A. Punk legend alice bag talks to fetish photographer Rick Castro. *Another Man*. Retrieved from http://www.anothermanmag.com/life-culture/10714/fetish-photographer-rick-castro-meets-la-punk-legend-alice-bag

Cisneros, S. (1994). *Loose woman*. Knopf Publishing Group.

Contreras, F. (2011). Girl in a coma: Rockers tackle their second language. *NPR*. Retrieved from https://www.npr.org/2011/10/19/141475757/girl-in-a-coma-rockers-tackle-their-second-language

Dominguez, M. (2017). "Se Hace Puentes al Andar": Decolonial teacher education as a needed bridge to culturally sustaining and revitalizing pedagogies. In D. Paris & H. S. Alim (Eds.), *Culturally sustaining pedagogies: Teaching and learning for justice in a changing world* (pp. 225–245). New York: Teachers College Press.

Downtown Boys. (2015). *Full communism*. New Brunswick: Don Giovanni Records.

Downtown Boys. (2017). *Cost of living*. Seattle: Sub Pop.

Downtown Boys. (2019, January 8). A wall is a wall, and nothing more at all. That means borders are inherently violent. It also means that walls are built by humans and can and must be torn down by humans. [Tweet]. Retrieved from https://twitter.com/DowntownBoys/status/1082820582016729088

Dugay, R. (2015). Downtown Boys' Victoria Ruiz and Joey DeFrancesco are not backing down. *Vanyaland*. Retrieved from https://vanyaland.com/2015/11/19/interview-downtown-boys-victoria-ruiz-and-joey-defrancesco-are-not-backing-down/

Fea. (2016a). *Fea*. New York City: Blackheart Records.

Fea. (2016b). *Zine album: Phase one*.

Galindo, D. (2016). *We are still here/Estamos aquí todavía*. Printed Matter, Inc.

Girls Rock Dallas. (2014). *Women who rock!* San Antonio: Muchacha Zine.

Habell-Pallán, M. (2005). *Loca motion: The travels of Chicana and Latina popular culture*. University Press.

Johnson, G. T. (2013). *Spaces of conflict, sounds of solidarity: Music, race, and spatial entitlement in Los Angeles*. University of California Press.

Kahn-Egan, S. (1998). Pedagogy of the pissed: Punk pedagogy in the first-year writing classroom. *College Composition and Communication*, 49(1), 99–104. https://doi.org/10.2307/358563

Las Cafeteras. (2012, July 12). "La Bamba Rebelde" by Las Cafeteras. Retrieved from https://www.youtube.com/watch?v=9xv-FjbXaqk

López, A. (1999). Our Lady [Digital].

Los Prisioneros. (1987). Poder Elegir. On *La Cultura de La Basura*. London: EMI.

Lunsford, A. A. (2009). Toward a Mestiza rhetoric: Gloria Anzaldúa on composition and postcoloniality. In S. Miller (Ed.), *The Norton book of composition studies* (p. 27). New York City: W.W. Norton & Co.

Macon, C. (2014). Interview: Downtown boys. *The Le Sigh*. Retrieved from http://www.thelesigh.com/2014/08/interview-downtown-boys.html

Malportado Kids. (2015). *Total cultura*. Brooklyn: Dead Labour.

Mashurova, N. (2015). Downtown boys, "Monstro": Life-affirming protest punk. *Impose Magazine*. Retrieved from http://www.imposemagazine.com/bytes/new-music/downtown-boys-monstro

Meraji, S. M. (2018). Through slavery, segregation and more, 'La Bamba' has been the sound of survival. *NPR*. Retrieved from https://www.npr.org/2018/10/14/655833317/la-bamba-american-anthem-ritchie-valens-los-lobos-survival

Mesa-Bains, A. (1999). Domesticana: The sensibility of Chicana rasquache. *Aztlan: A Journal of Chicano Studies*, 24(2), 157–167.

Miguel. (2015, September 3). Miguel – What's normal anyway (Acoustic) live for make room. Retrieved from https://www.youtube.com/watch?v=Icyi7Jjhg-U

Moraga, C. (1981). Theory in the flesh. In C. Moraga & G. Anzaldúa (Eds.), *This bridge called my back: Writings by radical women of color* (p. 23). Kitchen Table: Women of Color Press.

Pérez, C. (2017). *The first rule of punk*. Penguin Random House.

Pérez, E. (1999). *The decolonial imaginary: Writing Chicanas into history*. Bloomington: Indiana University Press.

PressureDropTV. (2017, April 26). Downtown Boys-Monstro. Retrieved from https://www.youtube.com/watch?v=gjg9ao2sU4I

Quintero, I. (2014). *Gabi: A girl in pieces.* Cinco Puntos Press.

Rebolledo, T. D. (1995). *Women singing in the snow: A cultural analysis of Chicana literature.* University of Arizona Press.

Roberson, L. S. (2015). *Grrrls in the underground: Punk feminism in composition studies* (Order No. 1595224). Available from ProQuest Dissertations & Theses Global. (1710770016). Retrieved from https://search.proquest.com/docview/1710770016?accountid=14784

Spheeris, P. (Director). (1981). *The decline of western civilization* [Motion Picture]. United States: Spheeris Films.

Tuck, E., & Yang, K.W. (2012). Decolonization is not a metaphor. *Decolonization: Indigeneity, Education & Society, 1*(1), 1–40.

Valens, R. (1958). La Bamba. On *Ritchie Valens.* Hollywood: Del Fi Records.

Vargas, D. R. (2012). *Dissonant divas: The limits of La Onda in Chicana music.* Minneapolis: University of Minnesota Press, Print.

Xingonasinthepit [@xingonasinthepit]. (n.d.) Posts [Instagram profile]. Retrieved August 1st, 2019, from https://www.instagram.com/xingonasinthepit

Ybarra-Frausto, T. (1989). Rasquachismo: A Chicano sensibility. In *Chicano aesthetics: Rasquachismo* (pp. 5–8). Movimiento Artistico del Rio Salado.

Unsettling Social Justice Teacher Education: An Intergenerational Exploration of Music as Healing, Survivance, and Pedagogy

SEAN D. HERNÁNDEZ ADKINS, LUCÍA I. MOCK MUÑOZ DE LUNA, TANIA VARGAS, AND BYLASAN AHMAD

Social justice in education, like almost everything in U.S. education, is white women's work—it has to be or it is nothing, simply because the majority of teachers/education majors are white women (Loewus, 2017). This chapter aims to unsettle the notion of social justice work in education and instead move toward a theoretical and pedagogical stance that dismantles colonial and white supremacist understandings of the world. We do so through an intergenerational and transnational exploration of the role that music can play in both reinforcing and unsettling white supremacy, and proposing an unsettling praxis and pedagogy drawn from our own experiences with music in different contexts. Why begin with such a condemnation of social justice in education? First, Leigh Patel (the first Dean of Justice and Equity in a School of Education) notes extensively how social justice in education "has been so thoroughly leeched of meaning that its constant utterances do the work of hierarchy and power" (2018, p. 102). From this, we draw from Eve Tuck's recent call for engaging with frustration as a productive, generative, and wise affective response to the failure of the field of education research and practice to result in material outcomes that result in reducing anti-blackness, dispossession of Indigenous peoples, and global warming (Tuck, 2018). We are frustrated and see no sense in engaging with niceties in order to placate a reader who professes interest in decolonizing practices but balks at the urgent need for [rematriation of stolen land] material change, and a deep unsettling of the university, of public schooling, of the field of education, and education research. We also heed Tuck and Yang's admonition that "decolonization is not a metaphor" (2012). As such, we position ourselves squarely as settlers on stolen lands with a project of unsettling fellow settlers, as opposed to the Indigenous project of decolonization (Mock Muñoz de Luna & Hernández Adkins develop this argument elsewhere; under review).

Here we present three distinct but interrelated stories that form a transnational connection predicated on a critical reading of music as a tool for unsettling praxis. An analysis of Latinx/Chicanx music forms the basis for this reading, and we use this to connect to the struggles of Syrian and Palestinian youth an ocean away fleeing civil war and the Israeli occupation—through reading these two contexts together, connecting music and migration across imposed borders, we hope to engage an analysis of music as healing (Anzaldúa, 2015), transformative, and as a tool for survivance (Patel, 2016b; Vizenor, 2008) that can be used across contexts, and as a way of heeding Cherrie Moraga's call that we are all refugees of a world on fire (2021)—that now, more than ever, transnational collaborations—however contingent—are possible and necessary.

In order to engage with these ideas, we first turn back to the necessity of unsettling the notions of social justice education that are so pervasive in the field of education today, and argue that this field needs to be profoundly, and materially, unsettled. At its core, white women's social justice education seeks equity for marginalized peoples by providing access and opportunity to inequitable systems (ex: Bell, 1997). Take for instance, the two most cited works that appear in a Google Scholar search for "social justice education"; both are edited and written by Lee Anne Bell and Mauranne Adams. *Teaching for Diversity and Social Justice*, now in its third edition, is cited over three times as the third-most cited text (roughly 1,700 citations versus 500 citations). Arguably, whiteness or age do not necessarily preclude significant and demonstrable acuity in transformational social justice. However, whiteness limits experience with racism and age curtails understanding of modern formations of oppression. For instance, these authors and editors have written about "equity (fairness)" (Critical Race Theory without mentioning the permanence of racism, intersectionality without Black women, and oppression, racism, sexism, homophobia without white supremacist heteropatriarchy (Adams & Bell). Taken together it is little wonder that efforts toward an education for social justice have gotten us no closer.

Let's break this down a bit further. Take the authors of *Teaching for Diversity and Social Justice*: two old white ladies. These women went to graduate school in the 1970s, before the spread of third wave feminisms (intersectionality, standpoint theory, positionality, borderlands theory, etc.). These women may have been trailblazers in their own institutions and/or families for achieving doctorate degrees and tenured jobs. But it is likely that they came from relatively privileged backgrounds, and they most certainly benefited from segregated schools, neighborhoods, and hiring practices. So, what does it mean to study a text in social justice education written by scholars who, by virtue of racist structures, didn't have to compete with Black or Brown scholars for their jobs? Now, funnel the lessons from their scholarship through the minds of cohorts of nearly all white and female future teachers in the 1980s and 1990s, when these professors were building their claims to prominence in the field. Those students, those young white women, mostly came from middle and upper-class families. Those new teachers for social justice entered schools that would soon begin to not only re-segregate but also pursue tracking strategies that initiated the school-within-a-school phenomenon. And yet, with little evidence that these authors' ideas have brought about any real social justice, their book is still foundational. The consequences of hanging on to this legacy are very real.

Until recently, white women's social justice education could only conjure solutions to social problems by improving the odds for marginalized students in a game designed for the white heteropatriarchy. It's the type of social justice that sends Black and Brown kids to classes for the SAT instead of working to uncouple the schooling system from all forms of standardized testing, which has been shown to increase social stratification at best and reify racist beliefs at worst. These are the limits of fighting for the buzzwords "access" and "opportunity." While such an analysis might be interpreted as quite harsh, it opens the door to understanding how social justice education became inconsequential by design. Social justice education is a settler colonial logic. This logic is taught and enacted by settlers to other settlers. And yet, many Black, Brown, and Indigenous scholars of education still use the term, perhaps out of a sense of having been excluded from the foundations of social justice education (see the Introduction; Tuck & Yang, 2018).

With this engagement has also come distinct challenges to the universality of social justice in the field of educational research. Some of the most compelling challenges—in our reading—have come from scholars writing in and through decolonial frameworks. In the introduction to their edited volume *Indigenous and Decolonizing Studies in Education*, Linda Tuhiwai Smith, Eve Tuck, and K. Wayne Yang note that "social justice is most conventionally conceived of in educational research as, 'How can we make schools (and society) less unjust?' Or, 'How can we improve schooling outcomes?'"; thus, social justice is focused on the reduction of harm and alleviation of the consequences of white supremacy and colonialism (2019, p. xiv). This conceptualization, although well-intentioned, does little to imagine the destruction of the systems that perpetuate these injustices; indeed, they uphold these structures (Dumas, 2018).

In *Decolonizing Educational Research*, Leigh Patel (2016a) calls for a moratorium on social justice research, and here we draw on her work to frame our own understanding of the need to unsettle the ubiquitous and muddled nature of the use of social justice in teacher education. Patel frames this as a pause in order to see what we need to reach beyond, to properly consider what narratives around social justice enliven structures that uphold oppression rather than dismantle it; time to "consider what tools of progress, however inadvertently, have become conduits and proxies (Perry, 2011) for settler logics and have themselves become part of the structure of settler colonialism." (Patel, 2016a, p. 88; see also Patel, 2018). Here we quote her at length:

> When viewed in relation to the complicated history of land, settling, and chattel labor, *platforms of justice that seek equal treatment for human beings are, at best, off-kilter.* Without direct engagement of the connections across entities set asunder and dispossessed by settler colonialism, the anthropocentric liberal humanism found in much of social justice reseats certain settler logics, with the far reach of justice being a subject of the state, at best a better treated subject of the state. (2016a, p. 89, emphasis added)

The turn toward social justice in teacher education has been an off-kilter project since its inception and continues to be so as long as there is no reckoning with how this project has become a henchman for the "heteropatriarchal racist logics of individuality" (Patel, 2016a, p. 90). Tuck and Yang (2016) note that we must be wary of "how white supremacy creates common tools that are often picked up, reused, and recycled by efforts considered otherwise as 'social justice.'" (p. 10).

And yet, we are not calling for a rejection of social justice; a pause, a suspension, a call rather to take stock, hold ourselves and the field accountable, and then reimagine what justice can look like in education. Indeed, it is imperative that we do so, because as Tuck and Yang (2018) argue:

> Social justice is the field of education. There is no legitimacy to the field of education if it cannot meaningfully attend to social contexts, historical and contemporary structures of settler colonialism, white supremacy, and anti-Blackness. (p. 5)

For those who have been dispossessed of land and lives, these questions of justice form the very theoretical and pedagogical foundations of their work in education. Historically, those people most attuned to injustice have been kept out of the traditional academic conversations on theory and pedagogy around "social justice"; thus, alternate forms of story-telling and knowledge production and relationships have flourished. This is where we situate our work envisioning an unsettling pedagogy for social justice in teacher education. More specifically, here are the words and practices we associate with each term:

> Unsettling education: collectivity, relationality, survivance, fugitivity, marronage, futurity, rematriation, equity, transnationalism/borderlessness, land-based, non-linearity, transdisciplinarity, healing, liberation, abolition, subversion, answerability, haunting
>
> Social justice education: meritocracy, individualism, liberalism, resilience, grit, access, opportunity, diversity, inclusion, multiculturalism, equality, empathy, self-regulation, rights, empiricism, white supremacy

How We Met and Why We Write

Our paths as co-authors were brought together through a social justice education course the three of us were involved in at our School of Education in the fall of 2018—Lucía and Sean were graduate TAs and Tania was an undergraduate student. The semester witnessed heights of white male privilege in the confirmation of a belligerent Supreme Court Justice (who we believe to be a perpetrator of sexual assault), the exposure of the despicable practices of child theft and concentration camps at the settler colonial U.S.-Mexico border, the entrapment by ICE of Samuel Bruno from a local sanctuary church and his immediate deportation (Flynn, 2018), and the continued brutalities of the Israeli settler state (Holmes, 2019; Israel demolishes Palestinian homes, 2019). Our School and University are in a time of tumult, with student and community activists pushing for a reckoning with the University's racist past and present; we continue to fiercely battle the removal of monuments to white supremacy throughout campus. While students want their removal, the administration has demurred and criminalized student protest (Villena, 2018). In our School of Education, we have pushed for our administration to serve as leaders for social justice—which is touted in our vision statement, alongside equity—and have been met with similar resistance: last year threats of charges for vandalism of state property were levied by the administration in response to students postering social justice-themed messages to the marble facades of the building. Students have been harassed by staff and labeled as troublemakers. Structurally, the course in which we met is offered only as an elective, and thus not required for the overwhelmingly white female student body soon to enter classrooms and schools. Over the past three years, there has been an exodus of faculty of color from our building—for instance, we now have only one Latinx faculty member remaining on staff—and the administration has also tried to take away space from the Latinx Education Research Hub (Blake, 2018), the only space in the School of Education dedicated to standing with (TallBear, as featured in Keene & Wilbur, 2019) marginalized members of our community. The world is indeed on fire.

Social justice then has become untenable for us in practice, and our critique stems from our experiences confronting its limits. What, then, are possible alternatives? How can we unsettle and re-imagine social justice, and what does this look like in practice? As we've asked ourselves these questions, we have decided to look beyond our textbooks and have sought out alternate forms of expression and healing. Reflecting on our own individual experiences with music has served as one way to unsettle social justice education—this next section introduces our individual voices and experiences as a means to access music as an unsettling praxis.

Nuestros Cuentos

Tania

My family migrated to the United States in the late 1990s from Mexico due to social and economic reforms. Learning of my family's migration to America has very much influenced my views on the existing immigration problems that the United States currently faces. Like many Mexicans in the 1990s, my family made the journey from Mexico to America in pursuit of a better life, particularly after NAFTA gutted Mexican agriculture and the ejidos (Flores Carmona, 2017; Stuesse, 2016). Many Mexicans risked everything in crossing through the desert and across the Río Bravo. They would then make homes in the southwestern region of the U.S.—for some, their ancestral lands—or the northeastern region. These regions encompassed states such as California, Texas, Arizona, Illinois, or New York (Zong & Batalova, 2018). Most Mexicans preferred to settle in regions where there was a possibility of work, or if possible, to stay within close proximity of other Mexican immigrants. These clusters of immigrants are often the result of large corporations advertising their jobs in Mexico and other parts of Latin America. For instance, poultry and pork processors recruited Latinx workers to the so-called Nuevo South as a method to break the unionization attempts by their historically Black workforce (Stuesse, 2016).

Many may ask, "What does this have to do with education?" Because immigrant families have kids and kids are guaranteed a public education in the U.S. Additionally, many people leave their country of origin because the lack of education in rural areas excludes them from the opportunities and mobility that education sometimes affords. They recognize this, but also understand that they have the skills that are beneficial for the trade/labor jobs which are integral to many nations' backbones, such as construction workers, factory workers, and landscapers, and understand that their time and effort are more valuable in different nations, especially neighboring nations that are more developed.

Furthermore, as is central to the ideology of the importance of family to Latinxs, parents consider the opportunities that will be available to their future children in both nations before deciding which would be best for both the present and the future. Although they may have been unable to receive a proper, formal education, their life skills and insight are equally as valuable as formal schooling, which could in turn be utilized for a better future for the next generation. For instance, in my case, my parents decided to migrate to the U.S. in order for me and my brother to receive a proper education and have better odds at success. However, it is hard to succeed if there is a lack of support in schools.

More than 43.7 million immigrants lived in the U.S. in 2016, constituting 13.5 percent of the total U.S. population of 323.1 million. As of 2017, immigrants and their U.S born children now numbered at around 86.4 million people strong (Zong, Batalova, & Hallock, 2018). In North Carolina, one in three school-aged children are either immigrants themselves or born to immigrant parents (Rong, Hillburn, & Sun, 2017). This relatively new demographic change has led to many nativist and exclusionary experiences for local Latinx students and families (Cervantes-Soon & Turner, 2017; Greene, Perreira, & Ko, 2017; Parkhouse & Freeman, 2017). As the immigrant population in the U.S. has increased and dispersed into new regions, so, too, has the need for schools to support these students and their families. However, Latinx students continue to be greeted by white-dominated schools that work to assimilate (read: colonize) these students. Instead, teachers and schools need to provide better academic and emotional support for Latinx students, assist immigrant families, and develop home-school relationships that benefit Latinx and immigrant students and families. These supports cannot simply work to conform Latinxs to the white, settler colonial schooling project—like the experiences I had in school.

I didn't have the full academic and emotional support that I needed at an early age. Since Spanish was my first language, I was tracked into English as a Second Language (ESL) classes so that I could learn English separately from my peers without being overwhelmed by the new language. Although I admit that it did help improve my English, ESL made me face an environment of segregation and isolation at an early age. Music helped me combat those feelings. In those moments where I felt the most out of place, I would listen to songs that would give me a sense of healing.

Most of the music I listened to was the music that my family listened to—corridos. Corridos are a "significant form of folk music and folk poetry sung by people of Mexican descent" (Rivera, 2018). Corridos are vehicles that pass along information pertaining to significant cultural, political, social, or environmental events. Many students of Mexican descent, and even other Latinx students, find a deep connection to corridos and write corridos themselves as an empowering and healing practice (de los Ríos, 2019). Listening to the lyrics and interpreting their meanings make me feel more connected to my culture and gave me a sense of hope. Hope that one day there will be a more interconnected society that promotes real inclusion and social justice. Hope that there will be no more wrongful deportations and discrimination against immigrant families. Hope that decolonization/unsettling dreams will come true.

The song that has made a huge impact in my life is the song "Corrido de Juanito" by Calibre 50. Listening to the song puts a lump in my throat. It is the story of my family; the story of many Mexican immigrant families. This song is a narrative that takes up the issue of migration from the perspective of this endearing character that could easily be any one of the millions of undocumented people living in the U.S. With fear and uncertainty, they have spent their lives hiding as if they were criminals, being discriminated against and oppressed, but always with their heads held high and proud of their roots. When my parents and I listen to the song together, our emotions are very sensitive. There are times when we cry together because it makes us reflect on all the sacrifices our family had to make to get to where we are now. It has not been an easy path for my family, but we have no regrets. Perhaps, this song reinforces how important it is to never give up because the benefits are on the way.

What would decolonized schooling have looked like for me, a U.S.-born mexicana? First of all, I wouldn't have been required to learn English—at least not unless the white students weren't also required to learn Spanish. Not only would there have been no ESL classrooms, there wouldn't be any tracking either—maybe not even grade levels. Structures of social exclusion would be made impossible by decolonization. I wouldn't have had to take End of Grade tests to progress through school. No SAT to get into college. Those forms of colonizer knowledge and merit would be made unthinkable.

One small step toward decolonization—an unsettling step—that teachers can make now is to include corridos in their curricula. Many educators have already taken up hip-hop as pedagogy (Emdin, 2016). Corridos could become the foundation of a new unsettling pedagogy—one specifically targeted at the notions of borders, nationalism, family, community, and monolingualism. Scholars and teacher educators should help detail that corrido pedagogy. If done with respect, a corrido pedagogy could help break down settler colonial schooling and make us all more free.

Lucía and Bylasan
We write from our time in Beirut, Lebanon working with a community school for Syrian and Palestinian youth. We are fiercely protective of our friends there and keenly aware of our role as interlocutors of their stories and lives. We know the traps and exploitative history of researchers and foreigners writing about refugee communities, and our friends have made clear to us what we can and can't tell about their lives to you, so here we present a story. It's based on a compilation of our experiences, and it is our truth, but we won't tell you everything:

Marwa stands in front of us, a steely look in her eyes. We're at the Center on a Saturday to teach English and classes have ended, so we're hanging out with the students, chatting about the week, and now—like most weeks—they've started showing us what songs and dances they've been working on during the school week. Most of the performances are groups of girls and boys, but this time it's just Marwa, standing up in front of us, all of our attention turned toward her. She's nervous, and her face is serious—but there's a look of determination that sends a clear message: *estoy aquí* / أنا هنا

But let's back up. Where are we? The Center is a community school started by a Palestinian refugee community in Lebanon for Syrian youth. Palestinians have been living in Lebanon since 1948 and continue to be at the mercy of the settler state Israel and the international community that has allowed a protracted refugee crisis. Almost 500,000 Palestinians live in Lebanon and the majority live in twelve refugee camps around the country. The camps were never meant to be permanent homes but have now existed for seventy years—they are overcrowded, lack infrastructure, electricity, and access to clean water. Many Palestinians are dependent on the aid provided by the United Nation Relief and Works Agency (UNRWA), which the United States has just stopped funding—a devastating blow to a community already radically marginalized. In the camp we work at, in the middle of Beirut, there are protests almost daily now of the U.S.; there is an anger and anguish that seethes through the pores of the land.

Since 2011, this camp has also become home to many Syrians fleeing the civil war in their country. The population of the camp has almost doubled—making an already precarious community strain under the pressure of more families, more bodies. Divides exist in between these two communities—Syrians and Palestinians, newcomers and long-time residents of the camp—histories deep and complicated, embodied in the children and young people sitting together in this cramped, cold room—heated by our bodies, by our movement. We don't pretend to fully know and understand these complications. We are outsiders, visitors in the camp and in the school. We've been working at and with the Center for the past five years, and have a deep love for the people here, but our understandings are glimpses, and come in fits and starts.

But here we are, once again, with Marwa looking at us as she stands in front of the room, which has now gone quiet in anticipation. And then, she begins—at first a whisper, her voice shaking slightly, but stronger as she continues. She is rapping, reciting words in her own rhythm, rhymes coming and going, and there is very little we understand. Between the two of us, only Bylasan speaks Arabic well enough to understand, but even then, the words fly by rapidly. But there is a refrain that is unmistakable. Marwa repeats: "عطونا الطفولة". *Danos nuestra niñez. Give us our childhood.* She continues and her words turn to her homeland, which is now her mother. Marwa says, "I know you're tired."

Marwa's refrain harkens back to a Lebanese song from during their civil war (1975–1990), and so in this moment something powerful is happening here. A Syrian, in a Palestinian refugee camp, is evoking the Lebanese Civil War. In an act of transhistorical, transnational connection, this young woman is forging together places, people, and time in a call for justice—evoking Anzaldúa's recognition of "The ability of story to transform the storyteller and the listener into something or someone else … " (1987, p. 88).

Steven Salaita (2016) has argued that the struggles of Indigenous people in the United States and Palestinians are intimately connected—and that decolonization in each context, although distinct and context-dependent, draws from similar relational onto-epistemologies to land and people. There are opportunities to learn from and with each other in the fight for inconceivable futures—engaging music is one such opening. Indeed, these connections are already being made by young activists, and musicians in particular—those who most clearly recognize the same fire burning the world over. Take for instance, the young people dancing the traditional Arab *debke* along the Gaza border as Israeli snipers gunned down protesters (RedPedGrl, 2018). Or the Palestinian rap group Ettijah, who in their recent song and video, Bala Hdood (Without Borders), emphatically rap in the last verse that "Black Lives Matter"—this proclamation and connection of struggles through music is a transnational move toward and beyond solidarities. Honoring the revolutionary tradition of rap music in African-American culture in a Palestinian context while stating that Black lives do indeed matter, all over the world, is a radical step toward solidarity and healing. The very idea of a world "without borders" transcends the myopic worldviews of colonialism, and music (and particularly young people's use of it) provides a potential theoretical/pedagogical tool to open such conversations, within and outside the academy—critical readings of Latinx music and Palestinian music, particularly in relation to each other, may provide a provocative unsettling step.

Sean

In early 2017 I was researching the literature on Central American immigrant students and their families in North Carolina. Naturally, this investigation led me to review reasons for and reaction to the recent uptick in centroamericanos at border crossings, especially the so-called "crisis" of unaccompanied minors apprehended at the Texas-Mexico border in 2014. In an article critiquing the crisis framing, David Hernández (2015) includes a small detail that marks my own methodological and epistemological turn. He notes, "US Customs and Border Protection launched a campaign ... [and] commissioned songs that aired on Latin American radio stations telling about the dangers and inevitable failure of migration to the United States" (p. 14). I not only already knew about some of the history of migra-corridos, but also have a deep and personal connection to immigration from these countries.

Firstly, I married into una familia hondureña who immigrated in the early 1990s. In the 1980s, mi suegro worked at the unofficial US military command center (alternately called Palmerola, Soto Cano, or Joint Task Force Bravo, among others) for meddling in sovereign countries. Around 1999–2000, los abuelos y trés tías initiated the greencard process. It wasn't until 2015 that they were granted permission to come to live in the U.S. While they waited, each of them, independently, knew someone who was murdered, kidnapped, or disappeared by the military or the gangs. As I write, un primo plans to take his wife and child to a port of entry in the U.S. to request asylum. Mi esposa y yo have offered to officially sponsor them, which may help their case, but it is difficult to be hopeful with the current president and my knowledge of the dangers of migration across three borders.

Unlike the 1988 song "Tres veces mojado" (and movie of the same name), the 2014 song commissioned by Customs and Border Patrol disrespects the visceral knowledge and testimonios of emigration from centroamerica to the US. "La bestia" is a corny pop-cumbia song that features a guitar solo that could only be described as imitating Carlos Santana in both sound and use of the pentatonic scale. The song itself dramatizes the well-known terrors of riding "the wretched train of death" known as la bestia north through Mexico. Furthermore, the Obama administration spent part of the $1 million Dangers Awareness Campaign to pay off at least 21 centroamericano radio stations to popularize the song (Ali, 2014; Walker, 2014).

Only the impudent boldness of settler colonial logics could conceive of commissioning and coercively popularizing a propaganda song three countries away in order to further its border protection policy called Prevention through Deterrence (PTD). Jason De León (2015) brilliantly analyzes the genesis and continued structure of PTD in his touted ethnography *Land of Open Graves*. In the text, De León details how enforcing border policies became inconvenient for the U.S. in the 1990s because it turns out that U.S. citizens who are Brown don't appreciate being viewed suspiciously by Border Patrol and Immigration and Customs Enforcement (ICE; formerly INS) officers. In order to move border control operations out of the public eye, Border Patrol effectively halted the movement of people across the southern border into populated areas without documentation. The Border Patrol explicitly sought to push undocumented migrations into the treacherous desert as a mode of deterrence—positing that the perils of desert crossings would outweigh the so-called push and pull factors for migrating without sanctioned documents. The Obama administration persuaded Mexico to recreate PTD along its border with Guatemala through development of Plan Frontera Sur (Abrego, 2018). Central American Studies scholar, Leisy Abrego, notes how this U.S.-aided militarization of the Mexico-Guatemala border "pushes Central American refugees through more dangerous routes" (p. 11).

This strategy of PTD was reinscribed and extended with the Obama administration's response to an uptick in unaccompanied minors from Central America crossing the Texas-Mexico border in 2014. The permanent anxiety of settler societies to losing their claims to stolen land (Tuck & Yang, 2012) leads to an absurd investment in border protection (Abrego, 2018; De León, 2015). For example, earlier in 2007, the Bush administration brokered the Mérida Initiative with Mexico in order to create a "21st-century border" that would protect U.S. interests (Abrego, 2018). When Obama and his administration were confronted by the seemingly unprecedented "crisis" of non-Mexican migrant arrivals, the paranoia of settler logics led to employing music to extend the PTD border strategy. Instead, centering the long-standing popular tradition of migracorridos in the classroom can work to disrupt the dominant logics of settler colonialism.

As Gloria Anzaldúa (1987) reminds us, mexicanos have a saying: "Out of poverty, poetry; out of suffering, song" (p. 87). As was seen in the days following the white supremacist massacre in El Paso, corridos remain a powerful source of healing (Brown, 2019). By juxtaposing a politically commissioned song over and against historical (i.e.: "Tres veces mojado" or "Somos más americanos" by Los Tigres del Norte) or current (e.x.: "El corrido de Juan" by Calibre .50, discussed above) migracorridos, educators can highlight the discrepancies in the depictions of and attitudes toward peoples seeking refuge. Like when using paired texts, students can make meaning from the differences in the songs' messages. Additionally, the embodied, emotional experience of music is one way "duality is transcended" (Anzaldúa, 2015, p. 102). Not only does teaching these migracorridos offer a narrative that challenges the dominant settler colonial framework, doing so also makes space for the healing power of music—which Anzaldúa later notes is part of "healing the split that originates in the very foundation of our lives" (p. 102).

Pedagogical Implications

Gloria Anzaldúa argued forcefully that we recognize the healing power of art, positioned as a form of "spiritual inquiry" (2015, p. 119). We contend that healing is fundamentally an unsettling praxis, particularly in white supremacist settler states predicated on the erasure of Black, Brown, and Indigenous (and queer, immigrant/refugee, disabled, otherwise) people, joy, and life. We similarly dare to imagine what it looks like when/if healing is offered as pedagogy. What does this look like in a college classroom, particularly one dedicated to teaching future teachers? How do the *cuentos* above inform an unsettling pedagogy that can be implemented in teacher education programs?

Drawing together these three encounters with music as a decolonizing force, we humbly offer an extension of the important work already being done in post-secondary classrooms (and far beyond!) around justice. Following the example of Del Vecchio, Spady, and Toomey—who note that addressing justice in our teaching practice is a *critical corollary* to writing about justice (2018, p. 123). We employ the thematic structure from their chapter on pedagogical applications of *Toward What Justice*, to similarly end our contribution to this reader with suggestions for further reading, listening, and lesson ideas that incorporate our own stories into an unsettling praxis for teacher education. Each section below corresponds to the themes of our personal narratives shared above—these themes, readings, and discussion questions are brought together to expand discussions on justice and education, with a particular focus on understanding borders, alongside music as a decolonizing tool for critical readings of Latinx (Indigenous) futures and solidarities. These are meant to be used in formal and informal education settings, and our hope is that they contribute to an unsettling praxis of healing across contexts and times.

Border-Crossers and Wake Work

How this unsettles:

> Marwa uses rap as a pedagogical tool both in making her knowledge and experiences central to learning, and in engaging with transhistorical and transnational themes in addressing justice and futurity. She asks: How will we heal? What will the future look like? Marwa provides us guidance as she invokes a transhistorical and border-crossing act of creation and resistance. She uses rap across contexts—and in performing for us, creates a collective experience focused on relationality with the land as teacher, mother. She at once calls for justice—a redress discourse somewhere between grievance and grief (Tuck and Yang, 2016) – while also invoking an inconceivable future (Tuck and Yang, 2018). In the suggested reading and listening, music is similarly engaged drawing from across transnational boundaries. How are these related to each other, and to the music of Latinx communities? Can we use music to create transnational, transhistorical solidarities across imposed barriers? Marwa provides an example of how this unsettling can be done within the space of a classroom; the readings and songs offered here are inspired by her praxis.

Theories:

> Decolonization (Tuck and Yang, 2012), Borderlands (Anzaldúa, 1987), Wake Work (Sharpe, 2016)

Themes:

> Collective mournability, haunting, refusal, rap as healing, transnational solidarities, futurity.

Learning objectives:

> Engage with the concept of wake work.
> Draw connections and distinctions between the Palestinian, Latinx and Black struggle for liberation.
> Understand haunting, futurity, and art as "spiritual inquiry".

Suggested readings:

Christina Sharpe: *In the Wake: On Blackness and Being*
Angela Davis: *Freedom is a Constant Struggle*
Gaza Writes Back: Short Stories from Young Writers in Gaza, Palestine
Mahmoud Darwish: *A Journal of Ordinary Grief*
Steven Salaita: *Inter/Nationalism: Decolonizing Native American and Palestine*
Gómez-Peña, Chagoya, & Rice (1998): *Codex Espangliensis*

Suggested listening:
La Santa Cecilia

"ICE el Hielo" (https://www.youtube.com/watch?v=0lNJviuYUEQ)

Shadia Mansour

"The Kufiya is Arab" (http://revolutionaryarabraptheindex.blogspot.com/2011/11/shadia-mansour-and-m-1-arab-kufiya.html)

Lupe Fiasco's album *Drogas Wave*

(Especially the songs: Manila, WAV Files, Down, Alan Forever, Jonylah Forever)
The 2018 album tells the story of the LongChains, a group of African people who either jumped or were thrown from slave ships. Fiasco writes on his reddit page: "When they were submerged in the water their earthly lives expired and they began a new life under and on the water. Some walked back to Africa while others stayed in the sea to help fight slavery by attacking and sinking slave ships ... The last of The LongChains still patrol the seas (and heavens!) to this day. 'Those who wouldn't become slaves ... instead became waves.' *-Attributed to Alan Kurdi.*"

Omar Offendum

"Crying Shame"(https://www.youtube.com/watch?v=LOpZrd8D-nQ)
"Close My Eyes" (https://offendum.bandcamp.com/track/close-my-eyes)

Ettijah

"Bala Hdood (Without Borders)" (https://www.youtube.com/watch?v=i7_RncXIgSU)

Discussion questions:

What does it mean to engage wake work? Who are we in the wake? Can we do so across transnational crossings?
How are these struggles for liberation in conversation with each other? How are they incommensurate?

What sort of transnational solidarities can be built across border-crossers? Those dispossessed of land?

Should we connect these struggles? What are the reasons for doing so? Are we all "refugees of a world on fire"? What are the challenges, or limitations?

Border Enforcement Is a Settler Colonial Logic

How this unsettles:

> La Bestia exemplifies the absurdity of border control, since the song's use displaces the geographical border between the US and Mexico to the radio waves of Honduras. It also allows for examining a recent manifestation of settler colonial logics, as well as the effects of those logics. When paired with any of the other songs, it reveals that Latinxs have a deep, cultural understanding of not only South-North migrations in recent decades but also the State-created fiction known as the border. Confronting this deep, cultural knowledge also points to understanding emigration as an act of both survivance and futurity. Additionally, when viewed through the knowing eyes of a refugee or asylum seeker, la bestia may be a site of haunting. Considering the thirty-year history of flight from centroamerica, la bestia and the desert could be sites of multiple hauntings—for those disappeared, dismembered, and dead. Exposing how those ghost-memories live on in centroamericanos en camino allows for an understanding on non-linear time.

Theories:

> Settler colonialism (Wolf, 2016; Speed, 2017), epistemologies of ignorance (Sullivan & Tuana, 2007), decolonization (Tuck & Yang, 2012), borderlands, Prevention Through Deterrence (De León, 2015)

Themes:

> Settler colonial logics, collective mournability, epistemicide, music, healing, borderlessness, empire, nativism.

Learning objectives:

> Identify settler colonial logics
> > Obtain understanding of survivance

Suggested listening:

> Eddie Ganz (commissioned by US Border Patrol), "La Bestia"
> Calibre 50, "Corrido de Juanito"
> Los Tigres del Norte "Tres veces mojado"; "Somos más americanos"
> Ricardo Arjona (feat. Intocable), "Mojado"

Suggested readings:

> Tuck & Gatzambide-Fernandez (2013). Curriculum, replacement, and settler futurity
> Davidson & Burson (2016). Keep Those Kids Out: Nativism and Attitudes Toward Access to Public Education for the Children of Undocumented Immigrants
> De León (2015). *Land of open graves: Living and dying on the migrant trail.*
> Abrego (2018). Central American refugees reveal the crisis of the States.
> Gomez-Peña, Chagoy, Rice (1998). Codex Espangliensis: From Columbus to the Border Patrol.

Discussion questions:

> What does it mean to enforce a border? What does it mean to enforce a distant border *for another country*?
> What must it feel like to board La Bestia? How is jumping onto La Bestia a metaphor for unsettling?
> How are the efforts by US Customs and Border Patrol analogous to social justice education?
> If US Customs and Border Patrol enacted an epistemology of ignorance by commissioning pop propaganda for centroamericanos, then how does social justice education do the same to students?

Reflection/Conclusion

Before final edits could be made to this chapter, the publication process and life itself was halted by the COVID-19 pandemic. While we haven't changed the framing of this chapter, we now recognize how terrifyingly close we were in 2019 to the world being both literally and figuratively on fire. We have seen massive swaths of Australia burn, untold miles of the Western U.S. go up in smoke, police precincts and other city structures across the U.S. reduced to ashes, and two devasting conflagrations in the Port of Lebanon; the metaphorical fires of (genocidal) forced sterilizations by ICE, shouts of "white power" and "heil Hitler" from armed caravans of white supremacists as they drive through our respective North Carolina cities, and the political chicanery at the highest levels to drastically alter the Supreme Court and refuse a peaceful transfer of power. However, these current events conclude, we recognize them now as the raging fires that threaten our very lives.

How will we find refuge from this world on fire? How will we heal? Can we? These questions may feel more daunting than ever before but returning to the wisdom of those who have come before us—those who have seen times perhaps harder than this—guides our thinking still. Cherríe Moraga and Gloria Anzaldúa, in good company with so many radical feminist women of color, remind us that art can heal us (Anzaldúa, 2015), language can protect us (Morrison, 1993), and theory can liberate us (hooks, 1994). Indeed, we would also be wise to remember that our Indigenous relations in North America have been living and surviving the apocalypse for 500 hundred years. Whenever we may have come to understand Indigenous survivance (Vizenor, 2008), it is not yet too late to imbue our pedagogies with a deeply unsettling project. Afterall, widespread fire opens spaces for literal and metaphorical new growth. Perhaps our unsettling project—now just beneath the surface—may emerge stronger than ever as the verdant, life-sustaining force that it is.

We end here with an invitation to scholars and educators to add their knowledge to the ones offered here—our list is necessarily incomplete, and we hope it will be a small contribution/provocation to already generative conversations. Finally, our stories and knowledges presented here are merely one part of a web of activists and scholars across the world who are engaging in the important work of decolonization. We gratefully acknowledge that our writing would not be possible without their work, and offer that anything written here also belongs to them, to you, and to everyone who dreams of an otherwise future.

¡Hasta entonces, la lucha sigue!

References

Abrego, L. J. (2018). Central American refugees reveal the crisis of the State. In C. Menjivar, M. Ruiz, & I. Ness (Eds.), *The Oxford handbook of migration crises* (pp. 1–18). Oxford: Oxford University Press. http://doi.org/10.1093/oxfordhb/9780190856908.013.43

Ali, L. (2014, July 31). La Bestia: Pop meets propaganda courtesy of U.S. border agency. Retrieved from https://www.latimes.com/entertainment/music/posts/la-et-ms-la-bestia-pop-hit-meets-propaganda-courtesy-of-us-border-agency-20140730-story.html

Anzaldúa, G. (1987). *Borderlands/La Frontera: The new mestiza.* Aunt Lute Books.

Anzaldúa, G. (2015). *Luz en el oscuro: Rewriting identity, spirituality, reality.* Duke University Press.

Bell, L. A. (1997). Theoretical foundations for social justice education. In M. Adams, L. A. Bell, & P. Griffin (Eds.), *Teaching for diversity and social justice* (pp. 1–15). Routledge.

Blake, S. (2018, September 12). UNC Latinx Education Research Hub losing on-campus space is nothing new, members say. *The Daily Tarheel.* Retrieved from: https://www.dailytarheel.com/article/2018/09/latinx-center-0912-education-research-hub-peabody-hall-unc-minorities-campus-carolina-collaborative

Brown, A. (2019, August 10). In El Paso's wake, a corrido honors the dead and points fingers at the villains. *Los Angeles Times.* https://www.latimes.com/entertainment-arts/music/story/2019-08-10/el-paso-shooting-corrido-walmart

Cervantes-Soon, C. G., & Turner, A. M. (2017). Countering silence and reconstructing identities in a Spanish/English Two-Way Immersion program: Latina mothers' pedagogies in El Nuevo Sur. In X. L. Rong & J. Hilburn (Eds.), *Immigration and education in North Carolina: The challenges and responses in a new gateway state* (pp. 195–220). Sense Publishers. https://doi.org/10.1007/978-94-6300-809-9_9

De León, J. (2015). *Land of open graves: Living and dying on the migrant trail.* University of California Press.

de los Ríos, C. V. (2019). "Los Músicos": Mexican Corridos, the Aural Border, and the evocative musical renderings of transnational youth. *Harvard Educational Review, 89*(2), 177–200. https://doi.org/10.17763/1943-5045-89.2.177

Del Vecchio, L., Spady, S., & Toomey, N. (2018). *Pedagogical application of Toward what justice?* In E. Tuck & K. W. Yang (Eds.), *Toward what justice?: Describing diverse dreams of justice in education* (pp. 123–146). Routledge.

Dumas, M. J. (2018). Beginning and ending with Black suffering: A meditation on and against racial justice in education. In E. Tuck & K. W. Yang (Eds.), *Toward what justice: Describing diverse dreams of justice in education* (pp. 29–45). Routledge.

Emdin, C. (2016). *For white folks who teach in the hood ... and the rest of y'all too.* Beacon Press.

Flores Carmona, J. (2017). Pedagogical border crossings: Testimonio y reflexiones de una Mexicana académica. *Journal of Latinos and Education, 8431*(April), 1–6. https://doi.org/10.1080/15348431.2017.1282364

Flynn, M. (2018, November 30). Feds deport undocumented immigrant whose church supporters went to jail to protect him. *The Washington Post.* Retrieved from: https://www.washingtonpost.com/nation/2018/11/30/feds-deport-undocumented-immigrant-whose-church-supporters-went-jail-protect-him/?noredirect=on

Green, M., Perreira, K. M., & Ko, L. K. (2017). Schooling experience of Latino/a immigrant adolescents in North Carolina: An examination of relationships between peers, teachers, and parents. In X. L. Rong & J. Hilburn (Eds.), *Immigration and education in North Carolina: The challenges and responses in a new gateway state* (pp. 53–80). Sense Publishers.

Hernández, D. (2015). Unaccompanied child migrants in "crisis": New surge or case of arrested development? In *Harvard Journal of Hispanic Policy* 27, 11–17.

Holmes, O. (2019, February 28). UN says Israel's killings at Gaza protests may amount to war crimes. *The Guardian*. Retrieved from: https://www.theguardian.com/world/2019/feb/28/gaza-israel-un-inquiry-killings-protest-war-crimes-army

hooks, B. (1994). *Teaching to transgress: Education as the practice of freedom*. Routledge.

Israel Demolishes Palestinian Homes Near Separation Wall. (2019, July 22). *Al Jazeera*. Retrieved from: https://www.aljazeera.com/news/2019/07/israeli-forces-prepare-demolish-100-palestinian-homes-190722032443910.html

Loewus, L. (2017, August 15). The Nation's teaching force is still mostly white and female. *EdWeek*. Retrieved from: https://www.edweek.org/ew/articles/2017/08/15/the-nations-teaching-force-is-still-mostly.html

Moraga, C. (2021). Refugees of a world on fire: Foreword to the second edition, 1983. In C. Moraga and G.E. Anzaldúa (Eds.), *This Bridge Called My Back, Fortieth Anniversary Edition: Writings by Radical Women of Color* (p. 255–260).

Morrison, T. (1993). Nobel lecture. Retrieved from: https://www.nobelprize.org/prizes/literature/1993/morrison/lecture/

Parkhouse, H., & Freeman, E. (2017). Citizenship without papers: A case study of undocumented youth fighting for in-state tuition policy. In X. L. Rong & J. Hilburn (Eds.), *Immigration and education in North Carolina: The challenges and responses in a new gateway state* (pp. 125–148). Sense Publishers.

Patel, L. (2016a). *Decolonizing educational research: From ownership to answerability*. Routledge.

Patel, L. (2016b). Pedagogies of resistance and survivance: Learning as marronage. *Equity & Excellence in Education*, 49(4), 397–401.

Patel, L. (2018). Justice as a lackey. In E. Tuck & K. W. Yang (Eds.), *Toward what justice?: Describing diverse dreams of justice in education* (pp. 101–112). Routledge.

RedPedGrl. (2018, July 2). This. Is. What. Refusal. Looks. Like. [Twitter Post]. Retrieved from: https://twitter.com/RedPedGrl/status/1013948532435443713

Rivera, D. N. (2018). Corridos. *Oxford Bibliographies*. Retrieved from: http://www.oxfordbibliographies.com/view/document/obo-9780199827251/obo-9780199827251-0166.xml

Rong, X.K. & Hilburn, J. (Eds.). (1017). Immigration and education in North Carolina: The challenges and responses in a new gateway state. Sense Publishers.

Salaita, S. (2016). *Inter/Nationalism: Decolonizing Native America and Palestine*. University of Minnesota Press.

Sharpe, C. (2016). *In the wake: On blackness and being*. Duke University Press.

Smith, L. T., Tuck, E., & Yang, K. W. (2019). Introduction. In L. T. Smith, E. Tuck, & K. W. Yang (Eds.), *Indigenous and decolonizing studies in education: Mapping the longview*. Routledge.

Stuesse, A. (2016). *Scratching out a living: Latinos, race, and work in the Deep South*. Oakland: University of California Press.

Tuck, E. (2018, April). *This is taking too long: Waiting on settler drives to mutual destruction*. In Symposium presentation at the American Educational Research Association Conference.

Tuck, E., & Yang, K. W. (2012). Decolonization is not a metaphor. *Decolonization: Indigeneity, Education & Society*, 1(1), 1–40.

Tuck, E., & Yang, K. W. (2016). What justice wants. *Critical Ethnic Studies*, 2(2), 1–15.

Tuck, E., & Yang, K. W. (2018). Introduction. In E. Tuck & K. W. Yang (Eds.), *Toward what justice?: Describing diverse dreams of justice in education* (pp. 29–45). Routledge.

Villena, C. (2018, December 18). Maya Little Isn't Done Fighting White Supremacy at UNC. *Indy Week*. Retrieved from: https://indyweek.com/news/northcarolina/maya-little-white-supremacy-unc/

Vizenor, G. (Ed.). (2008). Survivance: Narratives of Native presence. University of Nebrasks Press.

Walker, T. (2014, July 16). Hit song 'La Bestia' about Mexican death train released by US border agency to deter prospective migrants from making the trip north. *The Independent* https://www.independent.co.uk/news/world/americas/hit-song-la-bestia-about-mexican-death-train-released-by-us-border-agency-to-deter-prospective-migrants-from-making-the-trip-north-9608152.html

Wilbur, M., & Keene, A. (2019). Ep #4: Can a DNA test make me Native American? *All My Relations Podcast*. Retrieved: August 25, 2019.

Zong, J., & Batalova, J. (2018, October 11). Mexican Immigrants in the United States. *Migration Policy Institute*. Retrieved from: https://www.migrationpolicy.org/article/mexican-immigrants-united-states-2017

Index

activism 6, 7, 14, 15, 16, 145, 146, 147, 148, 150, 154, 156, 159, 182, 189, 190, 192, 194, 196, 197, 202, 203, 204, 206
African American 6, 10, 107, 124, 221
Alice Bag 188, 190, 192, 196, 202, 203
Américo Paredes 9, 136
Anibal Quijano 4, 114
Anthony Macias 10
Anti- colonial 16, 111, 137, 140, 153, 188, 189, 192, 193, 194, 195, 198, 199, 204, 206
Anti- colonial punk pedagogy 206
anti- racism
Didn't find
Applied Ethnomusicology 127, 130, 131, 135, 135, 137, 138, 141
Audry Funk 13, 103, 104, 105, 108, 109, 113, 116, 118, 121, 122

Black Atlantic diaspora 134
Blackness 108, 112, 124, 211, 214, 225
Boaventura de Sousa Santos 2, 29
Bocafloja 108, 112
Bomba 14, 127, 132, 134, 135, 196
Borderlands 2, 3, 8, 9, 17, 87, 91, 95, 97, 148, 190, 191, 192, 193, 194, 212

César Castro 140
Chela Sandoval 4, 9
Cherríe Moraga 195, 199, 212, 228

Chicana
Chicana Feminism 55, 191, 193, 205
Chicana feminist epistemology 57, 58, 68
Chicana punk, 15, 16, 188, 189, 190, 191, 192, 193, 195, 199, 202, 203, 204, 206
Chicana/ x/ o
Chicano Movement 14, 15, 64, 145, 146, 147, 148, 151, 152, 154, 155, 157, 158, 159, 160, 191
Chicano Movement music
Chicano Music 148, 149, 150, 160
Chicano/ a/ x
Chicanx viii, 10, 15, 18, 111, 112, 121, 130, 187–209, 212
Collective songwriting 23, 40, 141
Colonial 32, 33, 36, 56, 57, 61, 62, 64, 65, 72, 75, 81–83, 85, 87, 88, 95, 97, 99, 107–113, 122, 128, 130, 131, 132, 135, 136, 138–141, 148, 149, 151, 152, 155, 157, 158, 160, 184, 189, 191, 194, 197, 199, 204, 205, 206, 211
Colonial logics 12, 24, 32, 33, 34, 36, 222, 226
Colonial matrix of power
(also patrón colonial del poder) 1, 5– 7, 109
Coloniality 6–12, 17, 57, 84, 98, 99, 108, 109, 113, 115, 118, 122, 134, 160

Coloniality of power 5, 115
Colonization 1, 8, 10, 12–14, 16, 17, 56, 59, 62–65, 72, 82, 85, 87, 88, 90, 92, 95, 97, 108, 109, 114, 115, 117, 122, 145–147, 150–155, 157, 159, 160, 168, 183
Composition studies 193, 194, 196, 204
Comunalidad 23, 32, 33, 35, 37
Concheros 93
Conocimiento 59, 70, 168, 181, 182, 184
Convivencia 2, 27, 61, 65, 69, 70, 71, 76
Corridos (written twice in the galley) 9, 10, 14, 17, 127, 131, 135–138, 141, 145, 151–153, 168, 218, 221, 223
Creation-resistance 2, 17
Critical Latinx Indigeneities 192
Critical pedagogy – no entries
Critical race feminista methodology 27
Critical race theory 131, 212
Culturally sustaining pedagogies 8
Cura 13, 82, 88, 91–93, 95, 97, 119

David Saldívar (listed twice in the galley) 5
Deborah Vargas 10, 190, 200, 204
Decolonial
decolonial curriculum 15, 146, 150
Decolonial feminism 112, 113, 114, 115, 118
Decolonial hip hop 13, 14, 105, 109, 110, 117, 118
Decolonial imaginary 1, 3, 112, 150, 191
Decolonial pedagogy 7, 8, 128, 135, 194, 204
Decolonial teaching 14, 87
Decolonial turn 2, 108
Decoloniality 2, 3, 6, 11, 16, 32, 108, 114, 117, 122, 131
Decolonialidad 29, 37
Decolonization
Decolonization
Decolonizing methodologies 57, 58, 108, 180
Decolonizing pedagogies 7, 12

digital 13, 48, 83, 84, 85, 97, 98, 99
Divascape 190, 191
Downtown Boys 189, 192, 196, 197, 198, 199, 203, 204, 205

earth 13, 84, 85, 86, 87, 88, 89, 90, 91, 92, 93, 94, 95, 98, 119, 120
Ecology of knowledge 29
ecología de sabers 29, 37, 46
Education
Emma Pérez 3, 112
Epistemic colonization 183
Epistemologies of the South 12 (epistemologías del sur) 33, 37
Ethnomusicology 127, 128, 129, 131, 133, 135, 136, 138, 141
Eve Tuck 194, 211, 213

Fea 199, 200, 201, 203, 204
Feminism 13, 14, 16, 37, 55, 83, 109, 112, 113, 114, 115, 116, 117, 118, 119, 120, 122, 123, 138, 150, 191, 193, 202, 204, 205, 212
Feminismo decolonial 37
First Transborder Gathering of Indigenous Women Musicians 12, 23, 24, 25, 26, 38, 45, 46, 48
Francisco Aguabella 133

Gaye Johnson 10
Gaye Theresa Johnson 188, 204
Geopolitics of knowledge 5
Girl in a Coma 190, 200
Global North 1, 2, 11, 127, 128
Global South 1, 2, 127, 128
Gloria Anzaldúa 3, 4, 15, 60, 109, 192, 193, 195, 223, 228
Gregorio Cortez 136

Nahua Tolteca 83, 94, 97
Nahui Ollin 7
Nepantla 3, 67, 70

Oaxacalifornia 28
Oaxacan Brass bands 12, 26
Oppositional consciousness 4

Index 235

Palestine 225
Panche be 7
participatory pedagogy 14
Paulo Freire 114
pedagogical approach 14, 16, 145
Pedagogy 2, 7, 8, 14, 15, 17, 114, 127, 128, 130, 131, 132, 135, 140, 141, 145, 146, 160, 178, 187, 192, 193, 194, 195, 197, 204, 206, 211, 214, 215, 218, 219, 223
Pensamiento fronterizo 5
Pláticas 57
Punk 15, 16, 73, 129, 141, 187, 188, 189, 190, 191, 192, 193, 194, 195, 196, 197, 198, 199, 200, 202, 203, 204, 205, 206
Punk educator 206
Punta 134

Quilomboarte Collective 112

Rap 103, 104, 108, 111, 112, 114, 115, 116, 123, 152, 220, 221, 224
Raza cósmica 109
Rebeca Lane 108, 110, 114, 118, 119
Reconstruction 184
Refugee 219, 220, 223, 226
resistance
Rio Grande Valley (also see "El Valle") 14, 145, 146, 147, 149
rumba guaguancó 14, 127, 132, 133, 134

Sergio Navarrete 35, 36
settler colonialism 6, 9, 15, 105, 111, 129, 136, 149, 180, 214, 223, 226
Sincere Collaborative Intention 23, 27, 47

Healing 1, 8, 13, 15, 17, 59, 60, 81, 85, 88, 89, 91, 92, 94, 97, 99, 109, 110, 211, 212, 215, 216, 218, 221, 223, 224, 226
Higher education 8, 11, 12, 13–15, 17, 76, 105, 106, 109, 114, 129, 139, 148, 160, 173, 177–179, 198

Hip hop 10, 13, 14, 103–124, 129, 141, 218

Identity
Indigenous
In lak' ech 7

Jacinto Treviño 153, 156
José Limon 10
Juan Cortina 136, 153, 156 (also noticed Cortina is spelled "Cortinas" on page 153)
Juan Tejeda 10

Latin America 4, 6, 32, 49, 107, 109, 115, 116, 123, 127, 128, 137, 140, 142, 153, 192, 216
Latinx 13–16, 86, 103–105, 107, 108, 110–112, 117, 118, 121, 122, 124, 130, 181, 189, 190, 192, 194, 196, 197, 198, 200, 205, 206, 212, 216–218, 221, 224, 225
Linda Tuhiwai Smith 4, 59, 60, 108, 180, 213

Machista 104, 113, 115, 116
Manuel Peña 10
Margaret Walker 11, 180
Maria Herrera-Sobek 10, 130
Maria Lugones 37, 49, 113–115, 117, 123
Mariachi Corazón de San Antonio 179
Mariachi education 171, 178, 180, 182
Mestiza
Mexican American
Mexican American Studies 17, 66, 129, 181
Mexico
Michael Dominguez 8, 204
Michelle Habell-Pallán 191, 196, 204
Migracorridos 221, 223
Miguel Zavala 7
Mixe
Mujeres Trabajando 118
Multilingual 194, 195, 197, 198

Multimodal (not listed in the text)
Mundo Zurdo 60
Music
Music curriculum 168, 181, 182
Music methods 182
Music pedagogy 178
Musicking 32, 137

Social Justice (listed twice) 2, 3, 11, 13, 15, 16, 55, 59, 60, 61, 72, 73, 75, 76, 78, 81, 83, 84, 95, 180, 211–216, 218, 227
Somos Mujeres Somos Hip Hop 118
Son Jarocho 13, 14, 55–79, 127, 129, 131, 135, 138, 139, 140–142, 196.

teacher education 8, 15, 211, 214, 215, 223
Teatro de Artes de Juan Seguin 171
Technologies of crossing 9
Tequio 33, 36
Testimonios 39, 55, 57, 58, 59, 61, 68, 75, 76, 221
Texas Rangers 149, 153, 156
Tradition

Transborder collaboration 30, 32, 49
transnational communities (not referenced in the book)
transnational solidarity (not referenced in the book)
Transnationalism 215
Tyina Steptoe 10

U.S. settler colonialism 6, 149

wake work (not listed in the book)
Walter Mignolo 4, 5, 9, 32, 34, 108
K. Wayne Yang 180, 194, 213, 214, 222, 224, 226
White Backlash 106, 183, 184
Women musicians

Xica Media 13, 81, 83, 84
Xicanx

Yacatsol 81–84, 97–99
Yolanda Broyles-González 10
Yomaira C. Figueroa-Vásquez 11

Zapoteca 25, 34

Yolanda Medina and Margarita Machado-Casas
GENERAL EDITORS

Critical Studies of Latinxs in the Americas is a provocative interdisciplinary series that offers a critical space for reflection and questioning what it means to be Latinxs living in the Americas in twenty-first century social, cultural, economic, and political arenas. The series looks forward to extending the dialogue to include the North and South Western hemispheric relations that are prevalent in the field of global studies.

Topics that explore and advance research and scholarship on contemporary topics and issues related with processes of racialization, economic exploitation, health, education, transnationalism, immigration, gendered and sexual identities, and disabilities that are not commonly highlighted in the current Latinx Studies literature as well as the multitude of socio, cultural, economic, and political progress among the Latinxs in the Americas are welcome.

To receive more information about CSLA, please contact:

Yolanda Medina (ymedina@bmcc.cuny.edu) &
Margarita Machado-Casas (Margarita.MachadoCasas@utsa.edu)

To order other books in this series, please contact our Customer Service Department at:

peterlang@presswarehouse.com (within the U.S.)
orders@peterlang.com (outside the U.S.)

Or browse online by series at:

WWW.PETERLANG.COM

www.ingramcontent.com/pod-product-compliance
Lightning Source LLC
Chambersburg PA
CBHW061711300426